SCOTLAND'S
LOST INDUSTRIES

James Watt's Cottage, Kinneil Estate, Bo'ness.

James Watt's cottage on the Kinneil Estate at Birkhill was the birthplace of the Industrial Revolution.

SCOTLAND'S LOST INDUSTRIES

MICHAEL MEIGHAN

AMBERLEY

For Auntie Katie

First published 2012

Amberley Publishing
The Hill, Stroud
Gloucestershire, GL5 4EP

www.amberley-books.com

British Library Cataloguing in Publication Data.
A catalogue record for this book is available from the British Library.

ISBN 978 1 4456 0917 1

Typeset in 10pt on 12pt Sabon.
Typesetting and Origination by Amberley Publishing.
Printed in the UK.

CONTENTS

ACKNOWLEDGEMENTS

In writing this book, I have received enormous support from a number of people, particularly the local heritage organisations and retired staff groups and members who are keeping the history of their industries alive. In particular I would like to thank:

Iain Cameron for his help with the tobacco industry; John Campelton, David Air and N. Brinklies for information on North British Rubber and the rubber industry; Colin Findlay for his advice on Scottish Steel; Heather Martin for information on Singer; Raymond McLaughlin and James Friel for their for comments and general encouragement; John Paterson for information on Leyland Tractors, Bathgate; Pat Whitley of Sterling Resources for his invaluable information on granite and the shale oil industry; Winnie Stevenson for images and information on the Roslin Gunpowder Works and Widnell's carpet factory.

I am also indebted to the following websites for their information: rcahms.gov. uk; Scottishmining.co.uk; nbrinklies.com; wikipedia.com; wikimedia.com; www. derelictplaces.com; myweb.tiscali.co.uk/clydebridge; Particularly to www.gracesguide. co.uk. *Grace's Guide* is the leading source of information about industry and manufacturing in Britain from the start of the Industrial Revolution to the present.

IMAGE CREDITS

James Watt's Cottage – J&C McCutcheon Collection.
Empress of Britain – J&C McCutcheon Collection.

Aviation
R. H. Barnwell – J&C McCutcheon Collection; Cierva Air Horse – Imperial War Museum, Wikimedia; Prestwick Aerodrome – J&C McCutcheon Collection; Landing of R34 – Library of Congress, Wikimedia; Twin Pioneer, Borneo Airways – J&C McCutcheon Collection; Twin Pioneer publicity material – J&C McCutcheon Collection.

Carpets
Widnell's Carpet Factory – Roslin Heritage Society.

Coal Gas
Plaque to William Murdoch – J&C McCutcheon Collection.

Explosives
Roslin gunpowder works – Roslin Heritage Society; Nobel Works, Linlithgow – J&C McCutcheon Collection.

Iron and Ironworks
Newmains from Slag Hill – J&C McCutcheon Collection; Baird of Gartsherrie locomotive – J&C McCutcheon Collection.

Linoleum
Nairn's of Kirkcaldy – David Muncey and Forbo UK.

Vehicles
The Stonefield – Ray Land. Leyland Tractor line – John Paterson and The Nuffield and Leyland Tractor Club. Kelvin car – Mr George Bergius.

Papermaking
Photographs of the Kinleith salle and machinery images courtesy of Heriot-Watt University Heritage and Information Governance; Manufacture of dandy rolls courtesy of Woollard & Henry, Aberdeen; Caledonian Railway postcard – J&C McCutcheon Collection.

Railway Locomotives
North British Locomotive Works – J&C McCutcheon Collection; Machrihanish station – J&C McCutcheon Collection.

Rubber
Images of North British Rubber – David Air and Nbrinklies

Shipbuilding
John Elder – J&C McCutcheon Collection; *Empress of Britain* – J&C McCutcheon Collection; *Queen Mary* – J&C McCutcheon Collection; SS *Sunniva* – J&C McCutcheon Collection; SS *Camito* – J&C McCutcheon Collection; North British engine – J&C McCutcheon Collection; Men like these carry on the tradition – Wikimedia Commons; Men leaving Yarrow – J&C McCutcheon Collection; *Lusitania* and *Atalanta* – J&C McCutcheon Collection; Destroyers at Yarrow – J&C McCutcheon Collection.

Steel
Puddling furnace, Ravenscraig strip rolling mill – Wikimedia Commons; Clydebridge pan mill 1920s, Clydebridge 1970s, Jimmy Cunningham – Colin Findlay, http://myweb.tiscali.co.uk/clydebridge

Tobacco and cigarettes
Imperial Tobacco Limited for use of the image of the manufacture of The Three Nuns; *Queen Mary* – J&C McCutcheon Collection.

Vehicle Manufacturing
Argyll Motorcar – J&C McCutcheon Collection.

Coal
Cowglen, Thornliebank – J&C McCutcheon Collection; Colliers' Row – J&C McCutcheon Collection; Montgomeriefield – J&C McCutcheon Collection.

Granite Industry
Tormore Jetty – J&C McCutcheon Collection; Curling, Ontario, Canada – Wikimedia Commons

Limestone
James Reid, Lime Merchants – Howie Minerals Ltd, part of the Leiths Group of Companies.

Slate
Ballachulish – J&C McCutcheon Collection; Locharbriggs – J&C McCutcheon Collection

Turkey Red
New Lanark– J&C McCutcheon Collection

Fishing
Wick Fishing Season – J&C McCutcheon Collection; Trial Trip – J&C McCutcheon Collection; Herring Gutters, Stronsay – J&C McCutcheon Collection; Cullen Bay – J&C McCutcheon Collection; Preparing for Lewis – J&C McCutcheon Collection

The Scottish Merchant Fleet
SS *Perth* – The Dundee, Perth & London Shipping Company – DP&L Group Limited, Perth; TSS *Athenia* – J&C McCutcheon Collection; The Irrawaddy Flotilla – Paukan Cruises; Carron Line – J&C McCutcheon Collection; SS *Medina* – J&C McCutcheon Collection; SS Highlander – J&C McCutcheon Collection; Aberdeen & Commonwealth Line – J&C McCutcheon Collection; Allan Line – J&C McCutcheon Collection; SS *Benvalla* – J&C McCutcheon Collection

Whaling
SS *Sevilla* – J&C McCutcheon Collection; Factory Ship – J&C McCutcheon Collection; Landing a Whale, Harris – J&C McCutcheon Collection; Whaling Station, Harris – J&C McCutcheon Collection.

Shipbreaking
SMS *Hindenburg* – J&C McCutcheon Collection; *Mauretania* – J&C McCutcheon Collection.

INTRODUCTION

Scotland has a great industrial future, but not industry as we have known it. Our future is in areas like life sciences, microelectronics, petrochemicals, chemicals, oil exploration, alternative energies, agriculture, forestry, food and drink, education, tourism and finance. Scotland has a healthy mixed economy and has always had the entrepreneurs to make things happen. This book is not about the loss to Scotland of industry, for we are a flexible, dynamic, entrepreneurial country that responds to a changing world.

The idea for this book emerged from research for another book on Glasgow. While I was investigating the history of James (Paraffin) Young and the shale oil industry, I discovered that, while there are books on individual industries, there was not one which covered those Scottish industries which have disappeared. Not that I have in any way attempted to describe every last, lost Scottish industry. This is not a catalogue but a description of some of our lost industries and why they were lost. It is also a tribute to our manufacturing past.

Many Glaswegians of my age are naturally nostalgic about some of the lost or reduced industries like railway locomotive building, shipbuilding and carpet making. Particularly so if they have worked in those industries, like many of those that I have talked to. On the other hand, there are younger generations in Dundee, Glasgow, Paisley and other towns and cities of Scotland that have no idea of the factories and workshops, the foundries and pits that would have been part of their existence had they lived a couple of generations ago. I have set out to describe through words and images what it might have looked like.

When did manufacturing in Scotland start? That is a difficult question. As soon as two people get together to make something it can be called manufacturing. As soon as an entrepreneur employs someone else to make something, it can be called industry. The craft industries can also be called manufacturing.

Back at the end of the Stone Age, there was primitive industry producing artifacts in stone, wood, pottery and metal; this would normally have been for local, domestic consumption. As time progressed, along with the beginning of agriculture, the primitive extraction of coal, evaporation of salt, lime kilning, brewing, spinning and weaving would have been the beginnings of what would have been primarily local industries.

Much of this local industry was limited by the geographical isolation of Scotland. This was to change with developments in shipping. Scotland was in the forefront of these developments, particularly with Glasgow monopolising the American tobacco trade. Further adventuring brought trading in tea, flax, salt and cotton.

Because of this, even before the Industrial Revolution, Scotland was in a prime position to take an advantage in trading. The government of the time supported industrial developments. We had the entrepreneurs, we had the education and we more than anything had a spirit of investigation and experimentation which produced some of the best scientific brains of the time.

The Industrial Revolution started around 1760 in Scotland. You could almost say that the starting point for this was the great Carron Ironworks at Falkirk, from which began our great iron and steel industry which was to expand continuously into the second half of the twentieth century.

We had the coal, we had the ironstone, we had the shipping, we had the engineering expertise and the will. All this came together to drive Scotland forward as one of the world's great industrial nations. From that point we developed a huge shipping empire that delivered steam engines and a multitude of other products throughout the world, initially to support Great Britain's developing colonies.

I discovered that there are many and complex reasons why these industries disappeared. Some of them had had their time. Competition from other countries, often within our own Commonwealth, wanting to develop their own industries was common. Such was the case with jute. New, synthetic materials replaced linoleum and carpets, closing or reducing those industries. Synthetic dyes made in Germany saw the end of Turkey red. The whale was fished almost out of existence and petroleum replaced shale oil.

These industries are gone and while they should be celebrated there are always new industries coming along to take their place. Scotland had, and continues to have, a bright industrial future. It just won't be so dirty and so smelly, as you will find out here.

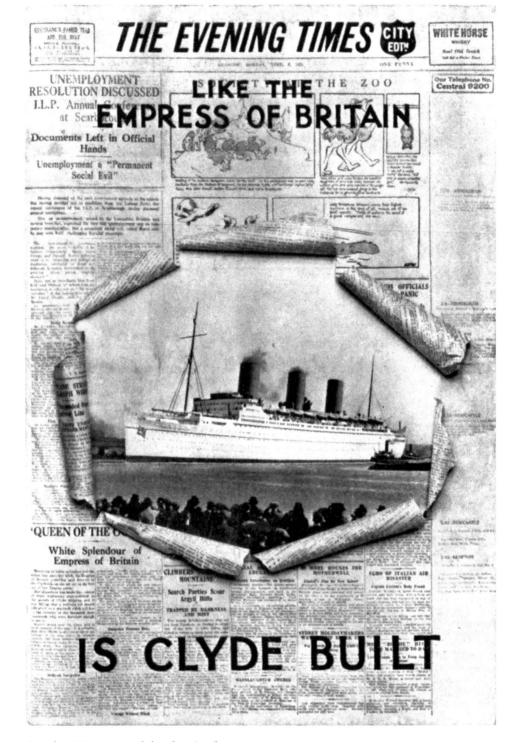

An advertising postcard dated to April 1931.

MANUFACTURING INDUSTRY

Wings Over the West – Aviation in Scotland

I would not like to offend either of the two camps supporting the first powered flights in Scotland so I will mention both as they represent the entrepreneurial and engineering skills for which Scotland is renowned.

While there are other claims without evidence, Harold and Frank Barnwell certainly were the first in Scotland in powered flight. Their motorbike-engined glider flew around 80 metres in a field in Stirlingshire in 1909 and the following year they managed over a mile. And here is the confusion, as this record is also claimed by Andrew Baird of Bute in the same year. His interest in flying took him to an Aviation Week in Blackpool in 1909 and on his return, he used his blacksmithing skills to build a monoplane. He flew this successfully over Ettrick Bay but landed heavily, buckling the undercarriage. It would be fairly reasonable to think that he was an early victim of 'fear of flying' as he never flew again.

However, the aircraft was seen by aircraft manufacturer Tommy Sopwith and it is said that he got permission and subsequently incorporated some of Baird's innovations into his aircraft designs, which takes us on neatly to the first serious builder of aircraft in Scotland, Sir William Beardmore, who built Sopwiths under license.

In virtually every area of industry in Scotland, the name of William Beardmore & Company is to the fore and this was also the case with aviation as they started aircraft developments in 1913, just before the First World War. Their first venture was the building of the Sopwith Pup at their Dalmuir factory. They followed that with a ship-launched version of the Pup, the Beardmore WB III, with a hundred being delivered to the Royal Naval Air Service.

The company was, as ever, happy to be involved in experimental work and such was the case with their 'Inverness' flying boat, built with a new metal 'stressed skin'. The first was produced for Beardmore by its inventors, the Rohrbach Metal Aeroplane Company of Copenhagen, but Beardmore's built the second one themselves. The design was unsuccessful and was scrapped. The Beardmore 'Inflexible' was a large transport aircraft with three engines also built at Dalmuir between 1925 and 1927, first flying in 1928 and appearing at RAF Hendon the same year. Unfortunately, the

R.H. Barnwell, brother of Frank Barnwell, at Hendon, *c.* 1913.

huge Inflexible lived up to its name. It was underpowered and received little interest, being scrapped in 1930.

In fact, between 1913 and its demise in 1930, Beardmores produced around twelve diverse aircraft designs, none of them as successful as the original Sopwith and its shipboard variant. To be fair, some of these were experimental and for evaluation purposes. These were still the early days of military flight and the Air Ministry and other services were looking at submissions from various manufacturers. Some had to be unsuccessful. On the other hand, Beardmores was very successful in producing a range of engines that powered their own and many other aircraft. I should also point out that other shipyards produced airplanes during the First World War, including Alexander Stephen of Linthouse and Barclay Curle of Whiteinch, who both produced aeroplanes for the Royal Aircraft Factory.

It was also an experimental time for airships and Beardmores was fully involved in developments in the field, building and operating the Inchinnan Airship Constructional Station, where they produced the airships R27, R32, R34 and R36.

As the First World War was drawing to a close, the possibilities of the use of airships began to be investigated. This resulted in the production of the R36 using ideas as well as components from a German Zeppelin which had crashed in England in June 1917. Although destined for military use, the airship was redesigned for civilian use, carrying fifty passengers and with folding beds in individual compartments. It used German Maybach engines salvaged from the downed Zeppelin

The R36 was the first ever airship to carry a civilian registration: G-FAAF. Launched at Inchinnan in 1921, it was built with a high degree of comfort comparable to that in ocean-going liners. It was indeed experimental and found use in a number of contexts, including by the Metropolitan Police as an 'eye in the sky' at the Ascot races. Journalists and police dined well together (not for the last time!) with the racing correspondents sending their reports by parachute to be picked up by dispatch riders and taken to Fleet Street.

While there were a number of incidents in flying and landing the R36, it nevertheless established that airships could be used successfully for commercial purposes. However, following the R38 disaster, and given her age, she was finally scrapped in 1926. She had, however, been given her place in history. (The R38 was a Short Brothers-built airship, which crashed at Hull in August 1921 killing forty-four out of a crew of forty-nine. More people had been killed in that than in the *Hindenburg* Disaster of 1937).

With the recession following the First World War, there were no further military contracts forthcoming so Beardmore exited the field. The Construction Station was closed. The massive company was also in trouble with reduced demand in all of its markets. It was forced to close in 1930 with part of its Dalmuir site becoming Royal Ordnance Factory Dalmuir.

G. & W. Weir of Cathcart and the Cierva Autogiro Company

Weir of Cathcart was and still is a famous name in Scottish engineering and its 1871 founders, George and James Weir, can be said to be two of Scotland's great entrepreneurs, inventing and developing pumps and equipment particularly for the great Clyde shipbuilding industry and surviving successfully today as the Weir Group, with its headquarters in Glasgow and operations in oil and gas, mining, minerals and power generation. It is one of Scotland's industrial success stories.

During the First World War, Weir's received contracts for the manufacture of aircraft and parts. These included the BE2 single seater biplane and the Airco DH9 bomber. These contracts gave them extensive experience which would be drawn on with the development of gyrocopters and helicopters.

Just as Scottish industrialists assisted Alfred Nobel in the development of Dynamite at Ardeer, so did James George Weir, son of James Galloway Weir, assist Juan de la Cierva develop his 'autogiro', invented by him in 1920. De la Cierva was a Spanish civil engineer and aeronautical engineer who moved to England in 1920 and with Weir's support started the Cierva Autogiro Company, under whose patents G. & J. Weir began to manufacture his aircraft in 1936. Cierva was killed in an air crash at Croydon Aerodrome the same year but Weir's carried on.

Production of a series of successful designs had begun in 1933 and by 1934 they had produced the Weir W2, a prototype for a production aircraft which they hoped would sell for around the same price as a family car at £355. However, the company decided at a late date to switch to helicopter production.

Developments in helicopters started in late 1937 with the first test flight of the Weir W-5 on 7 June 1938 in Dalrymple, Ayrshire. Designed by R. A. Pullin, it was flown by his son and was the first flight of a British-made helicopter.

It was followed by a two-seater machine in 1951. The Cierva Skeeter W14 was used by both the RAF and the Royal Navy. By the outbreak of the Second World War, Weir's had a major stake in Cierva but the war saw developments in other priority areas. Helicopter developments had to wait. In 1943, the virtually defunct Weir aircraft division became the Cierva Autogiro Company to develop helicopters for the Air Ministry, mostly at Eastleigh.

Cierva Air Horse.

They produced what was then the world's largest helicopter, the Cierva Air Horse. Tragically, the prototype crashed, killing Cierva's manager and test pilot Alan Marsh, the chief Ministry of Supply test pilot, as well as the flight engineer. The decision to abandon further investment in Cierva was taken and the existing contracts passed to Saunders Roe in 1951. Saunders Roe was to go on to become part of Westland Helicopters.

And for information, a Cierva Autogyro appears briefly in the hunt for Richard Hannay in the 1935 movie *The 39 Steps*.

Denny's Shipyard and the Blackburn Aircraft Company

While we are talking about wartime operations, we should also mention that the Blackburn Aircraft Company was in operation in Dumbarton. The company was established by Robert Blackburn in Yorkshire in 1914 and in 1937 he and Sir Maurice Denny of Denny's Shipyard cooperated in the building of a Dumbarton production site called Barge Park.

Aircraft manufactured here included the Blackburn B26 Botha, a reconnaissance and torpedo bomber which entered service with the RAF in 1939. While 580 aircraft were built, it was considered to be underpowered and was retired in 1944. It is said that it was actually used on the front line for only three months.

There was also the successful Short Brothers Sunderland flying boat, of which 739 were built, 240 in Dumbarton. It was to become the world's most famous flying boat. The Blackburn Shark B6 Reconnaissance biplane was also a product.

Following the war, the company was absorbed into Hawker Siddeley and the name disappeared completely in 1963. The Dumbarton factory closed in 1961.

Scottish Aviation

Scottish Aviation is the story of another entrepreneur, David F. McIntyre, who founded the company. Born in Govan in 1905, McIntyre was a quiet, inspired man with a love of aviation which encouraged him, along with the Duke of Hamilton, to become the first people to fly over Mount Everest as well as establish Prestwick Airport, Scottish Airlines and to build uniquely Scottish aircraft. David had served in the 602 'City of Glasgow' squadron of the RAF during the 1930s and had a hand in training RAF pilots through his Scottish Aviation Elementary Flying School. Scottish Aviation had been founded by him and the Duke of Hamilton.

With true entrepreneurial spirit, the purchase and rebuilding of the 1938 Empire Exhibition Palace of Engineering at Prestwick was a masterpiece. Here, during the war, 1,200 Spitfires were repaired and it was used for receiving and modifying aircraft arriving from America. Around 5,000 people were employed there during the war years.

Following the war, with the experience gained, they entered the world of aircraft manufacture with the Prestwick Pioneer, which was built to an Air Ministry specification but was not taken up by the RAF until a more powerful engine was fitted. As one of its roles would be in jungle areas such as Malaysia and Borneo, there was a requirement for a very short take-off aircraft. This was certainly achieved and demonstrated at a Farnborough air show when the Pioneer took off across the runway rather than along it!

Besides the RAF, Pioneers were supplied to the Royal Ceylon Air Force as well as the air forces of Oman and Malaysia. Squadrons of Pioneers were able to land and take off from airstrips only 180 metres long and were used to support anti-guerilla operations and evacuate casualties in jungle areas and in Aden in the 1950s and 1960s. The last Pioneers were used in Singapore before being withdrawn in 1969. The Royal Air Force Museum at Cosford has a survivor.

The concept of short-take off and landing, (STOL) had obviously been proved, for Scottish Aviation went on to develop the theme with the more powerful Twin Pioneer designed for both military and civilian use. The aircraft was a success with variants being sold throughout the world including to the RAF, which bought thirty-nine which were built in 1958 and 1959. The aircraft had a successful career as a commercial aircraft, particularly on rough airstrips, and for survey and oil exploration work.

Prestwick Aerodrome in the 1930s.

Following the collapse of the Handley Page Aircraft Company, Scottish Aviation undertook the building of the Jetstream Turboprop. Handley Page was the company which designed the Jetstream for the American 'feederliner' market but the development was too late to save the company, which was in financial trouble. The design was purchased by a consortium including Scottish Aviation in 1970 under the company name 'Jetstream Aircraft' and was to become a successful product, including the sale of twenty-six to the Royal Air Force, which used it for training pilots and observers.

The Scottish Aviation Bulldog was another production takeover, from the Beagle Aircraft Company which had gone into liquidation. First flying in 1969 but without any production aircraft ready, the company went bust. Again Scottish Aviation was to come to the rescue with a new company formed to produce the Bulldog, which was to go on to become a highly successful trainer, with the RAF purchasing 130 in 1972. There is an example in the National Museum of Flight at East Fortune.

In 1977, the Aircraft and Shipbuilding Act, a manifesto commitment of the Labour Party, effectively enforced the merger and nationalisation of a number of companies, one of which was Scottish Aviation, to form British Aerospace and British Shipbuilders. The Jetstream continued to be produced by British Aerospace after its takeover of Scottish Aviation. British Aerospace was to go on and purchase a number

The Twin Pioneer.

of companies to form BAE Systems, still very active today on the Clyde as a builder of warships.

Building of the Jetstream was maintained by BAE at Prestwick until 1998, when it was moved to England. BAE Systems Regional Aircraft still has a base at Prestwick and is presently involved in the maintenance and conversion of aircraft. Also at Prestwick is Spirit AeroSystems, which took over much of the manufacturing site in 2006. With 900 employees it is one of the biggest employers in the area and continues to produce major aviation components for Airbus and for Boeing.

So while complete aircraft are not manufactured, the spirit of David McIntyre lives on in some of the world's largest aircraft. Group Captain David Fowler McIntyre AFC was tragically killed on 7 December 1957 when his Twin Pioneer crashed in the Libyan desert. The pilot and flight engineer were also killed. He is remembered as one of Scotland's most important aviation pioneers.

Rolls-Royce of Hillington

Before we leave aviation we should mention another of Scotland's success stories, Rolls-Royce, which started producing aircraft engines in 1940 in Hillington and making a huge contribution to the war effort in the process. The Hillington plant in Glasgow was producing 400 Merlin aero engines a week by 1943, many of them destined for Spitfires and Hurricanes. In one month production reached 1,650 and overall during the war years they produced 23,600 engines, which was 14 per cent of worldwide output, an astonishing statistic.

The Merlin engine was an icon of British design and engineering and made a major contribution to the war effort. The Merlin's, originally the PV-13, first production version was in 1936 although it first ran in 1933. It was originally used in the Supermarine Spitfire, the Fairey Battle and the Hawker Hurricane. While it also powered the Avro Lancaster it was in the Spitfire that it made its name, first flying in 1936. Its early use helped its development up to the war when it proved its reliability.

Rolls-Royce Hillington had 16,000 employees and by the end of the war was one of Scotland's largest factories. Following the war, the factory continued in operation at Hillington refurbishing aero engines until its move to Inchinnan in 2005. The East Kilbride plant, which has also repaired aero engines for fifty-nine years, will close and its workforce will move to Inchinnan in 2015. At Inchinnan it presently employs 1,000 people in four plants making compressor blades and other components for a range of engines.

Merlin production at Rolls-Royce Hillington, 1942.

Landing of the R 34 at Mineola, Long Island, New York State, 1919.

Short Sunderland.

A Twin Pioneer of Borneo Airways making a test flight from Prestwick in 1960.

Scottish Aviation Jetstream.

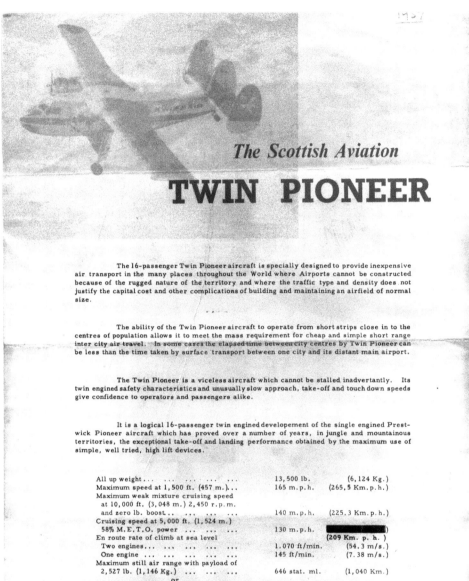

The Scottish Aviation
TWIN PIONEER

The 16-passenger Twin Pioneer aircraft is specially designed to provide inexpensive air transport in the many places throughout the World where Airports cannot be constructed because of the rugged nature of the territory and where the traffic type and density does not justify the capital cost and other complications of building and maintaining an airfield of normal size.

The ability of the Twin Pioneer aircraft to operate from short strips close in to the centres of population allows it to meet the mass requirement for cheap and simple short range inter city air travel. In some cases the elapsed time between city centres by Twin Pioneer can be less than the time taken by surface transport between one city and its distant main airport.

The Twin Pioneer is a viceless aircraft which cannot be stalled inadvertantly. Its twin engined safety characteristics and unusually slow approach, take-off and touch down speeds give confidence to operators and passengers alike.

It is a logical 16-passenger twin engined developement of the single engined Prestwick Pioneer aircraft which has proved over a number of years, in jungle and mountainous territories, the exceptional take-off and landing performance obtained by the maximum use of simple, well tried, high lift devices.

All up weight...	13,500 lb.	(6,124 Kg.)
Maximum speed at 1,500 ft. (457 m.)...	165 m.p.h.	(265.5 Km.p.h.)
Maximum weak mixture cruising speed at 10,000 ft. (3,048 m.) 2,450 r.p.m. and zero lb. boost..	140 m.p.h.	(225.3 Km.p.h.)
Cruising speed at 5,000 ft. (1,524 m.) 58% M.E.T.O. power	130 m.p.h.	(209 Km. p. h.)
En route rate of climb at sea level		
Two engines...	1,070 ft/min.	(54.3 m/s.)
One engine	145 ft/min.	(7.38 m/s.)
Maximum still air range with payload of 2,527 lb. (1,146 Kg.)	646 stat. ml.	(1,040 Km.)
or		
With long range fuel tanks and a payload of 2,045 lb. (928 Kg.)	916 stat. ml.	(1,474 Km.)
Ground run (zero wind) Landing... ...	135 yds.	(123.4 m.)
Take-off.. ...	132 yds.	(120.7 m.)
Take-off distance to 35 ft. (10.7 m.)...	265 yds.	(242.3 m.)

SCOTTISH   AVIATION   LTD   PRESTWICK   AIRPORT   SCOTLAND

Publicity material for the Twin Pioneer, produced by Scottish Aviation in 1957.

The Scottish Brick and Fireclay Industry

If any single object can be used to trace the history of the Industrial Revolution, it is the common or garden Scottish brick. While they may have become generally uniform in size, in fact they were not always so common. Bricks became quite unique as they were identifiable through the imprinting of the brickwork name in the indented area (or frog) of the brick.

This feature has made them strangely collectible. Besides Darngavil, my collection included Blantyre, Walkinshaw and Garscube, Hurlford and Nitshill. Sadly, my collection is now limited to eight bricks holding up a shelf of plants on our balcony. The larger portion was left behind holding up water butts and barbecues or in the paths of former Meighan residences. You can see a fantastic selection at Summerlee Heritage Park in Coatbridge, 'Scotland's Noisiest Museum'.

In 1869, David Bremner's *The Industries of Scotland* recorded:

> There are in Scotland 122 manufactories of brick, tiles, and articles of a similar nature; and in connection with these from 4,000 to 5,000 persons are employed. The manufactories are widely scattered over the country, the farthest north being at Banff and the farthest south at Dalbeattie; but the greater number are in Lanarkshire and Fifeshire.

The Brick, Tile and Fireclay Industries in Scotland, a 1993 publication by the Royal Commission on the Ancient and Historical Monuments of Scotland, records over one hundred brickworks operating in the late 1940s. Most of these were situated in the central belt with the heaviest concentration still in North Lanarkshire.

Many of the surviving works benefited from the house-building programmes following the end of the Second World War. By the end of the 1980s, however, through the lack of demand and high fuel prices, this figure had dropped to only

Traditional brick.

twenty works operating in Scotland. Closures were mitigated by the housing boom of the 1980s but the industry continued to contract, speeded by the growth of the use of concrete blocks, as well as rationalisation. By 2011, there were only five brickworks in operation in Scotland, including Caradale Traditional Brick at the Etna works in Armadale, as shown below.

House building is still the main customer for bricks and the industry in Scotland continues to be subject to fluctuations in the building market as well as tastes. Harled buildings don't need bricks and their use in building has continued to contract. The few remaining brickworks in Scotland produce mainly common bricks although 'heritage' bricks are produced for new 'traditional' buildings and for conservation. The mechanical processes are generally the same although improved processes have speeded up the system. Today's bricks may be very nice looking but I think that I prefer the quirkiness of those solid, named bricks of a bygone age.

The making of the common building brick was closely associated with coal mining and brickwork kilns were often found beside mines. As with brickworks, there are few mines left. My own memories are of playing in and around Dodds brickworks on the Royston Road in Glasgow. Here there was a clay pit beside the works from where the clay was dug and carried on barrows to the works. In the 1950s, little had obviously changed here from the first brickworks, which were manual operations in which clay was forced into moulds by hand, turned out and placed on flat barrows to be wheeled into kilns where they would be fired until ready.

Caradale Traditional Brick, Etna Works, Armadale.

The provision of both clay from the coal mine and heat from coal was a happy coincidence and resulted in the heaviest concentrations of brickworks around collieries. Nowadays, the kilning of bricks is done using gas.

Hand moulding was the first process and this was described by David Bremner:

All the bricks are hand-moulded, which is a very simple process, and is executed with wonderful rapidity. An expert moulder, with the necessary assistants to keep him supplied with clay, and to remove the moulds as they are filled, will make from 4,000 to 5,000 bricks a day. The moulder works at a table, on one end of which is a supply of clay, the other being left clear for his operations. The bricks are formed in a deal framework, resembling a small box with the top and bottom removed. A boy dips the mould in water and lays it on the table. The moulder, taking up a lump of clay, dashes it into the mould, presses it with his hands, and then removes the superfluous clay by drawing a piece of wood over the mould. His assistant, who has meantime laid down an empty mould, snatches up the full one and deposits the newly formed brick on the floor of the workshop. Thus the work goes on until the floor is covered.

With the need for improved efficiency, the use of hand moulds died out and simple extrusion machines came in. In this process the clay was pushed through a die and then wire-cut to size. The first of these was introduced in 1888 by John G. Stein at his Bonnybridge works. Stein was one of the two great men of brick production whose products were to contribute to the making of an industrial Scotland.

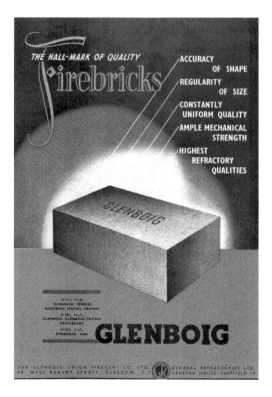

Glenboig firebrick advert.

A very special brick – Fireclay and Firebricks

As you pass on the rail line from Edinburgh to Glasgow, you may not know that near Polmont was another railway station or that Manuel Station was from where firebricks left the biggest firebrick works in the British Empire to be distributed throughout the globe.

It is probably true that the Industrial Revolution may not have advanced as quickly as it did without fire clay and the firebrick. The first industrial furnaces used sandstone or Welsh and English firebrick but there was a growing need for materials capable of withstanding high temperatures. The firebrick was the solution and is an essential component of blast furnaces, ovens and refractories as it can withstand temperatures up to 1,600 C. Fireclay was also used in the manufacture of crucibles and retorts.

The first extraction of fireclay in Scotland was very local, with possibly only one kiln or 'clamp'. With the introduction of Neilson's hot blast furnaces the industry began to take off. This and other processes needing high temperatures required a growing supply of refractory materials, as they are called, mainly firebricks.

Perhaps the man most associated with fireclay was John Gilchrist Stein, whose Stein Refractories went on to become the largest producer of firebricks in the British Empire.

John quit his first job as an apprentice at Winchburgh Brickworks when bosses refused to give the 20-year-old Stein his father's job as works manager – and was sacked from his second post at a rival brick works after a row over royalty payments.

But when Stein parted company with Cumbernauld Pipe Works, it was not as a bitter young man. Rather, it was as an ambitious individual determined to go one better than his former employer, James Dunnachie, who owned Glenboig Union Fireclay Company Limited and Cumbernauld Pipe Works. He was to become the owner of one of the largest brick making concerns in Scotland.

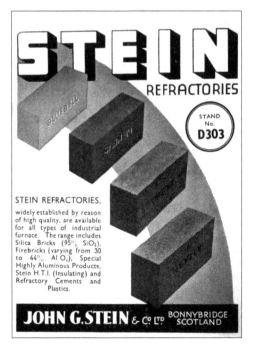

Stein refractory bricks.

Stein leased two acres of clay fields at Milnquarter, Bonnybridge, in 1887. He mined open cast clay and sold it to the steel industry. At the same time he started work on his first brick kiln which, in 1888, was capable of producing 5,000 hand-made bricks in a firing.

Stein continued to develop the business, opening the Anchor Works at Dunipace and installing a brickmaking machine at the Castlecary Works in 1899, and the Manuel Works at Whitecross in 1928. In 1932, 1,000,000 bricks were being produced every week. Milnquarter closed in the 1960s and Steins was taken over in 1971. The company continued to produce but closed its door in 2001. That huge area is now being re-developed as an environmental village.

Stein was interested in the welfare of his ever increasing workforce and built them houses to live in and a football pitch and bowling green to play on when they were not working. He also ordered and paid for a hall his workers used as a canteen and recreation room.

Stein had become the foremost brick manufacturer in Scotland when tragedy struck. In 1927, while inspecting the Castlecary works, he tripped over a brick and grazed his shin. The wound turned septic and his leg was amputated, but it was not enough to save his life, the industry losing an eminent figure overnight; his death signaled the end of an era.

Another large producer was Garnkirk Fire-Clay Company, six miles east of Glasgow. The company originally set out to mine coal but the existence of high quality fireclay prompted them to concentrate on that. This clay was considered to be as good as the English clay from Stourbridge. The principal seam was seven feet thick and at a depth of 50 metres:

Raw material is brought in, and finished goods are sent out by branch railways. 300 men and boys are employed, and 200 tons of clay and about an equal weight of coal are used daily. The clay is of a dark colour, owing to the presence of a small proportion of bituminous matter; but when that is dispelled by the action of fire, only silica and alumina remain, and it is the presence of these substances in certain proportions that decides the value of the clay. As it comes from the pits the clay is entirely devoid of cohesion or plasticity; and in order to bring it into working condition, it has to be ground very fine, and then mixed with water. Several powerful mills are used for this purpose. They consist of great iron rollers, which travel round a circular trough, and pass over the clay.

Fireclays occur under most coal seams and as such generally have to be mined rather than quarried. Fireclays are made up of kaolinite, illite and quartz. While most common bricks have a reddish tinge, firebricks generally have a cream appearance as they contain less iron. They generally also have a finer, smooth surface and feel and look 'harder'.

The Glenboig Union Fireclay Co. Ltd, which owned the Old Works and Star Works in Glenboig, was founded by James Dunnachie & Partners. The company specialised in the production of refractory ware, including furnace lining bricks and pipework for the iron and steel industry. They expanded through acquisition of other works between 1882 and 1919. These included the Cumbernauld Fireclay Works, Gartcosh

Works, Castlecary Fireclay Company, Faskine, Palacecraig Bricks, Coal Ltd and the Bonnymuir and Dykehed Works

Dunnachie's invention of a gas kiln for firing bricks was to promote his company's position in the brick world as they produced higher temperatures than before and gave considerable savings in fuel.

The workings of a clay mine can be seen at Birkhill Station, where the mine has been preserved at the terminus of the Bo'ness & Kinneil Railway. The mine was established by P. & M. Hurll Ltd of Glenboig, with production at its highest in 1952. Along with other clay mines it went into decline and the company went into liquidation in 1982. In 1987, it was opened by Falkirk Council as a tourist attraction. Within the mine you can see the 'stoop and room' method of mining in which columns of clay were left to support the roof. On the roof you can see the imprint of ancient riverbeds.

Birkhill Clay Mine Top Workings.

P. & M. Hurll Ltd – Urgent Ground Fireclay!
For Colville's Garnkirk Steelworks.

Piles of Carpets from Scotland

When I was a little boy living in Anderston in Glasgow I was, like many other young lads, a stamp collector, but with a little advantage for just up the road from me was Greig's Wool Warehouse and I would stop regularly at the huge roller door to look into the building where would be stacked huge bales of wool. I can still remember the oily and musty smell of the grey-looking material packed in jute and would look at the work going on in the building which had previously been a stable and still had the ramps and walkways up to the multi-storey stalls.

But the greatest attraction was the metal bin regularly placed at the front door. For within the bin were piles of old envelopes and, more importantly, foreign stamps, mostly from India and Pakistan, all to go into my stamp album. I must admit that my album had a bit more emphasis on the Indian Subcontinent. I was to learn much later about the connection between Greig's and Bridgeton in Glasgow. For Bridgeton was where my grannie lived and with my father and brother we would regularly walk past the great Templeton's Carpet Factory, explained to me as being modelled on the Doge's Palace in Venice. What I did not know then was that Greig's was a supplier of wool from both home and abroad to the carpet industry in Scotland. The demise of the carpet industry just as much affected other industries and the livelihoods of workers in those industries, including the sheep farmers, wool importers, jute manufacturers who supplied backings for carpets and the machinery supply industry.

A. F. Craig, Paisley, supplier of carpet-making machinery.

One of the reasons for writing this book is to explain how it once was walking through a city street in the industrialised towns in Scotland. On all sides of the street would be working factories, foundries, warehouses, commercial offices, stables, carters and, of course, public houses providing refreshments for the workers who would stream out of these mills and factories at the end of the working day.

And Templeton's was a prime example, based in Bridgeton with a dedicated station next to its Glasgow Green factory. Templeton's on the Green was not the only, but because of its situation and architecture, is probably the best remembered and loved of Scotland's great carpet factories. But there were others, some of them even bigger.

The carpet industry seems to have flourished in Ayrshire, which was already well know for the manufacture of 'Scotch' or 'Kidder' carpets produced on hand looms. These reversible carpets were flat woven and double cloth rather than made with pile and mostly sold to a Continental market. They were also made in Stirling, the Borders, Glasgow and Edinburgh.

The Ayrshire weavers quickly adopted to power looms when they were introduced and Kilmarnock became a respected centre for carpet manufacture, moving on to pile carpets of a high quality. The leading firm at that time was Gregory Thomson & Co. of Green Street.

BMK is a familiar brand, as is the little gamboling lamb which features in its advertising. What is rarely known outside the town famous for Johnnie Walker and locomotives is that BMK was a Kilmarnock company. BMK, otherwise Blackwood & Morton, Kilmarnock, was based in West Shaw Street in Kilmarnock, with its factory in Burnside Street and at other sites in the town.

The Blackwood family were wool, cotton and worsted spinners. One Blackwood brother set up a carpet factory at the Townhead Mills and produced carpets until 1909. Robert Blackwood & Sons was set up by Robert and taken over on his retirement by

BMK Kilmarnock.

his son William Ford Blackwood in 1900. In 1908, it combined with Gavin Morton to form Blackwood & Morton and became the largest carpet manufacturer in Kilmarnock. The company was soon producing army blankets during the First World War and by 1918 was producing Chenille (tufted) Axminster carpets.

With the coming of the Second World War they were prevented by war restrictions from making carpets but contributed to the war effort by manufacturing a range of products including blankets, shells and radio equipment. Following the war they were back in production and by 1974 were employing around 3,500 people producing Axminster, Wilton, tufted carpets and underfelt.

The company found itself in financial difficulties in 1981 and went into liquidation. It was subsequently bought by Stoddard Carpets and the factory closed. Hansard reported Kilmarnock's MP William McKelvey complaining in October of that year about the loss of manufacturing jobs in his constituency:

> In recent years the carpet industry has been in decline, mainly because of the massive influx of imports from North America and from the Continent. The North American carpets are most certainly subsidised and are being brought into this country and sold at a rate cheaper than that at which carpets can be manufactured here. They are being sold to the detriment of our carpet industry. Thousands of jobs have been lost ...

> ... In January and February this year, the figures showed an increase in imports of American carpets of 40 per cent and an incredible jump in Belgian imports of 96 per cent. The cost, of course, has been borne by our industries here, and in particular BMK in Kilmarnock, which is now in the hands of the receiver, who is desperately trying to find a buyer for a firm which had shown a loss in the previous six months of over £1.3 million.

But the good news, maybe not for Scottish manufacturing, is that the BMK brand is up and running again. It was relaunched in 2007 and it was such a well-known brand that possibly not many people knew it had gone. The company is now based in Leeds but I am glad to say that it has Royal Highland as one of its ranges.

There can hardly be a Glaswegian who doesn't know about Templeton's carpet factory, which has a rich history. James Templeton, its founder, was a Highlander from Campbeltown in Argyll, who with many thousands of his ilk left the poverty of the Highlands to find fame and fortune in Glasgow.

By the time he was twenty-seven James had set up a business in Paisley making shawls and with William Quiglay worked on a patent for the manufacture of woven soft pile chenille carpets. Buying out Quiglay, he was joined by brothers in-law and moved to King Street in the Bridgeton area of Glasgow to expand his business. Production started in 1839 and by 1851 the company was employing 400 people. By the start of the First World War it was reputed to be the biggest carpet manufacturer in the United Kingdom.

Templeton & Co. exhibited at the Great Exhibition of 1851 and the carpets on display were considered to be some of Great Britain's finest at a time when French carpet designs were seen to dominate all others. The designers used by Templeton is a list of famous names through the years, including Charles Rennie Mackintosh and Mary Quant.

Templeton's success can be attributed to his innovation. He introduced seamless carpeting and continued with what is sometimes considered a modern management technique – that of continually looking for improved methods and lowering cost of production. Templeton's achieved worldwide fame. When you see photographs and film of United States Presidents in the White House, they may be standing on Templeton carpets. In fact, Mary Lincoln, wife of the assassinated president, had been criticised for her profligacy in 1861, for buying an expensive Templeton carpet.

Templeton's on the Green is as Glasgow as its near neighbor, the People's Palace. It is said that the nearby residents in what was then a very desirable area objected to Templeton's building plans for a new factory a number of times so he was forced to come up with a dramatic design that would guarantee acceptance. He recruited architect William Leiper, who emulated the Doge's Palace in Venice to produce what must be one of the most unusual industrial buildings in Europe. Leiper is also known for Glasgow's Gothic Dowanhill Church, now home of the Cottier Theatre. The design of the factory also guaranteed its listing and survival as a business centre. Its opening in 1889 was tinged with sadness, as soon after a freak gust of wind combined with alleged bad building work caused a partial collapse of the main façade, killing twenty-nine workers. It was rebuilt and re-opened in 1891.

It is well worth a visit, as is the People's Palace and the restored Doulton Fountain. A stone in Glasgow Green also commemorates the place where James Watt was said to have come up with his ideas for a condenser for the steam engine, so starting the age of steam and allowing the power loom to produce carpets at Templeton's.

At the end of the 1960s, the Guthrie Corporation, a rubber plantation owner, was looking for a foothold in the British flooring market. They succeeded with a takeover of Templeton's in 1969. Guthrie's was ambitious and in 1980 they acquired a £1.5 million stake in Stoddards. It subsequently closed down the Templeton factory and transferred production to Elderslie.

William C. Gray of the Newton Carpet Works in Ayr had been another successful carpet manufacturer, making chenille Axminster rugs as well as traditional Scotch carpets.

In 1968 the *Glasgow Herald* reported on the takeover of Gray's by Templeton's. At that time both companies were profitable and Templeton's had just announced a £1 million extension to its Crown Street factory. Gray's continued to trade until 1971 when it succumbed to the difficulties in the carpet trade.

One company certainly understood the benefits of French design and that was Henry Widnell & Stewart of Bonnyrigg, who employed a famous French designer and artist, Pierre Langlade, during the latter part of the nineteenth century.

Widnells had its origins in the Lothians with a patent taken out by Richard Whytock for a tapestry carpet loom in 1833. With his partner Henry Henderson he began producing Persian and Turkish style carpets in Lasswade, becoming patent carpet manufacturer to the Queen. Whytock left the partnership to do other things. Henderson was joined by Henry Widnell to continue the business as Henderson & Widnell.

Henry Widnel & Stewart's carpet factory, Roslin Glen.

They must surely have been close to Templeton's when they exhibited at the Great Exhibition in 1851 where they won a gold medal for the quality of their carpets. Although there were some financial difficulties the company overcame these and expanded to a new site at the Bleachworks in Roslin Glen, just along from the gunpowder factory and below the famous Rosslyn Chapel.

Around 1873, George Stewart joined the equation, with the company becoming Henry Widnell & Stewart Ltd. It seems to have managed quite well for a long time but in the 1950s it was taken over by A. F. Stoddard of Elderslie, although it traded under its own name until 1983, when it closed its doors along with Stoddard's and Templeton.

Which takes us to Stoddard's, whom you can already see had a very important part to play in the history of Scottish carpets. Unusually, the originator of Stoddard's was not from the United Kingdom. Alfred Stoddard was an American silk merchant who arrived here in 1862, taking over the collapsed firm of J. & R. Ronald of Elderslie. With his contacts in the United States, Stoddard's was to become a huge enterprise supplying the home market, the New World and the Empire. They supplied the carpets for the wedding of HRH Princess Elizabeth in 1947. They had previously made carpets for the RMS *Titanic* and were called upon to replicate these for James Cameron's filming of the disaster in *Titanic*.

The carpet and other Scottish industries had been doing very well with exports to the Commonwealth, but after many years of accepting British goods the Empire was fighting back and the effects were to show that many British companies had taken their established markets for granted. By the end of the 1940s, Australia was a substantial market for all carpet manufacturers and Stoddard alone was sending 48 per cent of its product there, bolstered by the publicity from the Royal Wedding. However, the Australian Government, in order to balance its own books, imposed import tariffs on a range of products including textiles. This was to have a dramatic effect on the industry, resulting in questions in the House from those MPs representing the constituencies affected.

In fact, while the Government said that they had made representations to the Australian Government, the view seemed to be that the Australians had every right to balance their own books and we should not be interfering.

This was a tough time for the carpet industry but it was to get even worse. Entry to the European Common Market was just around the corner and it was likely that the competition from Europe would intensify. Stoddard's prepared for this eventuality by expansion, in 1959 taking over Henry Widnell & Stewart and building a new mill to increase its capacity in tufted carpet and operating it as Glenvale Carpets Ltd. It carried on in this way, acquiring other smaller carpet manufacturers in the 1960s.

They also saw the need to counter competition by buying into Europe through a joint venture with Dutch Bergoss Gerbre van der Bergh Koninklijke Fabrieken. A new tufted carpet mill built by them started manufacturing in 1962.

In the 1960s, the textile industry was Britain's largest employer with 1.5 million alone working in carpet manufacture. However, the industry was in decline. Stoddard was not able to expand its markets. Foreign subsidies and import tariffs were again in the way. Outsourcing of manufacturing processes by foreign competition to low wage economies was making the company uncompetitive. The introduction of synthetic materials for carpeting was also making life difficult for companies producing traditional carpets.

Stoddard's were forced to cut back on their European ventures and restructure. They tried diversification into mainstream textiles with disastrous results, having bought an overvalued company which they resold at a loss.

In many cases I have found that when an industry is under threat, the threatened companies merge to salvage something from the ruins. Stoddard merged with Templeton's, which had already been taken over by Guthrie's, and Kingsmead Carpets. But it was trends and not just competition which finally did for Stoddard's. Having fought off competition and barriers to trade, they were facing changing fashions away from carpets towards tiles, wooden and vinyl floors. The company restructured, with one base in Kilmarnock. However, debt was increasing and in 2005, with sales dropping and debt mounting to £9 million, the receivers were called in and the carpet industry in Scotland was at an end.

I am glad to say that while the industry may be gone, the history has not. With a grant from the National Heritage Memorial Fund, the University of Glasgow, the Glasgow School of Art and Glasgow Museums have jointly bought the archives of Stoddard International, which include the papers, designs and carpets of Stoddard's and James Templeton & Co. and other companies which had previously been absorbed.

I am glad to say that there are some remnants of this one great industry. Bonar Yarns of Dundee, part of Low & Bonar, continue to manufacture carpet yarns at their Caldrum Works. Low & Bonar is another of Scotland's industrial success stories, producing technical textiles.

THE NEW BUILDING WHICH FELL, KILLING NEARLY THIRTY PERSONS.

THE WEAVING-SHED, WHERE THE BODIES OF THOSE KILLED WERE FOUND

FALL OF MESSRS. J. AND J. TEMPLETON'S CARPET FACTORY, GREENHEAD, GLASGOW.

The aftermath of the collapse of the façade of Templeton's factory, as described in *The Illustrated London News*, 1889.

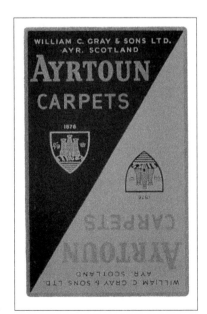

William Gray's Ayrtoun Carpets.

Heat and Light from the Ground – Coal Gas Manufacture

One of my most abiding memories of Glasgow in the 1950s is one in which the city is immersed in a dark 'peasouper' smog, with the only light coming from the dim gas lamps at the side of the road. This picture is thankfully long gone.

My first memory of coal gas was the acrid smell, which was recognisable anywhere in Great Britain. From its original discovery as an illuminant and for heating and cooking, it was only a few years before gasworks with their recognisable gasometers were evident in towns large and small throughout Scotland.

In the tenement flat where I was brought up in Anderston, Glasgow, we had a gas cooker and primitive electricity in our homes but gas lights on the stair landings. Glasgow Corporation employed 'leeries', whose job it was to both turn on the street lights and the stair lights using a pole with a lamp and a slotted key at the top end. They would open the gas tap with the key and light the gas with the lamp.

> My tea is nearly ready and the sun has left the sky;
> It's time to take the window to see Leerie going by;
> For every night at teatime and before you take your seat,
> With lantern and with ladder he comes posting up the street.

> Robert Louis Stevenson

There is debate about who exactly 'discovered' coal gas. It was probably known about as a natural phenomenon when coal was burning. The inventor of gas as an illuminant is acknowledged as another Scots inventor called Archibald Cochrane, Lord Dundonald, who illuminated Culross Abbey in 1787. He was most famous for the distillation of tar and did not take a great deal of interest in coal gas, a by-product of his tar production.

The person who championed its use was William Murdoch, who was born in 1754 in Lugar, near Cumnock, in Ayrshire. Around 1774, he was experimenting with the production of coal gas using a kettle as a retort to heat coal. He was the man who, in 1797, showed his system by lighting the workshops of Boulton & Watt, his employers (Watt being the Scottish inventor instrumental in improvements to the steam engine which kick-started the Industrial Revolution). This trial was successful and was extended to other factories in the area. His own house in Redruth was the first domestic residence to be lit by coal gas.

William Murdoch was a prodigious inventor. Besides identifying the practical uses of coal gas and making improvements to Boulton & Watt's steam engines, he produced Britain's first working model of the steam carriage. He invented 'iron cement', a compound used in the joints of steam engines. He invented a synthetic isinglass, a substance used to clarify beer in the brewing process. His most famous other invention was the sun and planet gear that converted the vertical motion of a beam into a circular motion. This was hugely important in the development of the steam engine and other rotary machines.

The memorial plaque to William Murdoch, on his house in Redruth, Cornwall.

The London Gas Light & Coke Company was the world's first public gas company. It was set up to provide gas for street lighting and domestic heating in 1812. In a very short period of time gasworks were common in most large towns and often as appendages to coal mines, where their primary purpose was to produce coke with coal gas as a bye-product. The first public supply in Scotland was in Glasgow in 1817.

Coal or 'town' gas was a product of 'gasification' in which coal was heated in retorts, basically big kettles. The resultant mixed gas of methane, hydrogen, carbon dioxide and carbon monoxide was piped to the customer. Belying the cosy domestic image below, the industry was a dirty, smelly and dangerous one. Coal gas was inherently dangerous, prone to explosion, and many people were accidentally gassed or used it for committing suicide as it was extremely efficient in that capacity.

But it wasn't only gasworks that produced coal gas. In many cases, the gas was a co-product of coking plants, coke being the product which was left over after the coal was heated and released its gases. Coke was a major raw material in smelting iron and is still used as such and as a fuel, mainly in industrial boilers and for steelmaking. Other by-products of the process were used in the production of nylon, dyes, antiseptics, fertilizers and benzol for motor fuel. This last and many of the by-products were important in sustaining Great Britain during the Second World War.

It was the discovery of natural gas which put an end to this very local industry and started the process of establishing a national grid, similar to that operated by the electricity companies. From the early days of the 1900s gasworks were generally operated by local councils, although there were some small private companies.

With the end of the Second World War and the introduction of Clement Attlee's Labour Government, many industries were nationalised, among them the coal gas

Riveters working on a gasometer using John Turnbull, Glasgow, hammers.

Arrol-Foulis hydraulic coke pusher from Dalmarnock Iron Works.

industry. 1,062 council and private gas companies were absorbed into Area Gas Boards, one of them covering Scotland. Each of these was further divided into divisions. There are many people to this day who still refer to the 'Gas Board' when they mean British Gas, which was the name given to the organisation when it was privatised by Margaret Thatcher's Conservative government in 1986.

The beginning of the end of the local gasworks was in 1959, when the British Gas Council showed that liquefied natural gas (LNG) could be imported safely when the *Methane Pioneer* docked at Canvey Island on the Thames with a cargo of LNG from the Gulf of Mexico. The success of the scheme in the local area, and with a pipeline to Leeds, showed that coal gas had competition.

Then, in September 1965, our very own natural gas was discovered around 3,000 metres below the seabed and forty miles from Grimsby. This was the first of many gas discoveries which signaled the end for local gas and coking plants. By the mid-1970s appliances in every house in Britain had been converted to run the new gas, which was clean and odourless to the extent that an artificial smell had to be injected so that people would know when a gas tap had been left on. While the term is only a memory, we first of all called this North Sea Gas.

It was also the first of the North Sea oil disasters. The barge which discovered the oil, the *Sea Gem*, collapsed two months after the discovery, on 27 December 1965, killing thirteen people. The enquiry after this disaster was instrumental in ensuring that oil and gas rigs had stand-by boats and Offshore Installation Managers (OIM), practices that are still in place today.

Conversion to natural gas was a massive investment and a huge project, including the decommissioning of redundant plant and the laying of thousands of miles

Man and Andrew Barclay (Kilmarnock) fireless locomotive at Provan Gas Works.

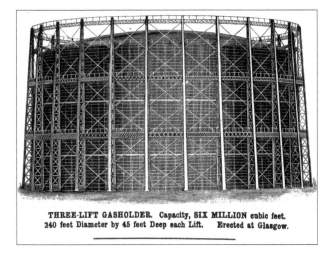

THREE-LIFT GASHOLDER. Capacity, SIX MILLION cubic feet.
240 feet Diameter by 45 feet Deep each Lift.   Erected at Glasgow.

The Secret of Fireside Comfort.

Above left: George Orme & Co. gasometer.

Above right: The secret of fireside comfort.

of pipeline. I particularly remember at night, the spectacle in the silent streets of Glasgow when the old gas was burnt off in huge fiery plumes through the manholes to allow the new gas to flow.

You can hardly call them remnants of this national industry, as some of the larger gasometers have been retained as storage for natural gas. These can still be seen in such sites as Dawsholm and Provan in Glasgow and Granton in Edinburgh. The retorts are gone, as is the smell. However, you can still get a whiff of how town gas was made at the wonderful Biggar Gas Museum operated by the Biggar Museum Trust.

> For we are very lucky, with a lamp before the door,
> And Leerie stops to light it as he lights so many more;
> And O! before you hurry by with ladder and with light;
> O Leerie, see a little child and nod to him to-night!

> Robert Louis Stevenson

A Blast from the Past – Explosives and Munitions in Scotland

On 21 March 1982, with a spectacle comparable to the famous Edinburgh festival fireworks, the end of the manufacturing of explosives in Scotland was signalled with an enormous explosion that lit up the Edinburgh sky. Luckily, no-one was hurt in this mysterious blast in a municipal dump. Investigations showed that the explosion was not the responsibility of an Edinburgh resident dumping dangerous materials but the buried remains of explosives left by the previous owners of the site, Hammond's Fireworks.

On clearing the site in 1970, a range of explosive and dangerous materials was discovered. Rather than move them through Edinburgh for disposal at sea, the decision was taken to bury the eight tonnes of materials in a concrete bunker. Following this, the site was used as a dump with waste materials being deposited on top of the layer of hardcore above the bunker. There are a number of theories about how it happened but the most likely seems to be the combination of hydrogen and methane exploding and causing a chain reaction, exploding the buried chemicals.

While Hammond's does not seem to have been a major producer, it did last for over 100 years and outlived other producers, some of them manufacturers of explosives for more serious purposes. Thomas Hammond had an interesting history. From Birmingham he moved to Edinburgh, where he set himself up as a fireworks manufacturer and pyrotechnic artist. He is recorded as having put on one show at the Royal Zoological Gardens. Unfortunately, his workshop in Chessel's Court, off the High Street, was the scene of a devastating fire in 1867 when two barrels of gunpowder ignited, causing a fire in which seven people died and ten were injured. Hammond was later to move to Powderhall and then finally to the site at Craigmillar. Following the death of Thomas Hammond, the company continued under his youngest daughter, Violet, but ceased trading with her death.

The manufacture of explosives is yet another industry that had wide geographic beginnings but which, over a period of time, died out with other industries or disappeared through merger and acquisition. Hammond's appears to have been a family company which reduced in the face of competition from larger producers and the hiatus of the Second World War. There is no record of the production of military explosives although it is likely that there was and the production of marine flares has been mentioned. Hammond's made traditional fireworks and the names would change in line with current topics. They obviously adopted futuristic ones with the Atom Bomb and the Atom Crasher. As a lad I used to buy little plastic bombs in which was placed a pistol cap. This would be thrown into the air and, as it had a weight in the nose cone, would come down to explode when it hit the ground. What fun. I wonder if that was an Atom Crasher?

Hammond's Atom Crusher.

Stobbsmills, Gorebridge, workers cottages *c.* 1916.

Black powder, and the similar gunpowder, has a long history in Scotland and was made in many areas. If you have the production of cannons, and Scotland was a major producer, then it would be safe to assume the production of gunpowder, particularly as it was simple, if dangerous.

Gunpowder is a mixture of charcoal, sulphur, and saltpetre (potassium nitrate). These would be milled together while damp into a powder graded according to its use. The milling process was particularly suited to Scottish conditions, where there was an abundance of water for milling as well as a damp atmosphere suitable for the process.

The first recorded gunpowder mill in Scotland was the Stobsmill, dating from 1793 on the Gore Water, Gorebridge, Midlothian. This was started by William Hitchener, John Hunter and John Merricks. The three partners had previously had turned down an application for a gunpowder mill in Surrey and turned their attention to Scotland, for unknown reasons.

This was a largish enterprise of ten wheels to power the mills and at one time employed sixty men. The mill provided blasting power for quarrying and mining as well as for sale to the Government during the Napoleonic wars and there is a record of the sale of 100 barrels of gunpowder at Liverpool in 1802. It was also, apparently, the first mill to supply blasting powder for mining. It seems therefore that these three men were entrepreneurs who could foresee the need for explosives for both military and industrial purposes.

It was an extremely dangerous occupation and two men (and a horse) were known to have died there in an explosion in February 1825, three more in September in 1827. The mill closed in 1861 and mostly fell into ruins, some of which can still be seen.

In 1804, John Merricks had left the consortium to set up his own business in partnership with John Hay in Roslin Glen – Hay Merricks & Co. In 1820, nephews of John Merricks joined the company and eventually became partners. The Roslin

Nobel Explosives' Roslin Factory.

gunpowder mill became a limited company and was taken over by Curtis's and Harvey's in 1898. The mill was a very similar set up and was to eventually have a long life, being taken over by Nobel Explosives but closed in 1954. During both wars the mills made significant contributions as a munitions factory.

There was another gunpowder mill in the area, at Camilty, which produced explosives for the shale oil industry in the area from 1890 to 1929. This was operated by the Midlothian Gunpowder Company, which employed around twenty people. Camilty was taken over by Curtis's & Harvey's in 1898, but the works were forced to close in 1929 due to miners' strikes. The workers at Camilty were then bussed to Roslin Glen which by then had been taken over by Nobel.

Some of the gunpowder from Camilty was taken to West Calder Co-op, where it was sold over the counter in bags. The origins of this was that miners of the time were expected to buy and store their own gunpowder and dynamite for shot firing. A number of co-ops also began to sell the ready-made cartridges. Miners did not then have to store the gunpowder in their own homes! Very recently, in 2012, in Sunderland, a house owner unearthed in his garden a stash of dynamite bearing the logo of Nobel's Glasgow office. It has been assumed that, as the house once belonged to a colliery manager, that this was a safe method of storage!

Before Nobel, Curtis's & Harvey's was the best known name in explosives in Scotland. Curtis's & Harvey's was established in Hounslow in 1820 and eventually owned 100 sites. As their first purchase, they took over Robert Sherriff's 1840 Clyde Gunpowder Mills Co. at Clachaig, Glenlean, Argyllshire, in about 1844. This was originally a black powder factory supplying blasting powder. It employed around thirty men, with an increase during the Crimean war. In 1893, it was given over in its entirety to the manufacture of Amerite, a new smokeless powder for sporting purposes. However, the site proved to be too inaccessible and production was transferred to Tonbridge and the factory at Glenlean closed in the early 1900s

Millhouse Gunpowder Works.

The Heritage Council of Victoria, Australia, records salvage from the wreck of the *George Roper* in 1883 'including previously transported gunpowder from manufacturers works at Glenlean to various ports'. The *George Roper* was a brand new ship and on its maiden voyage was transporting a range of goods when it perished. There seemed to be a sense of desperation of the owners to save the cargo. A salvage tug, the *Black Boy*, was sent out to save the vessel but this too sank. The *George Roper* also contained 10 tons of dynamite in 1,200 boxes. This possibly also belonged to Curtis's & Harvey's, which appear to have had a hand in the salvage operations.

With three other large mills, Argyll was quite famous for the production of high quality gunpowder. In 1876, Curtis's & Harvey's also took over the business of the Kames Gunpowder Co. at Millhouse, Kyles of Bute, which had been established in 1839. This factory produced blasting and sporting powders for both the home market and export and continued until 1921, ending production in Argyll.

Also in Argyll was the Loch Fyne gunpowder works established by Robert Sheriff in 1841. This was taken over by John Hall of Faversham in the 1870s. Unfortunately, it was destroyed by an explosion in 1883, killing the manager and causing severe injury and destruction. It had already been considered to be a danger before the explosion.

The works took advantage of the ready supply of charcoal which had previously been used for nearby iron smelting (also covered later in this book). These had since closed. The Explosives Act of 1875 ensured that such factories would not be too close to residential properties but as this factory predated the Act it was exempt. The need for the Act was amply demonstrated when the factory blew up. The works were never re-opened and all machinery was transferred to Hall's works at Faversham.

Nobel works, Linlithgow. Note the Walter MacFarlane cast iron fountain in the foreground.

At Melfort, ten miles south of Oban was the Melfort Gunpowder Works. The works were built in 1853 by a mining and ore company based in Ulverston, Harrison, Ainslie & Co. and closed after a relatively short period in 1874. Most mills of the time had impressive explosions and one here in 1860 killed six men. In 1867 the *Oban Times* reported the total destruction of the works, sending bales of hay a mile from the site.

Alfred Nobel in Scotland – An Explosive Growth
The name of Alfred Nobel to most people means the Nobel Prize, awarded to those considered to be worthy in such fields as peace, physics, chemistry, and literature.

Nobel Industries was founded by Albert Nobel for the production of nitro-glycerine and his invention, dynamite. Possibly for the same reasons as others before him, he chose the west of Scotland for his first factory. He needed an isolated spot but with good access to the sea as movement by any other method was virtually impossible for safety reasons. The great Ardeer factory was born.

Alfred Nobel was born in Stockholm in 1833. While nitro-glycerine had been invented in 1847 by an Italian, it was first produced in any scale by Nobel in Sweden. As often happened, his factory making 'Nobel's Blasting Oil' blew up in 1862 and manufacture was prohibited by the Swedish and other governments. Nobel had taken out a patent for dynamite in 1867 but had difficulty in persuading customers of its efficacy and safety, particularly since nitro-glycerene had been receiving a bad press. He was able to turn to Scottish industrialists who were interested and, after a meeting, the British Dynamite Company was born. The factory opened in 1871, with dynamite and nitro-glycerine being produced in 1873.

In order to overcome the problems associated with the liquid explosive, he experimented and finally arrived at the solid dynamite, patented by him and which was to revolutionise mining, quarrying and civil engineering throughout the world.

Nobel advert for the lady grouse shooter.

In 1877 the company name was changed to Nobel's Explosives Company and although Nobel died in 1896, his company continued to expand and by 1907 was the largest explosives company in the world. In 1918, Explosive Trades Ltd was formed to bring together most companies in the UK producing explosives. This included Curtis's & Harvey's which had a large involvement in Scotland having previously taken over a number of gunpowder producers. In 1920, the company became Nobel Industries, recognising the expansion into other areas such as motor accessories.

In 1926, the company merged with Brunner, Mond & Co., the United Alkali Company and the British Dyestuffs Corporation to form the Imperial Chemical Industries, or ICI, which was then one of Britain's largest companies, with the division of ICI Nobel. ICI Ardeer was to become one of Scotland's greatest factories, housing a dedicated station, bank and dentist. At its peak, Ardeer employed 13,000 workers (The United Alkali Company had previously been formed as a merger of forty-eight chemical companies including Glasgow's Charles Tennant).

During its life the factory introduced diverse explosives such as cordite, gun cotton, Gelignite and Ballistite, both these latter being Nobel patents. This was a smokeless powder, extremely important in the development of munitions. Ballistite produced gaseous explosions rather than smoke, making rifles and cannons more effective and useable. The smoke produced by lines of soldiers produced clouds of fumes and smoke, difficult to see through as well as producing an easy target for opposing forces. The new propellant also meant less fouling and therefore less jamming as there were less deposits left after explosion.

The factory continued to expand even after the cessation of hostilities following the First World War as new developments and inventions came forward and were developed by the recognised skills and innovation of the Ardeer chemists and workers. In particular, the development of nitro-cellulose had an impact as it was to be used in lacquer, particularly for the growing motor trade. Interestingly, the initial processes had similarities to the production of wood pulp for the paper industry and therefore machinery from Bertrams of Sciennes could be used (see chapter on the paper industry).

In 2002, the renamed Nobel Enterprises was sold to Inabata and subsequently passed to Chemring Energetics. They currently employ around 230 in the manufacture of explosives for aircraft ejector seats as well as flares. While not employing the kind of numbers from the heyday of explosives manufacturing, Chemring is a success story, contributing as it does to Scotland's position as a major supplier of chemicals. So all is not lost in the explosives industry as Chemring continues to produce detonators, plastic explosives, propellants and high explosives.

For very obvious reasons, the manufacture of explosives is confined to isolated areas where accidents will cause the least harm. This applies to Brock's Fireworks factory in Sanquhar, Dumfries. Brock's at its peak once employed 150 people and was a major employer in the area.

John Brock was an eccentric Londoner who set up the company in Islington in 1720 and is thought to be the earliest British fireworks maker. Apparently, he would wear a wide brimmed hat and cloak, giving the appearance of Guy Fawkes. By 1826 it was providing 'Brock's Benefits' fireworks displays in London, and these were to become an attraction at the Crystal Palace and continued until its destruction by fire in 1936. The company had a long history in several locations, moving finally to sites in Swafham in Norfolk and Sanquhar in 1971. The Sanquhar site had been the home of the recently closed Sanquhar & Kirconnel Coal Company's Gateside Colliery. Brock's was taken over by rivals Standard Fireworks in 1988 but is now back in Sanquhar with a small presence.

The Devil and his Porridge – Supplying the Military Machine

While some would say that the manufacture, storage and supply of gunpowder, bullets and bombs was a necessary industry ever since the gun and cannon was invented, and we had a major part in that, there was a new impetus to this in the First World War. It is sad to say that Scotland was part of the huge machine of war, supplying the explosives for bullets and bombs as well as the dynamite for the huge mines which were dug on the front lines.

Given the scale of the war, there was a necessity for the scientific management of the production of munitions and the Great War can be credited with the beginnings of modern management practice.

The production of munitions was divided into operations: the raw materials such as cordite were produced in National Explosives Factories and these were then transferred to National Filling Factories. During the First World War there were two main National Explosives Factories, with one of these in Gretna, codenamed Moorside. At the time it was considered to be the largest factory in the world.

The factory was built by the Ministry of Munitions for the manufacture of cordite and as a direct response to a shortage of shells in 1915 which caused a huge scandal. The site was twelve miles long straddling the English – Scottish border. By the start of production in April 1916, the workforce numbered 11,600 women 'Munitionettes' and 5,000 men. In 1917, production was running at the immense 800 tons of cordite per week. This was known as the Devil's Porridge and Gretna produced more than any other factory in Britain, although there were other companies such as Nobel producing cordite. The photograph on the next page shows Grace Ensell at HM Factory Gretna in her blue uniform. The term 'Devil's Porridge' was coined by Arthur Conan Doyle when he visited the site.

Grace Ensell – HM Factory
Gretna 'Munitionette'.

The factory had its own narrow gauge railway network, with thirty-four engines and a power station to provide the energy needed. Townships to house the huge temporary population were also built. The factory was demolished after the war and most of the land sold off in the 1920s, although some of the sites were put into use for ammunition storage.

While the National Explosives Factories (NEF) produced the raw materials, these would then have to be added to the shells and bullets, which were being produced by the Engineering Royal Ordnance Factories (ROFs). This was done in the National Filling Factories. There were around twelve NFFs, with one in Scotland near Bishopton called Georgetown after Lloyd George. By 1917 it was employing 10,000 people. It closed after the war. There was also a National Projectiles Factory at Cardonald in Glasgow, operated on behalf of the Ministry of Munitions by William Beardmore & Co. This was subsequently used by John Wallace & Sons for the manufacture of the Glasgow Tractor.

The government munitions factories were a response to the shortage of explosives but they were by no means the only producers. Nobel Explosives was busy producing, as were many more companies, including the eponymous Beardmore's.

Bruce Peebles, transformer manufacturer, made munitions in East Pilton, Edinburgh. During the Second World War, C. F. Wilson made shells in Constitution Street in Aberdeen. Metropolitan Vickers ran a factory in Motherwell and in Edingham, near Dalbeattie, built by Sir Alfred McAlpine with 3,000 Irish navvies, was another factory making cordite and nitro-glycerine. In fact, there would be hardly any Scottish manufacturing or engineering firm that was not engaged in war work.

The same was true during the Second World War when there was very much less production in Scotland, with four munitions factories being supplemented by the private firms. Nobel operated an explosives factory in Linlithgow which is now the site of a Tesco Store. BAE Systems took over ROF Bishopton and still maintains a munitions facility there while working with the local community to redevelop the site. ROF Dalmuir was leased to Babcox & Wilcox and is now the site of the Golden Jubilee Hospital. ROF Irvine was also closed.

Since the end of the Second World War there has been a general decline in the production of explosives, although Chemring and BAE Systems are involved in Scotland.

Scottish Iron and Ironworks

Growing up in Glasgow in the 1950s and 60s, my memories were that the birth of Scottish industry was in Glasgow and the Lanarkshire coalfields, for after all, that's where we had the great industrial enterprises of the shipyards, of the North British Locomotive Company and the Ravenscraig steel works. It was only very recently that I discovered that the beginnings of our great iron and steel industry were actually in the West Highlands of Scotland. In 1610, Sir George Hay had set up what is believed to be the first blast furnace, the Red Smiddy, at Loch Maree. This operated until about 1670. Hay was a politician, a courtier and an entrepreneur who also set up glass kilns and had a monopoly for its manufacture in Scotland.

However, the Bonawe (or Lorn) blast furnace was the first large furnace in, and now the best preserved in, Scotland and worth a visit. The works, which produced iron until around 1875, were established there by Richard Ford in 1752 because there was an adequate supply of wood for charcoal. The works were extensive and probably one of the biggest enterprises in Scotland at the time, with two tons of pig iron being produced each day. Pig iron was originally produced by smelting iron ore with a high carbon fuel like charcoal, with limestone as a flux to help the process. When molten, the resultant metal is poured out into two parallel sets of moulds set into sand on the floor of the foundry. These lines of moulds are connected by a thinner central channel, down which runs the molten metal to reach the individual moulds. This gave early foundry workers a picture of a sow with piglets feeding, resulting in the term 'pig' for the iron ingots produced.

The fact that more than 600 people were employed in the area making charcoal from oak is a good indication of the reasons for its existence. In reality it was accessible to the growing enterprises in the Clyde basin. Being on the coast, it was relatively easy to send goods by sea rather than by road. In fact, the ore for blasting was coming by sea from Barrow-in-Furness.

Walter MacFarlane sewage gas vent stack on Holburn Street, Aberdeen.

Also attracted by the natural resources was the furnace at Furnace. No, not a coincidence, for the village near Inveraray was originally called Inverleacainn. The furnace was established there in 1755 by the Cumbrian Duddon Company. The informal name for the village was adopted formally at some time. The furnace closed down in 1813.

These sites probably closed because of the exhaustion of wood for the production of charcoal. Possibly, too, it was the competition from the great Carron Ironworks in Falkirk which was established in 1759 and which was at one time the largest ironworks in the world. By 1814 it was employing 2,000 workers.

While the Bonawe and Furnace ironworks were fuelled by charcoal, the Carron Ironworks drew on the locally mined coal, which seemed inexhaustible at the time. The method of producing iron using coke from coal had been devised by Abraham Derby of Coalbrookdale, Shropshire, England. John Roebuck, Samuel Garbett and William Cadell though that they could emulate this and established their works on the banks of the River Carron to take advantage of the power of the water.

While ironworks might produce iron pigs (or ingots) to be melted down and processed elsewhere, the Carron ironworks was an integrated site in that eventually it was not just smelting the ore but producing cast iron products. Cast iron is where molten pig iron is poured directly into moulds to produce a wide variety of goods. Its close relation is wrought iron, which has very little carbon content; the hot iron can be wrought (worked) into the desired shape just as a blacksmith would do with horseshoes. It was this development and the spread of both these processes throughout Scotland's central belt that was to establish Scotland's place in the Industrial Revolution. Both cast iron and wrought iron were fundamental to shipbuilding and engineering. While cast iron manufacture continued, wrought iron was gradually replaced by the more advanced malleable iron and eventually by the introduction of steel. The term wrought iron has now been adopted for products such as decorative gates made from mild steel. And while we will later move on to look at the progression from malleable iron to steel we can concentrate here on cast iron, which remained a discrete industry.

The Carron Ironworks
Carron was one of the first and certainly one of the most successful British companies in the field. However, their initial forays into the manufacture of iron goods showed an early need for proper training of the workforce for they found it difficult to produce quality cast iron goods. I have read criticism of Scottish companies allowing their industrial secrets and techniques to be learned by other countries. In fact that is exactly how industry was started in Scotland, normally by English or French pioneers. In the case of the Carron Works, English smelters were engaged at a high cost to travel to Falkirk to work and to teach the locals how to smelt iron and make cast iron.The initial low quality was overcome and the success showed when they were contracted by the Board of Ordnance to produce what has become an iconic item in the history of Scottish manufacturing as well as in the Royal Navy. For the Carron Company was the birthplace of the Carronade and other cannon of the Royal Navy.

Typical iron foundry.

By the start of the First World War, the Carron Company was Europe's largest ironworks, producing pig iron for its own use and for export far and wide. From the pig iron they produced a range of domestic ironware including fireplaces, ranges and baths. It was one of the Scottish companies turning out the famous red telephone boxes and post boxes. When in Edinburgh, you can also see their presence in the many cast iron railings and balconies in the New Town.

Carron had its own shipping line, 'The Carron Line', and distribution networks. They were also known internationally for their range of cast iron cooking pots, 'The Falkirk', and sugar boiling vats. Although Carron diversified into stainless steel and plastics, it was suffering the same fate as many other companies. No-one wanted cast iron baths and the red telephone box was on the way out. Domestic ware, road signs and other street architecture were being produced in aluminium. European competition for cookers was growing and changes in fashion and architecture all had it on its last legs in the 1970s. It went into receivership in 1982. It was taken over by the Franke Corporation and still exists as Carron Phoenix making a range of sinks.

In 1786 William Cadell of Cockenzie, who had been one of the originators, was also involved in Carron setting up the Clyde Iron works in the West. Apparently this is actually where the Carronade was made and was reputed to be the most modern ironworks of the day. The ironworks there were the first to use Neilson's Hot Blast process. The works also made the transition from iron to steel production, being taken over by Colville's in 1931, modernised and integrated with the Clydebridge Steelworks.

The hot blast was a major innovation in ironmaking and invented by James Beaumont Neilson, inventor and foreman at the Glasgow Gas Works. The process involved preheating the blast air for the furnace. This reduced fuel consumption and coal could be used instead of coke. This all lowered the cost of production and gave

Cannon from the Carron Ironworks in Fort Queenscliff, Victoria, Australia.

the works a competitive advantage until the process was taken up under license by other ironworks.

This period saw a proliferation of ironworks to meet the demands of the Industrial Revolution, which is recognised as having begun around 1750. Some of these ironworks like the Clyde Works would make the transition into producing iron for steelmaking while some like Carron and its competitor MacFarlane would concentrate on manufacturing cast iron products.

Walter MacFarlane and the Saracen Ironworks

If you take a walk through Macquarie Place in Sydney, Australia, you will come across a canopy for a fountain. Although the fountain has been removed, the canopy is a link between Glasgow and Australia and between this new century and the end of the nineteenth. For this canopy came from Walter MacFarlane's Saracen Foundry in Possilpark, Glasgow, and was one of eight ordered for Sydney in 1870.

As the empire expanded and the colonies throughout the world grew and settled, they looked towards machinery, fittings and fixings as well as comforts and reminders from home. They also celebrated the establishment of their new homes and cities with statues and municipal ornamentation. They particularly wanted cast iron and where else would they get it but from their homelands? If there were foundries in the colonies then they were small or primitive. That would change but in the meantime orders were placed with British foundries. One of the most productive and celebrated was the Saracen Foundry in Possilpark, Glasgow.

'Keep the pavement dry'.

Walter MacFarlane was born in Clachan of Campsie, north of Glasgow, in 1817. His first employment that we know about was with a jeweller, William Russell, in the Trongate, in 1830. It is recorded that he furthered himself with evening classes in design. During this period he met his future wife Margaret, who was the daughter of his employer.

After three years in the jewellery business he started an apprenticeship with James Buchanan (blacksmith) in Stockwell Street. As this was a stone's throw from the Trongate it is easy to imagine the young Walter passing by the forge and being enthralled by the sight, sounds and smell of hot metal.

Around 1840, and presumably at the end of his seven-year apprenticeship, he moved to Moses, McCulloch & Co.'s Cumberland Foundry in the Gallowgate. Here he rose to the position of moulding shop manager and, in 1848, married Margaret.

Walter was a good friend of Margaret's brother, Thomas, and in 1851 went into partnership with him and another friend, James Marshall. They took over a disused brass foundry in Saracen Lane in the Gallowgate. By 1861, they were employing 120 people. By this time they had outgrown these premises and relocated to expanded premises in Washington Street, in Anderston. Their premises were designed by the architect James Boucher, who went on to form an association with the firm.

They weren't here very long, however, as a decision was made to move to a green field site. You can imagine from the firms where Walter worked that central Glasgow was a hive of industrial activity, much of it supporting the nearby Clyde. Washington Street in Anderston was such a place, full of workshops but also full of tenement buildings. The pressure on space must have been immense and you can possibly imagine the difficulties there may have been in casting large pieces in such cramped areas.

The final site for the Saracen Foundry was to be in the grounds of Possil House, near Maryhill. This was named Possilpark by MacFarlane and in 1872 was established one of the largest and greatest of Glasgow's and Scotland's industrial sites. I particularly remember the tower, which was a Glasgow landmark but has since been demolished. The new factory occupied twenty-four acres and employed 1,200.

The foundry continued in operation into the early twentieth century, but eventually saw a decline in the industry and demand for such ornamental cast ironwork. Much of the product of the foundry was going overseas. But the days of Empire were drawing to a close. In the colonies, foundries were being established and Scottish iron was not needed. Although there was still a call for some standard traditional products such as the classic red telephone box, tastes were changing and new materials were being developed. Iron was being replaced by steel. Electricity was replacing gas. Ceramic was replacing cast iron plumbing.

Walter MacFarlane and the Saracen Foundry may have gone but he has left us with solid reminders of Glasgow's style and enterprise throughout the world. In Brazil and Australia, in India, and at home in Scotland there are lasting reminders of his work. These are seen in staircases, banisters, bandstands, fountains and lamp standards, all illuminating the skill of the Glasgow iron worker.

The company became part of Allied Ironfounders in 1965, and was absorbed into Glynwed in 1966. The foundry at Possilpark eventually closed and was demolished in 1967. The company name was bought by Glasgow firm Heritage Engineering in

1993. With an extensive archive, this company specialises in the conservation and restoration of architectural ironwork, and continues to manufacture many of the original designs of the Saracen Foundry.

The Lion Foundry in Kirkintilloch was also highly productive. The Scots were ever enterprising and Walter MacFarlane should have found it no surprise if some of his workers set up in competition. This was the case in the 1880s, when three of Macfarlane's staff left to set up their own enterprise. Brown, Hudson and Jackson set up The Lion Foundry in Kirkintilloch and were later joined by designer William Cassells. The Lion Foundry outlasted Macfarlane's by twenty years, finally closing in 1984. The Lion Foundry had made similar products to Walter MacFarlane but specialised in products such as fire escapes and architectural facades. Lothian House at Tolcross in Edinburgh is an example.

The demand for architectural ironwork was in steady decline and the company concentrated on work for the GPO and local authorities. This included bus shelters, post boxes, telephone and connection boxes, all of which can be seen on Scotland's town and city streets. However, the use of aluminium casting was growing, as was the use of stainless steel. Their last work was for pillar boxes but this was not enough to prevent closure in 1984.

There were other foundries in Scotland meeting the demands for domestic, industrial and architectural purposes but through time almost all of these closed, leaving only a few small foundries, mostly providing for the heritage market. One of these is Ballantine's Bo'ness Iron Foundry. Established in 1856, it has been in continuous production ever since and is still owned and operated by the same family. Their range covers traditional cast iron works, from municipal bandstands to street lamps, drainage castings, fountains and balconies. The restored cherub on the Stewart Memorial Fountain in Glasgow's Kelvingrove Park is one of their smaller projects but

Original Macfarlane's 'pissoir' behind a church on The Black Isle.
It says 'Do not adjust your dress'.

Original cast iron panels from the Caledonian Railway's Glasgow Cross Station, now in St Vincent Place.

Colville & Gray's Clifton iron works, Coatbridge.

Newmains from Slag Hill, showing the ironworks and workers' housing.

A Baird of Gartsherrie private locomotive at Gartsherrie Ironworks.

one dear to my own heart as I used to paddle in the fountain as a wee boy. I was no wee cherub. Another cast-iron success story for Scottish industry.

'The Queer-Like Smell' – The Story of Linoleum

When I was in the cycling club at Harris Academy in Dundee we went once to Nairn's Linoleum works in Kirkcaldy. You could smell it as we approached the town. I don't remember much about the works but the smell was powerful, powerful.

Laurie Christie

Kirkcaldy was linoleum and linoleum was Kirkcaldy. If you mentioned linoleum now most people would think of vinyl flooring, which is not linoleum, and is part of the demise of that product and that great industry centred in Kirkcaldy and closely bound up with Dundee's jute industry.

In 1956, the Monopolies & Mergers Commission reported on the linoleum industry, which had been said to have being agreeing prices and acting as a cartel. In the event the industry was allowed to continue their agreements as it was not thought to be against the public interest. How different were conditions then before the European Common Market and the opening of competition across Europe. And in any case, it was all too late, as the linoleum industry was already on the way out as reported in the *Glasgow Herald* of September 1963:

Nairn's Tile inspection and sorting, 1958.

The recent news that the North British Linoleum Company are to cease production comes as no surprise to the industry. The difficulties that have confronted NB have not been confined to them alone. The whole of the linoleum industry has fallen on hard times due to the severe and still increasing competition from tufted carpet and plastic tiling.

Linoleum, so connected with Kirkcaldy and with Scotland, was actually invented in England by Frederick Walton, who took out a patent for it in 1863, giving it the name Linoleum. His patent expired in 1877 and others, mostly floorcloth manufacturers, got in on the act. Walton had failed to register 'Linoleum' as a trademark and failed in his action to prevent Nairn and others from using the term. By that time linoleum had become established in the same way that Hoover is synonymous with vacuum cleaners and Singer with sewing machines. In fact, linoleum is considered the first brand to have become a generic term.

By the same year, 1877, Kirkcaldy was already the world's largest manufacturer of wax floorcloth and was ready and willing to take advantage of Walton's patents. Within a short time there were more than a dozen manufacturers in the area and Kirkcaldy became the provider of lino to the world and could easily be identified by the smell of linseed oil pervading the town.

> There's a gey wheen boats at the harbour mou',
> And eh! dae ya see the cruisers?
> The cinnamon drop I was sookin' the noo
> Has tummelt an' stuck tae ma troosers. . .
> I'll sune be ringin' ma Gran'ma's bell,
> She'll cry, 'Come ben, my laddie',
> For I ken mysel' by the queer-like smell
> That the next stop's Kirkcaddy!

> From 'The Boy in the Train' by M. C. Smith

The manufacture of linoleum was well suited to the east of Scotland given the predominance of the jute manufacturing industry, for the linoleum companies were some of the biggest customers for jute. Besides jute for the hessian backing, the raw materials for linoleum were linseed oil derived from flax, wood flour of various grades, powdered cork, rosin (a form of resin) and chalk as a filler.

The process starts with oxidisation, in which linseed oil is mixed with rosin. By passing air through the mixture it thickens it, at which time it transferred to a 'smacker' that further heats and mixes the now viscous mixture. On cooling, this cement is turned into slabs looking like Turkish delight and is ready for the next stage.

These cement slabs are mixed with ground cork, wood flour and filler. At this point colour is added, 'marbling' being achieved by mixing in three colours. The granulated cement is then passed through sets of steel rollers (calendering), which converts the granules to sheets, which are then pressed onto a prepared hessian base.

The linoleum is then hung in continuous and moving loops to allow the sheets to be seasoned, or hardened, over a period of weeks. A final surface resists soiling and improves the look of the final product.

As to its uses, well, obviously as a floorcovering, which was both hygienic and easy to lay. I can vouch for this, having laid many rolls of the proper stuff in my youth. Real linoleum cuts very easily with a knife made for the purpose. However, it was also used substantially as a top for desks in Government departments as it was easy to clean and easy to write on. I seem to remember that it came in brown and battleship grey. We must also remember that making lino cuts was a very popular in school art periods.

By the time of the Monopolies report in 1956 there were nine linoleum companies in Great Britain, with six of these being based in Scotland: Barry, Ostlere & Shepherd of the Forth Works, Kirkcaldy; The Dundee Linoleum Co. in Dundee; Michael Nairn & Co. of Kirkcaldy; the North British of Dundee; and the Tayside Floorcloth Co. of Newburgh; and the Scottish Co-operative Wholesale Society, whose works were in sleepy Falkland. It was a substantial industry and all based in the Dundee area.

Barry, Ostlere & Shepherd Ltd was set up in 1899 to acquire the existing companies of Shepherd & Beveridge, the Kirkcaldy Linoleum Co. and John Barry, Ostlere & Co. It was acquired by Barry & Staines Linoleum but continued to trade under its own name in the Rosslyn and Lorne Linoleum Works in Kirkcaldy. The downturn in the business caused its closure in 1963 with the loss of 1,500 jobs.

At the St John's Works, Falkland, the SCWS began manufacturing floorcloth in 1919, and a department for making linoleum was opened in 1934. The factory stopped making linoleum in 1963, with the building subsequently being used for the manufacture of paper bags by Smith Anderson.

In Newburgh, was the Tayside Floorcloth Company, set up in 1891 by Thomas Stalker Greig, firstly as the Tay Oxyde Co. Like other lino companies, 'Tayside's' first produced floorcloth on which jute sheets were covered with putty or gesso to produce a painted finish.

Moving to linoleum, the business grew and by 1910 it was employing around 100. Given the state of the industry, it was a relatively long-lasting company which suddenly closed in 1978 after a fire.

The North British Linoleum Company was registered in 1927 but the premises were requisitioned for war purposes in 1941 and it was not re-established until 1947. It succumbed to the downturn in Linoleum sales in 1963.

By far the largest of the companies was Michael Nairn, which was established by him in 1828, manufacturing floorcloth and quickly moving to linoleum in 1877. Through the thick and thin of linoleum manufacture, Nairn's factory has been the longest lasting of the Scottish linoleum companies but lack of investment and out-of-date equipment brought it to its knees until it was saved by the take-over by the Swiss-based Forbo group which continues to make linoleum under the brand name Marmoleum. Sensibly, they have registered the name and in an act of kindness they have named one of their designs Walton after linoleum's inventor, dispossessed of his own invention.

Nairns – assembling patterned inlay. And yes, the girls are twins!

It is the only British factory and one of a very small number of factories in the world still producing traditional linoleum, which has become a very trendy and costly but still a very practical floor covering and which is made entirely of natural products. Nairns' long survival was probably due to the company's foresight in expanding overseas, taking a minority interest in the Dominion Oilcloth & Linoleum Co. Ltd of Canada. In 1926, they bought into a French company as well as taking over the Linoleum Manufacturing Company of Australia. In, fact they were the biggest exporters to Australia for many years.

They also had a presence in the United States, where Michael Nairn had established the American Nairn Linoleum Company in Kearny, New Jersey, in 1887. In the 1920s, they joined with a Pennsylvania distributor to manufacture a three-foot wide simulated grain floor covering used to border rugs. This they called Congoleum as the ingredients came from the Belgian Congo. The company was then renamed the Congoleum Nairn Company. Changed to Congoleum, the company still exists as a separate entity, still producing flooring materials but not linoleum. It is very proud of its Scottish roots.

But as we have seen, linoleum has mostly had its day. While it had great appeal, it was easily replaced by cheaper vinyl flooring. Where it had been used as a border in hallways where carpet runners or squares were used, wall-to-wall carpeting was coming in and was becoming more affordable. Laminate tops were replacing desk and other surfaces.

In kitchens and bathrooms, builders were putting in rigid or semi-flexible tiles which had a little PVC in them and which were easier to lay. Nairn did join the market for these but never got more than 15 per cent of sales. The other product was hard printed vinyl, which had printed designs on a flexible vinyl backing sheet. This product could easily be cut with scissors. Nairn's had a good share of this market and further improved this with cushioned vinyl, which had a subtle embossed surface and was softer underfoot. Congoleum Nairn in the USA had the patent for this and Nairn's were given the exclusive rights in the United Kingdom. Cushionflor was the only star in the Nairn portfolio.

An advertisement for linoleum, dating to about 1900.

However, the 1960s and 70s were a sad time for linoleum manufacture in Kirkcaldy. Some of the PVC plant which was installed did not work well and neither did new products tried at the plant. By the early 1970s, Nairn floorcovering production had reduced to Congoleum, linoleum and a felted carpet tile plant in Glenrothes. Nairn's were under pressure as other companies were offering the new vinyls in wide widths that Nairn could not afford to finance. Unilever came to the rescue in a move to become the market leader in floorcoverings.

While Unilever had invested new capital in a wide-width, cushioned vinyl plant, nevertheless losses had been made in each of the ten years of ownership; by 1985 they had reversed their policy of expansion into new fields and a decision was made to sell to Forbo. Forbo had a policy of acquiring suitable flooring market leaders and Nairn's fitted the bill. It came as a huge surprise to the existing management that Forbo, rather than concentrate solely on vinyl, had ambitions to produce quality linoleum, finally bringing Nairn's back to its roots where it continues to bring benefits to Kirkcaldy. The smell might not be so strong but it is definitely linoleum.

And on that final note, we have already seen that these great manufacturers and entrepreneurs were also great benefactors to the community. This was the case in linoleum too with the philanthropic Nairn family gifting both the Beveridge and Ravenscraig parks to the town as well as the Kirkcaldy Art Gallery.

Papermaking

The salle, the Fourdrinier, the presse-pâte, the potcher: terms which would be very familiar to the large number of people who once worked in Scotland's many paper mills. Some of the terms are also evidence that the industry originated in France.

I didn't know a lot about paper before I started looking into it but I think it was to picture huge rolls of paper coming off a production line or sheets of standard paper piling up ready for the photocopier. We may have moved towards industrial plants spewing out standardised rolls of paper of one type but it was not always like that. I am indebted to Charles Gibson, author of the 1898 *Romance of Modern Manufacture,* for starting my interest in paper manufacture, an industry in which I had never been involved.

I was fascinated by the range of papers once produced in Scotland, the purpose of many of these lost in the distant past, or going that way. Factories specialised in blotting or carbon paper. Do you remember fountain pens, or wooden pens that you attached metal nibs to, and scratched your school essays? You needed blotting paper for that.

There was of course paper for banknotes and share certificates, Edinburgh being in the forefront of the financial industry. There was gummed paper for stamps. There were early playing cards, wrappings for tea and sugar and waxed paper for bread, paper for board for packaging, paper for the great industrial expansion which demanded invoices, receipts and letters as well as tracing paper. And of course paper for school jotters and text books. Paper was involved in hat and shoe manufacture and for insulating electrical cables. Paper was required for backing for linoleum and still is for wallpaper. It was also needed for maps and charts, Edinburgh also being in the forefront of that business as well.

Papermaking was never geographically widespread in Scotland and was concentrated in a small number of places. The rise of papermaking was closely related to the growth of Scotland's printing, publishing and banking industries, all needing large amounts of paper, so it is no surprise that the first Scottish paper mill was in Dalry, Edinburgh, started in 1590 for 'manufacturing white writing and printing papers'. The later mills also grew along the Water of Leith, which flows through Edinburgh, and in the nearby Esk Valley.

Another reason for location was that the mills were large users of clean water, both for power and for the process. Closeness to ports for export purposes was also a factor. So too was the need to be near a ready supply of rags.

I am of an age able to remember rag and bone men, or at least I think they collected only rags and scrap metal. I still remember the incongruity of horse-drawn carts sporting tyres being driven round Glasgow's modern Nitshill in the late 1950s. Before the use of Esparto grass and wood pulp, the ragman was absolutely necessary to the manufacture of paper as the acquisition of rags of linen and cotton was an essential part of the process. Rags fetched very good money and there was great competition for them.

Essentially, paper is made from vegetable matter: cellulose fibres, originally from rags derived from linen and cotton, then esparto grass and wood pulp. The rags were either left to rot down to pulp or pulverised by machine. This was essentially a huge mortar and pestle, or a 'Hollander', a kind of mangle which shredded the material.

Papermaking was a slow industry to change. The adoption of steam machinery was slow and so was the move to continuous production. Until 1860, the making of paper was essentially a craft, with the pulp, with glue added, being poured into wooden trays with a wire bottom. From here, with some sleight of hand, the water drained off and what was left was paper. It was not until the advent of the Fourdrinier machine that the process was able to become continuous and move from a craft to a mass-produced product. The Fourdrinier machine was a French invention funded by the Fourdrinier brothers, stationers in London, and patented in 1801.

The basic but substantial difference was in the change away from the use of individual tray moulds to a continuous wire bed upon which the pulp is first of all evenly spread. The paper is then carried on the wire through rollers which squeeze water out of the paper before moving on to the dryer rollers and to the calenders. Calenders are a set of rollers that smooth and finish the paper.

The Water of Leith

The Water of Leith is synonymous with industry in Edinburgh. This narrow and fast river rises in the Pentland Hills and travels through Balerno, Juniper Green, Currie, and Colinton, flowing through and skirting the centre of Edinburgh to end in the Firth of Forth at Leith.

While the Water of Leith Walkway is now a tourist attraction and the river a haven for wildlife, there are few obvious remains of the industries which lined and which were eventually restricted by its banks. There were over eighty mills producing flour,

Fourdrinier paper making machines at Kinleith Mill.

wool, linen, snuff, spices and paper, some of these combining their output or changing to milling more profitable outputs as the economy changed. There were around seventeen paper mills of various sizes.

At Balerno, John Galloway's Balerno Bank Mill had been making 'tea' and 'grey' paper since 1805 before being taken over by him in 1925. Converting to esparto grass as the raw material, Balerno Bank produced high quality art papers as well as gloss papers for magazines such as *Country Life* and *Vogue*.

As with so many enterprises, efforts to update technology were behind the closure of Galloway's. The force behind the company, John Galloway had died in 1965. A new coating plant was giving problems and the company got into financial difficulties, finally winding up in 1971. The offices of Galloway's have been converted into flats and the milling buildings are replaced by a housing development.

Kinleith Mill was another of the more long-lasting mills on the Water of Leith. Begun in 1689, it was bought by Henry Bruce in 1844 and was taken over by the expanding Inveresk company in 1928, producing book papers. Featherweight papers were pioneered here by Henry Bruce. Due to what they said was foreign competition and the small size of the mill, Inveresk closed Kinleith in 1966 and moved its production.

Prior to 1735, paper for Scottish banknotes was imported. Boag's Mill at Colinton Dell is believed to have produced the first paper used for notes in Scotland. It subsequently converted to grinding spices and barley. It burned down in 1924.

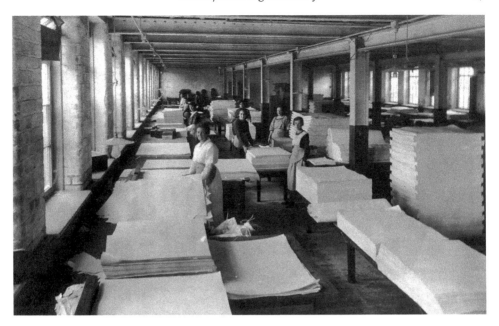

Kinleith Salle.

Woodhall Board Mill at Juniper Green converted to papermaking in 1792, which appears to have been a good year for papermaking. It was a long-lasting mill that produced packaging, mainly for the whisky industry, until 1984. It was another mill owned and closed by Inveresk.

Upper Spylaw was Scotland's fourth oldest papermill and was producing paper in 1682. It is said that the top floor of the mill housed an inn which was a smugglers' den and which was raided by Customs officers in 1776, when they found a haul of smuggled tea and brandy.

Other mills on the water were at Canonmills, Slateford, Colinton and Redhall. The last paper mill on the Water of Leith was James Inglis & Co., which was based at Canonmills. Their specialisms were board, crayon paper and wrapping paper. It had been owned by the Williamson family but was taken over by Stirling Fibre in 1987. It closed in 1989.

Penicuik: 'The Papermaking Town'
Another major papermaking area was Penicuik and the North Esk. Agnes Campbell started the first paper mill using water from St Mungo's Well. Production here started in 1709 and after successive ownership the mill was purchased by Charles Cowan in 1779. By 1796 it was the largest paper mill in Scotland, employing thirty people and producing up to three tons of paper a week. More mills were to follow and by 1914, the industry in all mills in the Penicuik area was employing 1,200.

The Cowan family was to become a benefactor of the town, with Alexander funding the building of the Cowan Institute, a school, social housing; the company also provided sick pay for all workers.

Edinburgh Advertiser, 19 November 1776

Papermill to let. There is to be let ... the Papermill at Pennycuik etc. with the whole machinery, houses and others pertaining thereto lately belonging to Mr Watkins and presently possessed by Mr. Spottiswood – The subjects and machinery are all of the best kind and in good order. There are 2 vats in the mill which is plentifully supplied with the very finest spring water conducted in lead pipes.

In 1803, a nearby mill was converted from corn to papermaking and was incorporated into the Valleyfield site as Bank Mill. Here high quality papers for banknotes were made.

Low Mill, on the river below Valleyfield, had been converted from a waulk or cloth mill in 1749 to paper manufacture. It was bought by Cowan in 1815, just after the Napoleonic Wars, and in 1832 it moved from hand-made papers when a papermaking machine was brought in.

Ownership of the Valleyfield Mills by Cowan's ended in 1965 when the company was taken over by the Reed Paper Group. The new owners sold it in 1974 and a housing estate now stands on the site.

The Esk Mills were converted from cotton mills by distillers James Haig and John Philp around 1805 and, following the Napoleonic War, taken over by James Brown, who introduced mechanisation. By 1832, the mills were producing printing and writing papers. They eventually moved on to coated papers and produced duplicator and copier paper, which was exported worldwide.

However in the 1960s, the machinery was becoming outdated. It seems that problems with the commissioning of new machinery caused production problems which affected cash flow. The mills went into liquidation and closed in April 1968 after 163 years.

Valleyfield Mills in Penicuik.

Finally, with the closure of Dalmore Mill at Auchendinny on the North Esk in 2004, papermaking in Midlothian, which had lasted 300 years, came to an end. Dalmore Mill, itself in existence for 170 years, produced high quality papers for such products as the *Encyclopedia Britannica* and pension books.

Also in East Lothian is Gifford, whose chief industry at one time was the paper mill at Yester that produced notes for the Bank of Scotland. It closed in the 1770s.

There were few paper mills in the west of Scotland. On the River Kelvin there is a record of one in 1690 at Woodside. James Duncan started a mill at Balgray on the Kelvin and was joined in 1746 by Edward Collins. There were water supply problems here so the business expanded to Dalmuir on the Duntocher Burn. This operated until the 1970s.

The Balgray site was to expand and install steam power and eventually became known as Kelvindale Paper Mills. This was to become a huge site with railway sidings. The site has now been redeveloped as housing.

Another paper mill on the Kelvin was started about 1750 by James MacArthur & Co. The firm became a limited company in 1890 before being taken over in 1934 and eventually became part of the Associated Paper Group.

On Glasgow's other tributary, the Cart, papermills were also established. Frenchman Nicholas Deschamps, who had worked in Edinburgh, established a mill at Newlands in 1682. His son-in-law, James Hall, started a mill upstream at Netherlee. These were both replaced by a mill at Millholm that lasted 200 years.

The Clyde Paper Co. at Eastfield, Rutherglen, was established in 1856 using the Fourdrinier machine. In 1926 it was voluntarily wound up and subsequently reconstructed, finally closing in 1971. Clyde Paper Mills were situated at Eastfield, Rutherglen. During its time it made a range of paper including arts, gum papers, 'calf' vellum, spool ticket papers, book-end and metallic papers.

Aberdeenshire

In Aberdeenshire, the industry became established around the Don with the Donside Mill, Tillydrone, opening in 1890. It closed in 2001 with the loss of 250 jobs. By 1920 the mill had been producing 400 tones of newsprint weekly. In order to compete and survive it moved into high grade coated papers, supplying high quality and art paper, with 40 per cent of its markets overseas. Its demise was blamed on high pulp prices and the strength of the pound. Like many other paper mill sites, it was cleared and is in the process of becoming an urban village.

The Davidson Mill in Muggiemoss was established in 1796 by Charles Davidson. Papermaking started in 1821 and before that, among other things, it was milling snuff. Although there was not a lot of innovation in Scottish paper manufacturing, it was the son, George Davidson, who came up with the idea for making block bottom paper bags and by 1857 Davidson's had cornered the market, becoming the biggest producers of paper bags in the world. A further innovation was the production of a grey paper which combined cedar dust with wood pulp. This could be used under carpets to prevent dust and discourage moths.

The company eventually moved over to paperboard manufacture. When it came time to look at new machinery to produce wider paperboard, the capital could not be raised. The mill closed in June 2005, defeated by the want of new technology and lack of capital to modernise.

The Culter Mills were established in 1751 by Bartholomew Smith on the Culter Burn. By 1897 it had 500 workers and was Aberdeen's longest surviving paper mill when it closed in 1981. It had been producing printing and writing paper. The Culter Mills was where the second Fourdrinier machine ever made was installed, the first in Scotland. With a Boulton & Watt engine, it was also the first steam powered paper mill in Scotland.

The mill was served by its own line to the site at Culter Station on the Deeside Line which is now a walkway. The mills are gone and new housing stands on the site. You can still see the weir and the aqueduct which was used for taking water to the mill.

The Thomas Tait Paper Mill in Inverurie was founded by the Tait family in the 1650s but it was in 1852 that they saw the potential for a paper mill. The company was a success and was owned by the Tait family until it was taken over by the America Federal Paper Board Company, which subsequently became part of International Paper. Thomas Tait was still on the United Kingdom Board of International Paper when he retired in 2000.

In 2008, the company said that the mill had become unprofitable and it closed with the loss of 400 jobs. It had been put up for sale with the stipulation that it would not be sold to potential competitors. None came forward.

> It appears that International Paper failed to reach an agreement with any of the potential purchasers. We believe it was its policy all along to close the site and replace lost production in Scotland with paper produced in Brazil, Poland or Russia.
>
> Trades Union Official 2009

In Tillicoultry, on the river Devon, Samuel Jones, who had a paper mill in England, founded the Devonvale Paper Mill in 1921. It merged with Wiggins Teape in 1964 and by 1967 it was employing a fifth of Tillicoultry's working population. Jones was well known for making gummed papers including British and international postage stamps. It closed suddenly in 1972 and the factory is now a furniture retailer.

The parent company, Samuel Jones & Co., became independent from Wiggins Teape in 2010 and has also sadly gone into receivership. Samuel had opened his first mill in London in 1810 and from 1905 produced gummed paper used for stamps and similar products.

Caldwell's was one of the more modern paper mills. The mill was built in 1914 and was owned by the Inveresk paper company from 1928 until 1981, when the mill was taken over by Georgia Pacific. By that time Inveresk had owned a number of Scottish mills, including Carrongrove and Stoneywood in Denny. Caldwell's, and others were subject to a management buy-out in 1993. However, the mills became unprofitable in the next ten years. Depending on exports, the company suffered through unfavourable exchange rates and several mills were closed as a result.

The building has lain derelict ever since and an inevitable fire partially destroyed it in 2010. There are currently plans to demolish this huge landmark, which has dominated the Inverkeithing skyline for a century.

At Caldercruix, near Airdrie, Thomas, Robert and George Craig founded a mill in 1848 and extended it in 1890. The mill was powered by two of the largest waterwheels in Scotland and was famous for the production of blotting paper made from rags. It was the world's largest producer. Like other mill owners, the Craigs benefitted the growing Caldercruix community with new houses and an institute. The mill closed in 1970 and has since been demolished.

The Craig family also owned the Moffat Mills near Airdrie, having moved the entire production from their Newbattle Mill. The Newbattle Mill on the Esk had originally been operated by Archibald Keith, and from 1825 by James Craig. It closed in 1890 when tenant and landlord could not agree a lease. 300 employees lost their jobs although some transferred to Moffat Mills and Caldercruix. James Craig had patented a machine for the boiling and washing of rags. The Moffat mills closed in 1963, when they were sold and converted to a whisky distillery for Inver House.

For anyone who knows St Andrews and Leuchars, the Curtis Fine Papers mill and its historic clock at Guardbridge will be familiar. The demise of the Guardbridge plant in 2008 has been the most recent loss to the paper industry in Scotland. Like other Scottish manufacturing plants, Guardbridge was subject to increases in raw material and energy costs, and lack of availability of credit. At the end it had a turnover of £35 million and employed 260 people but could not sustain further losses. Guardbridge provided uncoated fine paper for home and international markets.

The company was originally started as the Guardbridge Paper Company by the Haig whisky family, who were already involved in the Dalmore Mill on the Esk. They had operated it as the Seggie whisky distillery. The distillery, which had produced malt and grain whiskies at different times, had suffered through poor demand and lack of credit. It had closed in 1860. Production of paper started in 1872 and grew steadily, with the village of Guardbridge growing along with it. By the late 1950s it was employing 620. In order to consolidate and protect Guardbridge, Dalmore Mill was closed in 2004 with the loss of 127 jobs. This and other management measures did not work. The final straw came when the sale of land at the paper mill fell through. This resulted in the sudden closure of the Guardbridge Mill. The paper mill had experienced the same problems as the distillery, with the same consequences.

Kilbagie at Kincardine, also in Fife, is another paper mill that once was a distillery. Founded in 1720 by John Stein, Kilbagie was said to be the largest in Scotland at the time and produced until 1845. Kilbagie was famous as the site of the first continuous still, invented in 1826 by Robert Stein. It went bankrupt, said to be because of excessive customs dues.

After some time as a fertilizer factory, James Weir started the production of esparto-based fine papers in 1875, on machines supplied to the mill by Bertrams of Sciennes, a 92-inch machine being the largest in the country at the time. In 1941, there were four machines at Kilbagie and they were also producing newsprint.

Gestetner had been a customer and eventually bought the mill in 1965 and then modernised it. Ownership changed to an Australian firm, the Pratt Group of Melbourne, before being taken over by Inveresk in 1995, to produce fine papers.

One commentator has described Inveresk as the undertaker of the Scottish paper industry. Having taken over a number of companies, it shut down mills in

Musselburgh; Carrongrove in Denny; Caldwell's in Inverkeithing; Westfield in Torphichen; and Kilbagie. Inveresk closed Kilbagie in 2001. The plant is now partly a waste management site.

It was in 1964, with a huge fanfare and a slot on Pathé News, that the first paper mill in the Highlands was introduced to Corpach, beside Fort William. The new mill represented the Harold Wilson Labour Government's 'White Heat of Technology' and was part of a drive to introduce heavy industry into the Highlands and Islands. While it did increase employment in Lochaber it was to be a relatively short-lived industry, finally closing in 1981 after a long and slow run-down. In 2006, the site was taken over by BSW Timber with plans to move their existing sawmill in order to double their output.

Just like other industrial plants in the Highlands, the coming of the Mill was to bring infrastructure changes. The employment of around 1,000 meant the creation of new housing schemes, new roads and improvements to the roads and railway, which were to carry 375 tons of logs daily as well as taking the product out. Although some wood was imported, much of it was from the West Highlands, especially Inverliever Forest at Loch Awe. 10,000 trees a day went into the digesters to be pulped. In May 2008, *The Herald* reported:

> It was a symbol of a failed industrial strategy for the Highlands and Islands, and yesterday the 210-ft powerhouse at the former Corpach pulp mill was demolished in an explosion. It is to make way for a £25m development to create the UK's largest sawmill operation, safeguarding 88 jobs and creating another 45. The mill, near Fort William, was supposed to help transform the economy of the West Highlands when it opened in 1964 and employed up to 1,000 people before it closed in 1981.'

In 2000 there were some sixteen paper mills in Scotland, manufacturing products ranging from packaging materials to graphics papers, carbonless copy papers, paper bags, coated papers and board. By October 2009, twelve of these had closed and at the publication of this book there are four. What we are left with is a small number of factories rather than the extensive and varied range of paper manufacturers. In order to survive the ups and downs of the exchange rate you need economies of scale. Papermills have necessarily become bigger, efficient and faster. But we should praise the resilience of these companies which have survived, possibly against the odds, and we have also have a new one from the ashes of an old mill which we can start with as we say hello to the survivors:

Arjowiggins at Stoneywood in Aberdeen is a producer of art, craft and technical paper. Its most famous and very recognisable paper is Conqueror. Stoneywood Mill was established in 1770 by John Boyle and Richard Hyde, passing soon to Alexander Smith, an Aberdeen wigmaker. At the beginning of the nineteenth century it was taken over by Alexander Pirie, the first of a number of Piries to own the site. It was he who started the manufacture of fine papers and introduced powered machines as well as the first Stoneywood watermark. 'Pirie 1802'.

Close to the Don, it produces around 60,000 tonnes of paper annually. The mill also hosts one of the largest craft shops in Scotland, the Papeterie, selling materials and running classes. The company is owned by Arjowiggins SAS, based in Paris. That seems appropriate given the French heritage of the Scottish papermaking industry.

Tullis Russell is an employee-owned company with its papermaking plant based in Glenrothes in Fife. It was started in 1809 by Robert Tullis, a printer in Cupar, who made small quantities of hand-made paper. It was taken over in 1924 by the Russell family before the groundbreaking change to one of the largest employee-owned companies in the UK. It is an independent company and one of Scotland's industrial success stories, giving an inkling of what might have been. The company today employs 500 people making high quality board for packaging, cards and book covers. It exports up 160,000 tonnes of paper and card to fifty countries worldwide.

In Irvine, paper production started at the Caledonian Paper Mill in 1989 in what was then Scotland's largest inward investment. Production of coated magazine papers runs at 280,000 tonnes annually at the plant, which is owned by Finnish multinational UPM-Kymmene. Timber from many sources is pulped onsite, combined with imported pulp, mixed with Cornish china clay

Fettykil Paper Mill was started by Charles Anderson, an Edinburgh lawyer, in Leslie, Fife. Anderson was an entrepreneur and inventor who saw a market for paper bags and designed the first automated bag-making machine. While it was successful for 146 years through innovation and investment, it nevertheless succumbed to the costs of energy prices and went into receivership with the loss of 100 jobs. The packaging arm, Smith Anderson Packaging, survived to continue to produce packaging for home and international markets. At the time of its closure Smith Anderson was one of Scotland's oldest and longest surviving manufacturing companies and was the only paper mill to use waste paper as its raw material with no additions.

The good news here was that the plant was re-opened in 2010 by Fourstones, the Northumbrian-based paper maker. It has been re-named Sapphire Mill and there are hopes of creating around 100 jobs over five years. They will be manufacturing tissue for industrial use. Fourstones also uses locally-sourced waste paper. The products include hand towels and 'couch rolls' for medical and beauty salon purposes, hardly the romance of modern manufacture but a worthwhile enterprise. I hope it survives the statistical odds.

Before we leave the world of paper, we should celebrate not just the manufacture of paper but of paper machinery. We can look at two companies, one now gone and one still in existence. Bertrams of Sciennes, founded in Edinburgh in 1821, was one of the foremost manufacturers of papermaking machinery and branched into other areas of engineering. Bertrams Ltd, Sciennes, was established by two brothers, George and William, from an Eskbridge family that had been involved in both papermaking and making papermaking machines. The younger brother, James, founded James Bertram & Son in Leith Walk. The two companies sold papermaking machinery throughout the world, and of course, just as in other industries, this allowed for the manufacture of paper in other countries as well as the copying of the papermaking machinery. A familiar story!

The engineering firm of John Hall in Dartford, Kent, was a leader in paper mill engineering and it was here that the brothers were trained. It was William who started the enterprise with George taking a position at the Dalmore Mill. Edinburgh, being the centre of the papermaking industry, was ideal for siting a works to manufacture paper machinery. As the business prospered, George joined William and the Bertram's story started.

It was Bertram's who supplied the first Scottish-made Fourdrinier machine, to Trotter's Broomhouse Mill near Chirnside. With the cost of paper being dramatically reduced by mechanisation, the demand for the machines grew and Bertram's continued to expand. A steam engine and boilers were installed and the workshops expanded. There is a record of a machine being shipped to Moscow.

Over the succeeding years, the two Bertram firms combined and continued to develop and innovate, inventing and developing papermaking machinery but moving into other areas, such as rubber manufacturing equipment, linoleum mills and shipbuilding equipment. In 1961, they were employing 350 staff in the widest of engineering activities. By 1980, the company was in trouble. The papermaking industry was in decline and other work could not compensate. Bertram's finally closed in 1985. At Sciennes, there are now flats where the factory stood.

I think we should conclude this chapter on papermaking with a success story. While paper manufacture has suffered considerably over the past thirty years, there is one company which has outlasted many of its customers and which is the only supplier of dandy rolls in Scotland and which exports worldwide. I had never heard of dandy rolls until a friend with whom I was discussing my forthcoming book told me that he used to work in a factory in Aberdeen that made them.

I suppose that we are more familiar with the term 'watermark'. Well, it is a dandy roll which applies the watermark to paper. Watermarks became increasingly important to the industry, both as a mark of quality of the paper but also as security, increasingly complex marks being incorporated into the design. As manual production gave way to the Fourdrinier, so the manufacture of rollers incorporating designs into the wire became necessary and these were called dandy rolls, first invented by paper engineer John Marshall of Dartford in 1826. Because of the very specialised nature of this process, only a small number of companies specialised in it. One of these was Woollard & Henry.

The company was founded in 1873 by Ernest Woollard to build and maintain dandy rolls. It was and is still based in Aberdeen, once one of Scotland's centres of papermaking. In the 1930s, Dick Henry took a 50 per cent stake in the company, creating Woollard & Henry. The company expanded in the 1960s and 1970s with export markets in Scandinavia, India and Europe.

In 2002, the company was sold to the employees and is an independent business. While it continues to make dandy rolls and other papermaking equipment, particularly for the banknote industry, it has now diversified into the oil industry, producing transfer capsules to move personnel from rig to supply vessel. They now export to twenty-seven countries worldwide and achieved the Queen's Award for International Trade in 2009.

If you would like a detailed account of the papermaking industry in Scotland, at least up to 1861, then A. G. Thomson's *The Paper Industry in Scotland* is the ideal text. On the other hand, if you would like to know about the people in the industry and their experiences then *Papermaking on the Water of Leith*, published by John Donald, is a great wee book.

Edinburgh's position in the financial world meant that paper was needed for banknotes such as this one, printed for the Union Bank of Scotland.

Paper mill workshop with wood-protected MG (Machine Glazing) machines.

Caledonian Special Train of Paper from G[r]
on account of Union Transit Co Glas[

An official postcard produced by the Caledonian Railway showing the bulk transport of paper.

A potcher, by the way, is a vessel in which rags are stirred and bleached after being washed. The presse-pâte is a machine consisting of strainer plates through which the pulp is sucked. This stops the finer impurities and the pulp flows on to the wire-cloth in a thick web. The salle is the room or warehouse where finished papers are prepared for dispatch.

Railway Locomotive Manufacturing

There are hardly any of my father's generation left in Glasgow. If you met them, they would tell you that an exciting and common site was the transportation of brand new railway locomotives from the works to the Glasgow docks, where they would be lifted into ships ready for transport to all corners of the world. The locomotives would have been hauled on a low loader by steam traction engines, making an amazing spectacle in the Glasgow streets.

For Glasgow was a locomotive maker to the world and while I may have missed the movement of the locomotives, nevertheless, having been brought up in Anderston, in Glasgow, as a young boy I played around the docks where the locomotives were loaded, particularly at Finnieston where the great crane still remains as a monument to those thousands of engines manufactured in Glasgow and sent worldwide. The crane remains as a Category A listed building and as a monument to Glasgow's industrial past.

A locomotive for Egypt being shipped aboard the steamer *Burma*.

Drawing Office, North British Locomotive Works, 1887.

The picture on the previous page shows one locomotive from the North British Locomotive Company in Springburn destined for the Egyptian State Railways being shipped aboard the steamer *Burma* at Plantation Quay in Glasgow in 1949. The SS *Burma* was owned by a Glasgow company, Paddy Henderson's British & Burmese Steam Navigation Company.

This was one of a consignment of fifty locomotives for the Egyptians, who were one of the NBL's best customers. NBL had previously supplied forty locomotives to Egypt in 1928.

The North British Locomotive Company was to become the largest builder in the world and was formed through an amalgamation of three of venerable and successful Glasgow engineering companies: Neilson & Co., Dubs & Co., and Sharp, Stewart & Co.

I was brought up in Anderston in Glasgow in the 1950s. Anderston is a transformed area and it is hard to imagine the scale of industry where there are now office blocks and which is now transected by the Kingston Bridge. Then, Anderston was a bustling industrial, residential, commercial and industrial area with foundries, warehouses, factories, tenements and model lodging houses sharing streets. In 1960 it was also the site of one of Scotland's worst disasters. In Cheapside Street, which ran from Anderston Cross down to the Clyde at Broomielaw, the Arbuckle Smith whisky bond went on fire, killing eighteen firemen and salvage workers. I was there and saw it.

It was in McAlpine Street, just along from Cheapside Street, that Neilson & Co. was formed in 1836, primarily for the manufacture of stationary and marine engines. The company was set up by William Neilson and James Mitchell but was substantially financed by James Beaumont Neilson, inventor of the 'hot blast' process for smelting iron. From McAlpine Street the company soon moved to Hyde Park Street in Finnieston.

While the company had some initial difficulties resulting in changes in ownership, Walter Montgomerie Neilson, eldest son of James Beaumont Neilson, who had joined the company in 1838 as an apprentice, wanted to take the company into locomotive building. At that time, Scottish railway companies had to go to England for them. Walter's ambition came to fruition in 1843 when the first 0-4-0 engines were built for Scottish customers but very soon engines were being dispatched to India.

This was a hugely successful time for the company under first James Reid and then Henry Dubs, who was made a partner. Under his management the company moved to Springburn, retaining the name Hyde Park Works. From here came the thousands of locomotives destined for the world's railways.

Henry Dubs must have had ambitions of his own for he set up his own company in Queens Park. Henry Dubs was an interesting chap and possibly with a temper, certainly single-minded. He was German, originally Heinrich Dûbs, but anglicised to Dubs. I wonder if he knew it is an old Scots word for boggy ground? Anyway, Henry originally worked at the Lancashire Vulcan Foundry when he arrived in Britain. The Vulcan Foundry Co. was a locomotive builder so Henry was clearly building up experience of loco building. From there he moved to another loco builder, Beyer, Peacock & Co., from where he was dismissed in 1857.

He was obviously good as he was taken on by Neilson & Co. the following year. He obviously didn't get on with Walter as he left in 1864 to set up on his own. However, maybe it was Walter that had problems as Henry took with him a number of key staff when he set up the Glasgow Locomotive Works, later to be called Dubs & Co. Henry must have caused a bit of a stir in Glasgow industrial circles when, in 1866, he employed women tracers in the drawing office.

The new company was now in competition with Neilson and very quickly achieved success and a reputation. In 1867, they were producing locomotives for India, Europe, Russia and New Zealand. By 1903, when they became part of North British, they were employing 2,000 people and building 160 locomotives a year. Henry Dubs died in 1876 and was succeeded by William Lorimer.

Another founding company of the NBL was Sharp, Stewart & Co., which began in 1828 at the Atlas Works in Manchester as Sharp & Roberts. Like other locomotive companies, they started with stationary engines but entered locomotive building with the *Experiment* for the Liverpool & Manchester Railway in 1833. It was a bit of an experiment as it was withdrawn soon after it started service. However, they pressed on, with modified engines being sold to Irish and Scottish railway companies.

This was a time of enormous expansion in the railways and therefore locomotive building. The success of Sharp, Stewart's brought pressures on space at a time when the lease on their Manchester factory was running out. It so happened that Walter Neilson's unsuccessful Clyde Locomotive Company was up for sale. This, combined with access to the Clyde as well as lower wage rates, saw the company opt to move to Glasgow. There must be a tradition as they took the name Atlas Works with them when they completed their move in 1888. Very soon they were outstripping their Manchester production figures and selling locomotives to Asia, South America and South Africa. At the merger in 1903 Sharp, Stewart was as big as Dubs with 2,000 people employed producing 150 locomotives a year.

The big three locomotive companies in Glasgow were beginning to see increased competition from home and abroad. Of particular worry was the Baldwin Locomotive Co. of Philadelphia, which had the cheek not only to start selling locos in India, a traditional market for Glasgow engines, but they were also beginning to sell in Great Britain. We will see in the chapter on tobacco that when the Americans were interfering in the British market, home producers would gang up on them. This was exactly what happened in 1903.

The big three decided to combine their efforts and technologies and in 1903 the great North British Locomotive Company was formed and became the world's largest locomotive builder. Its capacity was 700 locos per year, a figure it never achieved, although 570 in 1905 was credible. By 1909, it had produced 3,000 locomotives and by the First World War had produced the staggering sum of 5,000 when, besides producing 1,400 locomotives, the North British became part of the huge munitions operation.

Between the wars, locomotive manufacture experienced the same difficulties as many other areas of engineering and manufacture. The changing demands resulted in redundancies with work being concentrated at the Springburn and Queens Park works. The Great Depression had a major impact with no locomotives being built at all in 1932. The company was then operating at a loss. Again, like many other firms, the Second World War was to revive its fortunes temporarily when it again survived by supplying locomotives and munitions to the Ministry of Supply.

It was after the Second World War that the company ran into trouble. Immediately after the conflict, when countries were repairing their infrastructures, the order book at North British was looking good for both steam and diesel engines. However, the forthcoming move from steam to diesel was to bring challenges and ultimately saw the downfall of this great company. Once known for its quality, it achieved a reputation of providing pretty worthless diesel engines. This was a situation not entirely of its own making.

While there had been experiments with diesel locomotives as early as the 1930s these were generally underpowered compared to steam engines, which continued to improve technically. When there may have been an opportunity post war to convert to diesel or electric, the decision was a long time coming as Britain was a nation with a lot of coal and coal-produced steam. While other countries were reconstructing after the war and running their railways on diesel and electric, the nationalised railway companies were continuing to invest in steam locomotives.

When decisions on conversion were finally taken, the railways, starved of investment, were in a dire state. Cheap imported oil had become available and in the 1960s the change to diesel was implemented. However, it was too late for North British Locomotive. They were slow in investigating diesel and when they signed a deal with a German company to manufacture diesels under license, it all went wrong. Manufacturing and operational problems caused breakdowns. Many of the locomotives had to be returned by British Railways for repair under warranty.

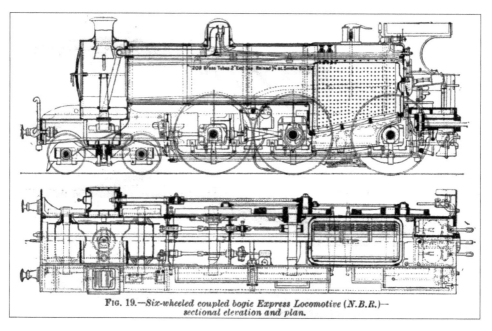

FIG. 19.—*Six-wheeled coupled bogie Express Locomotive (N.B.R.)*— *sectional elevation and plan.*

Six-wheeled express locomotive, one of ten for the Glasgow & South Western Railway designed by James Manson, Locomotive Superintendant.

A similar picture emerged with their electric locomotives. Ten locomotives sub-contracted by General Electric to the company entered service in 1960–61. Again, after long periods in and out of action for repairs, they were refurbished in 1972 but finally withdrawn between 1978 and 1980.

On top of this, the company had been selling the locomotives at a loss in order to stimulate profit on future sales which, not surprisingly, did not materialise. North British became bankrupt in April 1962 and the manufacture of locomotives in Scotland was over, nearly.

Nearly, because one of railway locomotives' lasting success stories is Barclay's. Andrew Barclay was one of a small number of Victorian Scottish engineering companies which survived war, fire and flood to enter the twentieth century still making railway engines. While it is now under new ownership and presently refurbishes rolling stock, it is still a testament to the quality of what it has produced, particularly in the niche market of small locomotives.

Andrew Barclay, based in the Caledonia Engine Works, was set up by Andrew along with Thomas McCulloch in 1840 to manufacture mill and mining machinery. The first setback came when money from the sale of his patent for a new gas lamp didn't materialise. In 1859, having suffered from the loss of his first enterprise, he embarked on locomotive building, producing the first of a line of 4-coupled saddle tank locomotives.

In the 1870s, having expanded into a second company run by other family members, the new and original companies again got into trouble and were bankrupted. With great tenacity, the business was again relaunched as Andrew Barclay, Sons & Co.

The company continued making mining machinery, including a winding engine at Elliott Colliery in Wales, which ran without repair from 1905 to 1981. They also manufactured locomotive engines in increasing numbers and specialised in small industrial locomotives for mining, quarrying and other operations. For example, the locomotive in the photograph in the chapter on coal gas is a Barclay's fireless steam locomotive at Provan Gas Works. A fireless steam locomotive has a steam reservoir rather than a boiler. This reservoir is charged with superheated water which turns into steam as pressure drops. The engine works like a conventional steam locomotive using the steam above the heated water. When the water runs out the reservoir has to be recharged. Clearly, these locomotives have particular uses in gasworks, mines and distilleries and Barclay's were the largest maker, producing 114 between 1913 and 1961.

The company continued its success into modern times, acquiring, in 1930, engine makers John Cochrane of Barrhead and when the North British Locomotive Company was in trouble they picked up the goodwill when it closed in 1963. Goodwill can include trademarks, patents and copyrights.

Another phase of the company began in 1972 when it was acquired by Hunslet of Leeds, which had also been a maker of steam shunters for over a hundred years. The name was changed to Hunslet Barclay in 1989. Following yet another bankruptcy, the company was taken over by Brush in 2007 becoming Brush-Barclay which was again taken over by Wabtec and operating as Wabtec Rail Scotland. The company continues in business in its home town of Kilmarnock, refurbishing rolling stock with a staff of around 100.

Over the years Barclays made over 2,000 steam locomotives, a fair contribution to Scotland's industrial heritage. Around 150 of these still exist in a number of heritage railways and museums and some are still operation as is this one at the Bo'ness & Kinneil Railway.

If you have been reading other chapters in this book then it will come as no surprise to you to learn that Sir William Beardmore again makes an appearance in the field of locomotive building. Always ready to diversify, in the 1920s, even when the competition was struggling, Beardmore's built the relatively small number of just over 300 locos, 200 for home railway companies and 100 destined for India. Along with Armstrong Whitworth of Newcastle-upon-Tyne, who also entered the market, they were in a good position to compete with established builders after 1918 as they had new equipment installed for the war effort as well as a frontage on to the Clyde at Dalmuir. While small in relative terms, the production was constant up to the failure of Beardmore's in the early thirties.

By virtue of the fact that a steam locomotive is a boiler on wheels, it is no surprise to learn that other engineering and shipbuilding companies also attempted to emulate the success of the big three and the NBL. The railways companies also built their own locos but none reached the scale of the output from the North British Locomotive Company.

Braeriach, built for the Wemyss Private Railway serving Methill docks.

Machrihanish railway station with a Barclay-built o-6-2T.

The North British Locomotive Works, Hyde Park, Glasgow.

Rubber – The Industry That Didn't Bounce Back

I went to school at Boroughmuir just above the canal and the smell of rubber from the North British was overpowering. My auntie worked there and she had sole responsibility for sealing rubber diving suits. A friend of hers put her hand into a heated press that was used for vulcanising wellies. Her hand was vulcanised instead!

An Edinburgh worthie

When Glasgow is called the industrial capital of Scotland it is easy to easy to forget that Edinburgh too had its industries, in every way as important to the economy and way of life of people in Scotland. The whaling and fishing industries in Leith were extremely important. To a lesser extent than the west there was also car manufacture and ship building. It was also a centre for the papermaking and printing industries. But perhaps the largest and most forgotten is the rubber industry. This is possibly because its existence along the Union Canal has been wiped out by the breweries which occupied the site there until very recently, where flats are now going up to serve the growth of Edinburgh in finance, education and Government.

Rubber was key to the Industrial Revolution and very little could have been achieved without it's availability for tyres, drive belts, conveyors, hoses and thousands of other products which would have been in use before the invention of plastics, which have mostly replaced rubber except in areas where it simply won't do, such as tyres. But let's start with the continuing story of one of its most well known products, at least as far as the festival-goer and 'green welly brigade' is concerned. For one of the products of the Edinburgh rubber industry was the welly boot, first produced at the North British Rubber Company's Castle Mills on the banks of the Union Canal at Fountainbridge in Edinburgh. The Castle Mills had had an earlier history as an unsuccessful silk mill but between silk and beer came rubber.

The history of the North British Rubber Company began in 1856 with Henry Lee Norris and Spencer Thomas Parmelee, who set up Norris & Co. to manufacture Indian rubber products including boots and galoshes (rubber overshoes which I once wore myself). Norris and Parmelee had come from the United States to operate Charles Goodyear's manufacturing patent. While better know for tyres, Goodyear had been behind a number of patents for making rubber.

In 1857, the North British Rubber Company was subsequently established and its product range was increased. The new products included conveyor belts, much used in the mechanisation of the mines. Tyres were an essential part of the growing lorry and car industry. Other rubber goods included essential domestic products such as hot water bottles, combs, belts and the famous North British golf ball. At the beginning the company employed only four people, but by 1875 there were 600 working at the Castle Mills.

The range of products mushroomed and included cartridge tubing and rubber for the explosives industry, gun sight covers, surgical sheeting, water beds and collapsible baths. There were gymnastic shoes and pontooniers' stockings! These were possibly for soldiers who fought in swampy areas. Surely one of the most unusual products

THE NORTH BRITISH RUBBER Co. WORKS FIRE BRIGRADE 1949.

A. WILSON. J. FORSYTH. J. ARRIGHI. W. MACKAY. W. HARPER. T. LEARMONT. H. DOCTOR. W. BEATTIE. G. CRAIG. S. TWEEDIE. R. THOMSON.
T. BROUAN. A. CROSBIE. J. RUTHERFORD. S MORRIS. T HALL. G. NEWTON. R. LEISHMAN. F. MEECHAN. H. DOCTOR. J. WILSON. J. GLADSTONE. J. RUSSELL.
J. GILMOUR. C. KELLET. J. ROSS. G. ANDERSON. Mr. MARSHALL. T. WINTON. R. BOA. J. CARRICK. (LIEUT) (CHIEF ENGINEER) (CAPTAIN) (LIEUT) (LIEUT)
D. LOTHIAN. R. MITCHELL.

Firemen at the North British Rubber factory wearing North British boots.

was the Baptist Minister's baptismal suit made so that the minister could go into the water fully clothed and come out dry. The top half looked like a very smart grey suit with seals at the cuffs and a white band at the neck to look like the minister's outfit of those days. The bottom again looked like a proper dark grey suit with galoshes. A clever seal at the waist kept everything watertight. Apparently, it wasn't a best seller but it was a special item and shows the diversity of the product range at the time.

This book explains the enormous contributions that Scottish industries made to the efforts of the Allies in both world wars and it would be difficult to judge which industry made the biggest contribution but if keeping your feet warm and dry was essential in the trenches, then the North British Rubber Company was very important. They were tasked by the War Office to produce a boot that would withstand the conditions on the front line. The Wellington boot that they came up with was the envy of the enemy. The company laboured on twenty-four-hour operation to eventually produce 1,185,000 pairs. These were seen as a major factor in keeping the army fit and healthy.

By the end of the Second World War, during which 9,000 people had been employees, the Wellington or 'welly boot' had become accepted footwear, particularly as rationing and manufacturing restrictions had affected the supply of boots and shoes. On construction sites the boot was in use and has become essential safety equipment for working with cement and concrete.

In 1955, along with the Royal Hunter, the company introduced the Green Hunter, which wasn't an immediate success, possibly until Hunter was awarded the Royal Warrant by the Duke of Edinburgh in 1977. It was shortly to become a fashion accessory for the 'Sloane Ranger' and demand shot up when Diana Spencer was photographed wearing a pair in her engagement photographs.

Production of the welly and other rubber products had transferred from Edinburgh to Heathall in Dumfries, to the factory previously inhabited by the Arrol-Johnston Car Company, and in 1966 the company was bought by Uniroyal Limited. The Castle

Gas mask production. Note the use
of the Singer sewing machines.

Mills site closed, with production moving to Uniroyal's site at Newbridge. In 1986, the ownership of the company moved to the Gates Rubber Company of Denver, Colorado, with the Newbridge plant closing in 1997.

During all of this, the footwear part of the company had been subject to a management buyout and in 2004 Hunter became an independent company for the first time.

The company, based in Dumfries, got into trouble in 2006 and was rescued from administration. However, the factory was outdated and a decision was made to close it, making staff redundant but relocating the headquarters of the company to Edinburgh, from where it operates today. Like many other manufacturing companies, it sources its products from the Far East and Europe but supplies the Hunter welly throughout the world and not only to those brave souls attending T in the Park.

The North British was not the only company in Edinburgh. The other manufacturer was the Victoria India Rubber Company of Leith Walk, which was established in 1879. They also made waterproof boots and shoes and supplied fabrics for airships and balloons. While they may have supplied rubber fabric for the airships of Sir William Beardmore's Airship Construction Station at Inchinnan, Beardmore also had a rubber mill in operation.

I recently learned that another major product of the Victoria Mills was the printer's blanket. Given the large number of printing companies, this is not surprising. The printer's blanket is used in offset printing, in which an inked image is transferred from a plate to a rubber blanket, which is then applied to the printing surface.

It came as a surprise to me to learn that not only was Edinburgh the home of the welly but also where the pneumatic tyre had its origins, albeit with a very confusing start. A patent for the pneumatic tyre had actually been taken out by Robert Thompson of Stonehaven, a world-travelling creative genius who had, among other inventions, come up with a process of igniting explosives using electricity. Thompson was only twenty-three when he took out a patent for 'aerial wheels', effectively pneumatic tyres, in France and the USA in 1846 and 1847. His tyres, fitted to horse-drawn carriages, actually worked but he was frustrated at that time by the lack of thin rubber.

It has always been generally accepted that the pneumatic tyre was invented by George Boyd Dunlop, himself a Scotsman. He patented the pneumatic tyre in 1888 but it was only two years later that it was realised that Thompson's patent pre-dated it, the confusion possibly being in the name of the earlier invention. This invalidated Dunlop's patent although he went on to found the Dunlop Pneumatic Tyre Company in Dublin, which became the best-known rubber company in the world.

Thompson's patent had by this time elapsed and there was then a free for all in the manufacture of tyres. Which takes us back to Norris & Co. who, using Charles Goodyear's patents for making rubber, started their manufacture in Edinburgh. One of their brand names was 'The Clincher'. However, the company seems to have lost out in 1907 when Norris left the company. His place was taken by William Erskine Bartlett, who patented the car tyre as we know it today. The new Dunlop Tyre Company purchased the Bartlett patent from the North British Rubber Company in 1907. You might imagine what that patent might be worth today?

The North British was instrumental in the development of the pneumatic car tyre, having first of all produced solid tires for traction engines. In 1946, they entered into an agreement with the United States Rubber Company which helped keep them technologically advanced. As a result of this the US Royal Tyre was produced and in 1956 the US company acquired a controlling interest. In 1966, the company changed its name to Uniroyal and acquired a site at Newbridge, Midlothian, to produce tyres and other rubber and plastic products. As a result, the Castle Mills finally closed in 1973.

There were other tyre manufacturers interested in manufacturing in Great Britain. One of these was India Tyres who, in 1927, took over a major part of what had been Sir William Beardmore's Inchinnan Airship Construction Station and started making tyres.

In 1933, the Dunlop Rubber Company took a controlling interest in the company and owned it for fifty years, employing around 2,500 people at its peak. The company closed in 1981, blaming unfair competition from subsidised tyres from Europe.

In 1930 the company had commissioned an art deco office block which was used by the company for 50 years until its closure in 1981. Following years of neglect it has now been restored and is back in use and takes its place along with the Alexandria Argyll works and Templeton's Glasgow carpet factory as one of the three finest industrial buildings in Europe.

India of Inchinnan was not the only Scottish company to be acquired by Dunlop for, in 1906, it took over the Scottish Tyre Company of Broad Street, Bridgeton, Glasgow. The company had been set up by Colonel J. S. Matthew, who was a pioneer of the Scottish motor car and involved as a director of Argyll Motors. On its absorption into Dunlop, Matthew became general manager of Dunlop in Scotland.

Another victim of the recession in the 1970s was the Goodyear Tyre & Rubber Co. (GB) Ltd of Drumchapel, which closed in 1979 amid bitter recrimination about whether it was the workers' attitudes and low productivity that had brought closure or whether it was the industry cutting back supply in a market that was overstocked. Whatever it was, the factory closed with the loss of 680 jobs to bring difficulties to an area about to suffer from the closure of Singer's sewing machine factory around the same time. The 1970s was a time of huge industrial conflict, which brought us a national miners' strike and the three-day week. There was huge deprivation in many

'The Clincher'.

India of Inchinnan.

areas, not the least in Clydebank, which had already suffered through the loss of shipbuilding and engineering.

I would hope that the end of rubber is not in sight as of May 2012. Showing the continuing precarious nature of tyre manufacture in Scotland, Michelin announced the temporary suspension of work at its Dundee factory, which currently employs 860 people. Michelin, now Scotland's only tyre manufacturer and Dundee's largest industrial employer, blamed the current state of the European economy as well as the mild winter which has reduced the demand for its specialised tyres. Michelin was new to tyre production in Scotland when it opened its factory there in 1972 and has clearly weathered the storms that have beset other manufacturing companies.

If you are interested in the history of rubber, you could do no better than have a look at the website of those who once worked at the North British Rubber Company and who, with a spring in their step, keep the spirit of rubber alive: www.nbrinklies.com.

North British tyres.

North British parade.

Victoria Rubber balloon fabric.

Sewing Machines

A sewing machine seems to be a very singular product to be bothered with in a general book on manufacturing but, after the mangle, it was probably the first domestic mechanical device available and at one time, the world's best known sewing machine manufacturer owned one of Scotland's largest factories, at Kilbowie, Clydebank. Not only that, it has a very particular place in Scottish labour history.

There can be very few people who have not heard about the Singer Sewing Machine. In Glasgow, although times are changing and memories are fading, there are still many people who could tell you that Singer had a huge factory in Clydebank producing their machines. In fact the workforce was so large that they built the still existing special station called 'Singer'.

The word 'Singer' became synonymous with the sewing machine just like Hoover did with the vacuum cleaner. There was clearly a lot of competition for both these machines and it is generally accepted that survival of the fittest could be applied to the process of becoming the most famous and the most successful.

Isaac Merritt Singer and Edward Clark set up I. M. Singer & Co. in 1851 and renamed it the Singer Manufacturing Company in 1865 after having established its first massive factory in New Jersey in 1863. It was to go on to become America's first multinational company.

By 1867, Singer was looking for export markets and the UK was clearly an option given the vast number of vessels plying between America and the UK, and the UK was a gateway to Europe. In 1856, they already had a branch office in Buchanan Street in Glasgow. Their factory at Love Loan, High John Street, near Queen Street Station

Singer Sewing Machine factory Clydebank, *c.* 1900.

in Glasgow, was the first outside the US, possibly because Singer's general manager of the time was George Ross McKenzie, who was born in Scotland but emigrated in 1846. He is credited with the expansion of, and success of, Singer worldwide. By his retirement the company was selling half a million machines each year.

Using machines and parts shipped from New Jersey, thirty machines were being produced each week in 1867. Very soon, expansion took the firm to James Street in Bridgeton where, by 1871, it was the biggest factory in Britain and by 1880 it was employing 2,000 workers. Continued demand and expansion required a green field site, this time on the other side of Glasgow at Kilbowie, Clydebank. Singer's factory, built by Sir Alfred McAlpine, was opened by George Ross McKenzie in 1882. It was the most modern factory in Europe, incorporating advanced features such as a sprinkler system and fireproof doors, the same features which were to become commonplace in Glasgow warehouses, factories and department stores in later years.

Mckenzie was to go on to become the company's fourth president. He was said to be a pious, driven Scot who was a hard taskmaster and who ran the company as if it was his own, crossing the Atlantic fifty-five times on Singer business. He 'entered the company as a mechanic and retired a millionaire'.

A situation at the factory in 1911 led to one of the most memorable of Scotland's labour disputes and contributed to the image of the 'Red Clydesider'. Between March and April, twelve female cabinet polishers protested against work changes introduced as part of the new 'Scientific Management' principles. To them, this would have meant an increase in work and a decrease in wages. In what might now seem like an extreme reaction, the entire workforce of 11,000 went on strike in sympathy.

This was a time of extreme industrial unrest in Scotland with a fourfold increase in strike days compared to the decade leading up to 1910. Trades Union membership increased dramatically in the years leading up to the First World War. The factory owners were suspicious of the motivations of trade unions given the political and social unrest in Russia at the time and used strong methods to prevent disruption to work. At the same time, Scientific Management, introduced by Frederick Wimslow Taylor in the United States in the 1880s and 1890s, was actively being considered in Great Britain. Taylor was the advocate of 'the one best way', which could be found by analysing the work. His approaches included what has become known as 'time and motion' study, the practice of breaking jobs down into component parts and setting standard times for each part. The idea of the white-coated time and motion man is still an image despised in Scottish working history and responsible for any number of industrial disputes.

On the other hand, his efforts, combined with those of Henry Ford, are said to have made a major contribution to armaments factories during the First World War and this set the scene for modern management practice, theory and a move towards further experimentation leading to less intrusive and demeaning practices than are considered to have been advocated by him.

But, back at Singer's, the solidarity shown by otherwise disparate groups of workers within the factory is attributed to the influence of both the Industrial Workers of Great Britain (IWGB) and the Socialist Labour Party. In the face of solid support, Singer's closed the factory and threatened the workers with moving it elsewhere in Europe as well as blacklisting those on strike. This was no mean threat as industrialists were solid in their dislike of organised labour, breaking strikes with intimidation and using 'scabs' to replace striking workers. Following this ultimatum, the strike came to an end after a ballot. The workers voted to return unconditionally on 10 April 1911. They had achieved nothing except solidarity. The company however retaliated against the strikers, sacking all of the leaders and members of the IWGB. Among the 400 sacked was Arthur McManus, who would go on to become the first chairman of the Communist Party of Great Britain in 1920.

The Singer factory braved the ups and downs of two world wars, contributing substantially to the war effort. During the Second World War it made parts for Lancaster bombers, bombs, shells, mines and 60 million rifle components as well as bullets, bayonets and tank tracks. It had its own Home Guard unit to defend the plant; C Company 2nd Battalion, Dumbartonshire, Argyll & Sutherland Highlanders. Sadly, the unit couldn't stop the attacks on the nights of 13 and 14 March 1941 when, during the 'Clydebank Blitz', around 440 bombers dropped their deadly loads on Clydebank and the surrounding area, devastating the town and killing 528 civilians and seriously injuring 617. 35,000 lost their homes in one of the worst attacks of the war. Singer's got off relatively lightly with damage to the famous clock tower and a huge fire when incendiary bombs set light to the timber yard. Thirty-nine Singer workers lost their lives at home, but the work went on with the factory resuming full production within six weeks. Several members of C Company were awarded the George Cross for their bravery.

The Singer Clock.

Singer shop.

Sewing machines continued to be made after the war. The textile industry was booming, as was domestic demand. By 1965 Singer was employing 16,000 workers. However, the next decade saw a massive drop in demand. Competition began to emerge from Europe and the Far East, Japan particularly, which had converted its munitions factories to make sewing machines and other non-military products. The introduction of plastics and new technologies was also moving away from sewn textiles. Singer responded by the introduction of modernised lightweight machines and diversification but the decline continued.

By 1970, the workforce had dropped to 5,000 and continued dropping. Modernisation, diversification and streamlining production had limited effect on falling sales and financial problems. While both management and trades unions put up a brave fight to prevent closure, the end came when President of the company Joseph Flavin confirmed the growing fears of the workforce. The board of Singer's in the United States had decided that the factory should be closed, and closed it was, in June 1980. The buildings were demolished in 1998. The company still exists as the Singer Corporation and is part of SVP Worldwide, which also owns the Pfaff and Husqvarna brands.

From the Great Michael to Govan – The Story of Scottish Shipbuilding

> It was remarked by one speaker that 40,000 men are now employed in shipbuilding on the Clyde, and that the Clyde shipyards could reconstruct the British Navy in two years.
>
> Report in *The Illustrated London News* of November 1876.

Changed days! In 1876, Glasgow was considered the Second City of the Empire and 100 years after the start of the Industrial Revolution it was already in the forefront of developments in shipping, shipbuilding and marine engineering. A further 100 years and shipbuilding was dead in the water with, ironically, only successors to HMS *Nelson* being built in Glasgow, by BAE Systems. BAE is also in Govan, from where was launched the HMS *Nelson*, a twin-screw, iron corvette which was built by John Elder & Co. at the Fairfield works.

HMS *Nelson* was destined to sail for the Australia Station to serve the interests of the Empire in its colony there. While the new HMS *Nelson* clearly had the lines of a traditional man o' war, she was an ultra modern ship with new compound, vertical engines, the first to be fitted to a naval vessel. She had four 18-ton guns and eight of 12 tons, giving an enormous firepower. Since the launch of HMS *Nelson* we can track the growth of shipbuilding in Scotland.

However, it was not on the Clyde that ships of any size were first built, but in Newhaven on the Forth, where was constructed the *Michael* in 1504. The 'Great' *Michael* was ordered by King James IV of Scotland to meet his requirement for a suitably flamboyant flagship. At the time of its construction it was the largest warship in Europe, much larger than its English counterpart, Henry VIII's famous *Mary Rose*, launched in 1510.

The building of the *Great Michael* was reputed to have used up all the remaining timber in Fife, with more being imported from Norway. This would be explained by the fact that the walls of the ship were ten feet thick in parts. With 120 gunners and twenty-four guns, she was a formidable ship. There is a suggestion that one of her guns was the famous Mons Meg, still to be seen in Edinburgh Castle. However, she was a very expensive ship to run and was soon sold on to Louis XII of France. And so was established the great tradition of building naval vessels which continues today. But there were other vessels serving many different purposes.

Much of the growth of shipbuilding was fuelled by the 1707 Treaty of Union, which opened up England's markets to Scottish entrepreneurs and adventurers. In this book we look at the Tobacco lords and their success in importing tobacco. Mills and factories were opening and we were beginning to build the machines that drove the Industrial Revolution. All of this required ships to bring in the raw material and export the finished product. And where else would the enterprising Scot go but Scotland, as we had the skills and the engineering experience.

This tradition in shipbuilding was to last until the 1970s. Scotland was to become the shipbuilder to the world and at the centre of this was the Clyde and her shipbuilding entrepreneurs. One of these was John Elder, whose yards were to

Launch of HMS *Nelson* at Govan in 1876.

form an unbroken line of naval shipbuilding from HMS *Nelson* to the latest Type 45 frigates, which are the now the only ships of any size being built in Scotland and these at the former Fairfield yards now operated by BAE Systems in Govan.

The business had been founded by Charles Randolph, who was joined by John Elder to form Randolph, Elder & Co., which took over the Govan Old Shipyard in 1858, building their first ship, the *Macgregor Laird*, there in 1861. In 1868, they changed their name to the Fairfield Shipbuilding & Engineering Company and built new offices, designed by John Keppie with assistance from the young Charles Rennie Macintosh.

In 1919, Fairfield, one of the great names of Scottish shipbuilding, became part of the Northumberland Shipbuilding Group until it was taken over by Lithgows of Port Glasgow in 1935.

The years following the Second World War were a boom time for Scottish shipbuilding as countries replaced their destroyed fleets and came to Scotland to do so. A major criticism of the shipbuilding industry is that it failed to invest in new technology after the war but Fairfield took this opportunity to do so, embarking on a major £4 million investment programme planned over several years to minimise disruption.

However, like many other yards, tough times were ahead as other countries were already ahead in all-weather construction and were building massive tankers in more technologically advanced yards. In 1963, Fairfield went into liquidation and was sold by Lithgows in 1965.

John Elder.

However, the modernised yards were reopened as Fairfield (Govan) Ltd. The Fairfield Experiment was an attempt to implement new management and production techniques to shipbuilding. This was to last until the new company became part of Upper Clyde Shipbuilders, which collapsed in 1971 following a famous 'work-in'. The closure saw the company become Govan Shipbuilders and was enveloped in the new nationalised British Shipbuilders in 1977.

On de-nationalisation in 1988 the Norwegian Kvaerner group took over and the yard was named Kvaerner Govan and finally passed to BAE Systems in 1999. The Fairfield story is not unique as it mirrors the fate of many Scottish shipyards too numerous to detail. This is an account of only some of them.

During its long history, like many other yards, Fairfield produced many famous ships. These included the Cunard Blue Riband liners RMS *Campania* and RMS *Lucania*. One launched by Fairfield was the first British ship sunk by the enemy during the Second World War, the RMS *Athenia*, which was torpedoed in 1939 and led to German fears that, as it carried American citizens, it would bring the United States into the war.

The *Athenia*, out of Glasgow bound for Montreal, was carrying around 1,700 passengers and crew. There were over 300 Americans on board when it was sunk. It caused outrage in America and Canada.

Another very different disaster showed the danger to which those in the shipbuilding industry were exposed day in and day out. It was a dangerous business with work being carried out of doors, sometimes in freezing conditions when it was impossible to touch metal with bare hands or the skin would be taken off. There was always the danger of falling from scaffolding or being burned by rivets or of any number of

Fairfield Shipyard, Govan.

things falling from cranes and scaffold.

At Alexander Stephen's Linthouse yard, the steam coaster *Daphne* was launched on 3 July 1883. The steamer was built for the Glasgow, London & Londonderry Steam Packet Co. and at its launch was carrying nearly 200 men and boys due to continue their work when the vessel was in the water.

Normally, in this kind of launch, two huge chains would be fixed to either side of the vessel to slow and stop the vessel as it slid towards the Clyde. On this occasion one of the chains failed to move and the current, catching the ship, capsized her. She sank immediately and was completely submerged by the high tide.

The death toll was 124 men and boys. Their deaths were witnessed by the many onlookers on the banks of the Clyde. There is a memorial to her in Govan. The ship itself was refloated and repaired but renamed the *Rose* and later sold on to work a Mediterranean route.

Next down the slipway is William Beardmore & Co. The name of William Beardmore is probably slightly less well-known than John Brown but it is a name that runs through virtually every facet of Scottish engineering, including aircraft, airships, vehicles, munitions and shipbuilding.

Sir William Beardmore of Parkhead Forge had been in the engineering business since 1886 and took over Robert Napier's Govan shipyard in 1900. Beardmore's was already a specialist in making massive propeller shafts and other marine forgings so shipbuilding was a natural progression. The purchase of the Govan yard was followed by the building of his Naval Construction Yard at Dalmuir, also on the Clyde. This was the most modern shipyard in Britain and well suited for warship construction. Production included the 1914 light cruiser HMS *Inconstant*, which took part in the Battle of Jutland in 1916.

Beardmore's also built the Dreadnoughts HMS *Conqueror* and HMS *Benbow*, as well as the first flat-topped aircraft carrier, HMS *Argus*.

Following the First World War, the company had been quite successful in the merchant field, building a number of tankers as well as three transatlantic liners for the Lloyd Sabaudo Line of Genoa. The first, the luxurious SS *Conte Rosso*, was the first new transatlantic liner to be built after the war.

At Dalmuir, activities had grown to employ 13,000 workers and encompassed the manufacture of armaments. However, the shipbuilding arm of Beardmore's suffered just as much as its other activities in the recession following the First World War and the shipyard closed in 1931.

Beardmore's Dalmuir Yard was right next door to John Brown of Clydebank. John Brown's yard at one time exemplified the quality of Scottish shipbuilding and its finest ambassadors were the *Queen Mary* and the *Queen Elizabeth 2*.

I have found that the growth of engineering and shipbuilding has often been through the entrepreneurial and adventurous nature of the Scot who, having learned a business, would go on confidently to set up their own. This was the case with John Brown's, which was started by James and George Thompson, who had previously worked for shipbuilder Robert Napier. They opened their first yards at Anderston and Cessnock, launching their first ship, the *Jackal*, in 1852. This was followed by the SS *Jura* in 1854 and the SS *Russia* in 1867. The SS *Jura* was to cement a long relationship with the Cunard Steamship Company.

The launch of the fast cruiser *Inconstant* at Beardmore's Naval Construction Yard.

Thomson's first yard, founded in my own Anderston in 1847, was called the Clyde Bank Foundry and this name was taken with the company, now run by sons, to Dalmuir further down the river. The shipyard, its workers' houses and the town which sprung up round it was to become one of Scotland's first new towns – Clydebank. John Brown & Co., a steel company from Sheffield, bought the company in 1899 and so was established the engineering giant and town that has become synonymous with Clyde shipbuilding and which suffered some of the worst ravages of the Second World War in what we now call the Clydebank Blitz.

Like William Beardmore, John Brown's yard was extremely busy during the First World War with naval ships and by the end of the war they had produced more destroyers than any other British shipyard. In the interwar years, the company suffered like most other shipyards and engineering works and only survived by the construction of the RMS *Empress of Britain*, the RMS *Queen Mary* and the RMS *Queen Elizabeth*.

But this was not all plain sailing. Construction of the *Queen Mary* (or hull no. 534) had started in 1930 but the Depression saw work being halted in 1931 and the workers laid off. Cunard applied to the British Government for a loan to finish the ship and it was granted on the understanding that Cunard would merge with the White Star Line. The merger took place and, with a great sigh of relief in Clydebank, work re-commenced and she was launched in 1934. The *Queen Mary*, which was called the Grey Ghost because of her wartime colours, went on to make a major contribution as a troop ship during the Second World War.

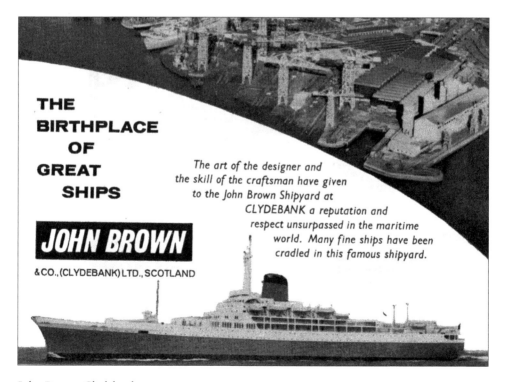

John Brown, Clydebank.

John Brown's shipyard unfortunately suffered a similar fate to others on the Clyde. With falling orders it was taken into Upper Clyde Shipyards, which failed in 1971. John Brown's shipyard was sold by liquidators of UCS and operated by Marathon Oil and then UiE, who built oil rigs from 1980 to 2001, at which time the yard finally closed.

Fairfield, John Brown and Beardmore can actually be classed as relative latecomers to shipbuilding on the Clyde if we consider the long life of Scotts of Greenock. Scotts Shipbuilding & Engineering Co. was founded by John Scott in 1711 and finally ceased shipbuilding in 1993. Between times it was a solid constructor, initially of fishing boats, then naval vessels and passenger liners.

Having been experimenting with submarines, it was tasked by the War Office to build submarines during the First World War. This continued during the Second World War. HMAS *Onslow*, built for the Royal Australian Navy and launched in 1968, is a testament to the skills of the Scottish shipbuilding industry. It is on display in the Australian National Maritime Museum and walking through it gives you a sense of the range of machinery and equipment supplied by Scottish engineering companies, including the periscope from Barr & Stroud of Anniesland, where I served my engineering apprenticeship at the time of the launch of the vessel.

These few shipyards are only a sample of the wide range of shipyards in Scotland. And while the Clyde clearly dominated the picture, nevertheless there were others in Scotland.

Empress of Britain, one of the finest ships built by John Brown.

Queen Mary.

The launch of the world's first purpose-built cruise ship, the SS *Sunniva*, at Aberdeen.

Aberdeen, with its importance as a fishing port, hosted a number of shipyards and between 1790 and 1990 several thousand fishing boats had been built. John Lewis & Sons, established in 1907, produced 'Pocket Trawlers' and its most famous launch was the first factory stern trawler, the *Fairtry*, for Scottish fishing company Christian Salvesen. The innovative vessel allowed for filleting and freezing fish at sea with the frozen blocks of fish bound for Ross's and Birds Eye fish fingers. I remember these blocks of fish arriving at Ross's in Aberdeen as it was next to a factory where I was working at the time.

From 1790 to 1957, Alexander Hall was a famous name in Aberdeen shipbuilding, building mostly fishing vessels but with twenty-six steam tugs completed for the Admiralty during the Second World War. It was one of the companies which failed to modernise after the war and was taken over by another Aberdeen company, Hall Russell, which was the last of the Aberdeen shipyards and which closed in 1992 with the loss of 300 jobs due to lack of orders.

In Dundee, the Caledon Shipbuilding & Engineering Company was founded by W. B. Thompson in 1896. It built frigates, tankers, ferries, lighthouse tenders and one aircraft carrier, HMS *Activity*. Most of its output is unremarkable but among these was the infamous SS *Californian*, which was said by both a ship's carpenter and engineer on board to be in sight of the *Titanic* as she was going down but the ship failed to respond to distress signals.

The SS *Californian*, the largest ship ever built in Dundee at that time, continued in service, being commandeered by the Royal Navy in 1915 and sunk by a U-boat off Greece in the same year. The wreck has not yet been found.

In 1968, the Caledon shipyard, with falling orders, merged with Henry Robb of Leith to form Robb Caledon Shipbuilding Limited, with the Dundee facility closing in 1981.

Henry Robb was founded in 1918 and expanded through acquisition, concentrating its shipbuilding in Leith in the 1920s. Robb's Victoria Shipyard built a range of vessels, mainly for the Royal Navy and for ferry companies. The SS *South Steyne*, launched by Robbs in 1938 for the Manly Ferry route, is the largest steam ferry still in use, albeit as a floating restaurant in Sydney's Darling harbour.

In 1968, Henry Robb and Caledon formed Robb Caledon Shipbuilding. The merged company was one of those that was nationalised in 1977 under the Aircraft & Shipbuilding Act to form British Shipbuilders. The Dundee yard closed in 1981 and Leith in 1983. The Victoria Shipyard is now home to Ocean Terminal and the John Brown-built Royal Yacht *Britannia*, a fitting tribute to British shipbuilding and engineering.

It is estimated that at one time there had been around 700 shipbuilding companies in Scotland, although with about 50–60 operating at any one time. In 1876, 50,000 were employed in the shipyards. At various times we produced 20–50 per cent of the world's shipping. During the Second World War, five ships were being completed in Scotland each week and we built some of the world's greatest liners.

Amazing statistics. So how did it all end? The demise of Scottish shipbuilding probably produces as much acrimonious debate as Scottish Independence and Scottish football, possibly because it was the last of our great industries and mirrored what had already been lost in other industries.

The end was already in sight as the yards were struggling in the 1960s. The Geddes Report had been commissioned by Tony Benn's Labour Ministry of Technology. The resulting Shipbuilding Act of 1967 recommended the rationalisation and integration of shipbuilding and aircraft manufacturers in order to successfully compete in a global market. It was thought that what was needed was economies of scale, investment and horizontal integration.

Among the groupings created with Government backing were Upper Clyde Shipbuilders (UCS), Scott Lithgow on the Lower Clyde and Robb Caledon on the East Coast. UCS, even with a substantial order book, was becoming unprofitable and went into receivership in 1971 and started perhaps one of the most contentious periods in Scottish industrial history.

The Conservative Government of Edward Heath refused state aid to the company and this resulted in severe cashflow problems. The workforce, headed by Jimmy Reid and Jimmy Airlie, took the unusual decision not to strike but to carry out a work-in. They would complete the jobs that they had started and they would do this with dignity. Jimmy Reid spoke to the men demanding discipline: 'There will be no hooliganism, there will be no vandalism and there will be no bevvying!'.

Amazingly, the tactic worked. The work-in had attracted enormous publicity and was supported by demonstrations and donations including one of £5,000 from Beatle John Lennon. The Heath government restructured the enterprise and created Govan Shipbuilders. Yarrow had already withdrawn from the merger and was again independent. John Brown's was sold to Marathon Oil.

There is one argument that the UCS work-in was a resounding success in forcing the Conservative government into a U-turn and stopping a general move towards a free market economy in which there would be no state intervention. This was to be short lived as these policies were again adopted by Margaret Thatcher, some said without any regard to the future wellbeing of those industrial areas that would be affected.

However, before that was to happen, it was recognised that British industry was in a dire state. The Labour manifesto for the 1974 election made a commitment to nationalise shipbuilding and the aircraft industry. The success of the Wilson campaign brought into being British Shipbuilders and British Aerospace in the Aircraft & Shipbuilding Industries Act of 1977. In Scotland, these included the Ailsa Shipbuilding Co. of Troon, Ferguson Shipbuilders, Govan Shipbuilders, Hall Russell, Scott Lithgow, Robb Caledon and Yarrow of Scotstoun. These represented the last of the shipyards of a once great shipbuilding nation.

It was to get worse. Margaret Thatcher's British Shipbuilding Act of 1983 returned the nationalised companies to the private sector. However, the closure of unprofitable and unsupported shipyards continued through the 1980s and 90s and now we are left with only one shipbuilding company, albeit highly successful.

For we are back where we started in Govan, where the assets of Yarrow Shipbuilding Limited were taken over by BAE Systems Surface Ships, which continues to make technologically sophisticated ships for the Royal and other navies of the world. This is one of Scotland's industrial success stories, showing what can be achieved by innovation, investment and good management. The yards at Govan and Scotstoun together employ 5000 in a company that is already planning for the next generation of naval ships.

Barclay Curle Ltd.

The launch of Elders & Fyffes' *Camito* at Barclay Curle.

Clydebank shipbuilding yard.

A North British diesel marine engine.

Men like these carry
on the tradition.

Men leave Yarrow's shipyard at the end of the day in the 1900s.

THE LARGEST.&SMALLEST.TURBINE STEAMERS IN THE WORLD.
BUILDING AT BROWN&COY'S. CLYDEBANK.

The *Lusitania* and *Atalanta* under construction at John Brown's, 1906.

Yarrow's shipyard, with the destroyers *Miranda*, *Landrail*, *Minos* and *Maily* at various stages of construction.

The Scottish Steel Story

One of my first job interviews was at Colville's Clydebridge Steelworks in Cambuslang around 1967. I didn't get the job, possibly because I was late for the interview. However, I did go on to 'get a start' as an apprentice in Coatbridge, the 'Iron Burgh', at the end of the Monkland Canal which once linked Glasgow with the heart of the Scottish coal, iron and steel industry. It was described by an observer in the 1890s:

> There is no worse place out of hell than Coatbridge. At night the blast furnaces on all sides are blazing volcanoes where smelting is continued on Sundays and weekdays, day and night – without intermission.

In our section on ironmaking we saw that the beginning of the iron industry in Scotland was in Falkirk, at the Carron Ironworks. In 1786, they expanded to the Clyde Iron works in Cambuslang, Glasgow, where the famous 'Carronade' cannon was made and where Neilson pioneered the hot blast process of smelting iron in 1828. The invention of the hot blast transformed the cost and efficiency of ironmaking. Lanarkshire, with its deposits of coal and ironstone, was from then to become the centre of iron and steelmaking in Scotland, Coatbridge becoming the 'Iron Burgh' and Motherwell 'Steelopolis'.

**The Colville Group of Companies
Iron and Steel Manufacturers**

Developments within the Group have increased our production capacity and with this our need for technically and scientifically trained men. To the school leaver we offer the opportunity of practical training allied to a suitable course of study at a College of Further Education to prepare him for a satisfying and interesting career.

For full details write to :-
The Group Education & Training Officer, Colvilles Ltd., Park House, Park Street, Motherwell.

COLVILLES LIMITED

Colvilles Limited.

While Lanarkshire was to go on to be a major producer of steel, in fact we were slower than England to produce iron which could be 'puddled' to produce malleable iron, such as was being produced in England and Wales. Malleable iron was the link between iron and steel.

Puddling was a process invented by Henry Cort in Hampshire in 1784. This process involved stirring molten pig iron in a reverbatory furnace in order to burn off the impurities. The reverbatory furnace is long and low with the flame, smoke, and therefore the carbon, being kept well away from the metal. The molten metal has maximum contact with the air and this burns off the carbon. At a stage when the mass was at the right consistency to be worked, it was gathered into a ball and then rolled in a process also invented by Cort. This process arranges the molecules within the mass, giving it strength and making it malleable and thus amenable to rolling.

Steelmaking, on the other hand, is a different process, taking previously smelted and carbon-rich pig iron and converting it to steel through further smelting. Oxygen is blown through the liquid metal, lowering the carbon content. Secondary steelmaking is where scrap steel is the raw material.

Large scale steelmaking in Scotland started with that great entrepreneur Sir Charles Tennant, who established the Steel Company of Scotland in 1871 at Hallside, primarily to make use of the iron ore from his pyrites mines at Tharsis, north of Huelva, in southern Spain. William Siemens had developed the open hearth furnace and conducted experiments to see whether the process could be applied to the Spanish mineral. While it was less successful with the iron from Spain, nevertheless the open hearth process was generally successful with Scottish ore and suddenly Scotland was making steel.

The new steel was about 50 per cent more expensive than malleable iron but was more reliable. It was also more reliable than Bessemer steel. The Bessemer process was patented by Henry Bessemer in 1855. The process involves blowing air through the molten steel and this removed impurities. However, while the process was adopted in England and elsewhere, it was found not to be successful with Scottish ores.

The steel produced by Scotland's open hearth furnaces was approved by the Royal Navy's Chief Naval Architect in 1876 and this opened the floodgates. By the early 1880s, virtually every ship on the Clyde was being built with Scottish steel, with Hallside being in the forefront of production.

For a time, the Steel Company had a monopoly but increasingly and quickly as demand from shipbuilding and engineering grew, other companies became involved in producing malleable iron converted to steel.

The Glasgow Iron & Steel Works was located in Motherwell and Wishaw. Steel production started at Wishaw in 1885 using Bessemer converters. These were not successful so conversion to open hearth started in 1894. In 1902, the Motherwell works were closed, with production concentrated in Wishaw where, by 1914 and the outbreak of war, the works were producing steel for ships and boilers as well as a range of architectural and other steel.

This was the time at which the enterprising William Beardmore was acquiring companies. In 1879, Beardmore had built three open hearth furnaces at Parkhead Forge. The Glasgow Iron & Steel Company was in his sights. Beardmore's teamed

THE PARKHEAD FORGE

Thomas Shanks of Johnstone Lathe cutting a casting at Parkhead Forge.

up with Swan, Hunter & Wigham Richardson of Wallsend to acquire the company. However, the purchase of the company was at the beginning of a trade depression. There was oversupply in the steel industry with Beardmore's making a loss in 1921 and 1922. Steelmaking was concentrated at Beardmore's plant in Mossend, keeping the blast furnaces at Wishaw open. These closed in 1930 at the time of another general depression.

Also involved as a major player was Baird's, which had for a long time been involved in coal mining but entered iron smelting with the adoption of Nielsen's hot blast in 1830. By 1843, they had sixteen furnaces at the Gartsherrie Iron Works, producing 100,000 tons of iron a year. In 1938, the company merged with the Scottish Iron & Steel Company to form Bairds & Scottish Steel. Eventually the company would be nationalised but not before they had become the only other serious contender to the place of Colville's in the Scottish steel industry.

Colville's was one of the great names in Scottish steel and engineering and laid the foundations for what was to become Europe's largest integrated steel foundry and rolling mill at Ravenscraig, near Wishaw. The closure of Ravenscraig in 1992 brought the end of a long tradition of major steelmaking in Scotland.

David Colville, born around 1811, was from Campbeltown where his family was involved in whisky distilling and coastal vessels. In 1840, David set up as a provision merchant in the Trongate in Glasgow. It might be a bit of a jump but in 1861 he moved to iron, joining Thomas Gray to set up Colville & Gray. By 1871, through two dissolved partnerships he had set up on his own, eventually running twenty furnaces and joined by his sons, Archibald and John.

Still producing malleable iron, Colville sent his younger son David to learn the business of steelmaking under William Siemens at the Hallside Works of the Steel Company of Scotland. David was so impressed with the process that he persuaded his father to establish steelworks at Dalzell in Motherwell under the close supervision of Siemens and these went into production in 1880. Dalzell steelworks was to become world famous for the production of steel plate for battleships, ocean liners, locomotive and marine boilers and pressure vessels, all areas where steel of the highest quality is required. Colville's was subsequently to become a huge producer of steel and a household name.

Clydebridge pan mill, 1920s.

Sons David and Archibald Colville were men of steel and their expertise was called upon by the Government to oversee the expansion of steel production in the West of Scotland. Colville's were to eventually take over two steelworks in the West; Glengarnock in Ayrshire and the Clydebridge Steelworks in Glasgow.

In 1930, Colville's, centred on the Dalzell Steel & Iron Works in Motherwell, had become a limited company. In 1936, they acquired the Steel Company of Scotland, the Lanarkshire Steel Co., Smith & MacLean Ltd and the Clyde Alloy Steel Co. With Glengarnock, Hallside and Clyde Iron they were now a huge enterprise. In 1937, they embarked on a rationalisation programme which was eventually to culminate in the plans for the Ravenscraig integrated steelworks.

Rationalisation was certainly required. Even before the start of the Second World War, there was increased competition from Europe. Costs were rising and outdated machinery was coming to the end of its life. British ore fields were worked out and there were raw material shortages as companies had to source from abroad.

The 1950s was a boom time for Scottish steel, mostly due to re-armament and the reconstruction of the British infrastructure. Mills were rolling continuously and improvements in smelting and casting had increased efficiency. By 1958, Colvilles alone was employing 17,000 and the weekly steel output was rolling at 40,000 tons. However, the home advantages of cheap coal and ore had come to an end. Coal prices had risen 134 per cent between 1950 and 1967. The pressure of demand had prevented companies from investing in new equipment and technology and equipment was outdated.

The iron and steel industry recognised the need for investment and rationalization but this did not come in the form the industry wanted. They saw the need for a single strip mill rather than the two that were announced by Harold MacMillan's Conservative government in 1959. For political purposes, a mill in Wales was announced at the same time as the plans for Ravenscraig. Neither mill was ever to work at full capacity.

Worldwide, nations had been reconstructing after the Second World War and making major investments in industrial infrastructure. France, Belgium, Luxembourg and West Germany were joined by Japan as competitors in a shrinking market. Thomas Miller, Chair of Motherwell Bridge & Engineering Co., had remarked in 1958 that much of the lack of progress in steel development as well as survival had been due to a lack of cooperation between companies scared of losing their own identities and secrets. This had certainly not seemed to be the case in the early days when the pioneers had been keen to share their ideas. In any event, the industry was fragmented and apart from the construction of the Ravenscraig Mill, it was working on the same cautious principles of the 1930s. Rationalistion was on the cards.

In 1949, the Labour Government headed by Clement Atlee decided to nationalise the iron and steel industry. The Iron & Steel Act was enacted in 1951, with the government acquiring all shares in the largest eighty iron and steel companies. The argument behind this was that the existing arrangements for the supply of steel produced a system that could restrict output, therefore raising prices, and generally impede progress in technical developments, one of the most frequent criticisms of industry following the Second World War.

The nationalised companies proved very difficult to manage and, in any case, by 1953 the new Conservative government had returned ownership of sixteen of the seventeen companies to the former shareholders, mostly the original holders. Colville's was returned to its former owners in 1955 having had an approval of major investments by the Iron and Steel Board in 1954. By 1957, Ravenscraig had a number of coke ovens, a blast furnace and three steelmaking furnaces. A strip mill was completed in 1959. Major new infrastructure included the building of three huge offloading cranes at General Terminus at Tradeston, on the Clyde. I often watched the offloading as the ore was dumped by the cranes in the midst of great clouds of 'stoor'. The ore was then transported to Ravenscraig via the Glasgow Harbour Railway. In 1954 alone, Scotland imported 1,436,000 tonnes of ore from Sweden, Newfoundland and North Africa. The Glasgow Harbour Railway, General Terminus Quay and the ore handlers have now all disappeared, replaced by business parks and housing.

While the original nationalisation of steel companies was unsuccessful, Harold Wilson's Labour government tried again, successfully establishing the British Steel Corporation (BSC) in 1967. The Act encompassed 90 per cent of steelmaking in Great Britain and in Scotland, the new BSC included Colville's.

Unfortunately, it seems that BSC had not only inherited old technology but old attitudes to investment. It was also subject to the high oil costs of the 1970s. By the middle of the 1970s, BSC was making a loss despite the concentration of manufacture in five areas, including Scotland.

The inexorable loss of business to Scotland eventually led to the closure of Ravenscraig and the end of steelmaking as an industry. With the return of Margaret

Clydebridge, 1970s – pouring iron into an open hearth furnace.

Thatcher's Conservative government, British Steel was privatised in 1988. It subsequently merged with Dutch steel maker Koninklijke Hoogovens to form Corus, which was subsequently acquired by Tata Steel of India in 2007.

Ravenscraig Steelworks had employed 5,000 at its peak. The strip mill closed in 1991 with the loss of 770 jobs. Steelmaking finally finished in 1992 with the loss of the remaining 1,220 jobs. It is estimated that there were around 10,000 jobs directly or indirectly linked to the works. The closure of a number of other companies was caused by, or related to, the closure of Ravenscraig. Among these were the Clydesdale Steelworks in Mossend and Clyde Alloy of Craigneuk as well as Anderson Strathclyde, famous for mining and tunneling equipment.

Open hearth furnaces had all been closed in Scotland in the 1970s and steelmaking was concentrated at Ravenscraig. With the existence of continuous casting (concast) at Ravenscraig, slabbing and billet mills were closed at other plants. Eventually, the finishing mills and other works depended on Ravenscraig. Therefore, when Ravenscraig closed, the other works lost their source of steel slabs and billets. Dalzell now gets slabs from Scunthorpe.

The closure also mirrored the social and personal tragedies of other major industrial closures. The effect on families in the area was devastating. Many of the workers there had gone to work in the steel mills straight from school and had no other skills other than those needed to produce and roll the steel. Marriages and family life suffered. Ravenscraig had taken on 200 apprentices a year and that disappeared too. I was working in Craigneuk at the time of the closure and I can confirm that there was a general air of despondency and bewilderment at how a successful plant producing quality steel could ever close.

While steelmaking is no longer carried out in Scotland, on a positive note, there is still a processing side. Steelmaker Tata, which had acquired Corus, still continues to operate the Dalzell and Clydebridge plants. Dalzell is a heavy plate rolling and processing plant, taking slab from Tata's Scunthorpe plant for processing. Clydebridge carries out heat treatment on plates rolled at Dalzell and Scunthorpe to produce plate that can be used where strength and toughness is required. The workforce at Tata numbers around 270, including an apprenticeship programme. It is a joy to see the long steel trains passing through south Edinburgh on their way to Dalzell. It gives the feeling that there is still some heavy industry left in Scotland.

You might not exactly experience the smoke, smell and stoor of industrial Lanarkshire as I knew it but if you visit the Summerlee Museum of Scottish Industrial Life in Coatbridge you will get some sense of the industry in the area. Set at the end of the Monklands Canal, in the remains of the Summerlee Iron Works, it has excellent displays of our industrial past as well as Scotland's only heritage tramway. Remains of the Summerlee Ironworks can be seen from a viewing platform. If you would like to read about the history of steel in Lanarkshire you could do no better than visit Colin Findlay's website:http://myweb.tiscali.co.uk/clydebridge/.

Puddling furnace.

Jimmy Cunningham, first hand melter at the L open–hearth furnace, Clydebridge.

Up in Smoke – Tobacco and Cigarettes

I don't know how many times I must have passed the bust ensconced in its niche in the entrance hall to the Mitchell Library, in North Street, Glasgow, the very same street of my youth. I visited the Mitchell Library often, firstly with my father, who was studying at Glasgow University and then to read the great volumes of back issues of *The Sunday Post* containing 'The Broons' and 'Oor Wullie'. Later, I was to study there myself as a school pupil.

To generations of studying Glaswegians the Mitchell Library was and is a friendly face and a place of learning and support. Before the expansion of the Glasgow universities and colleges, the Mitchell might be the port of call when no space could be found in the home to study. More recently, the library is again busy, not just for lending but for family research, internet access or to pour over its extensive collection of newspaper and family history archives. For 'The Mitchell' is still the largest municipal reference library in Europe.

It is strange that on the many times that I passed that bust on the way to the front door for a smoke, I did not reflect on the name Mitchell and his legacy, built on an empire dedicated to cigarette manufacturing. Strange too that the Mitchell must have been one of the only buildings in Glasgow in which smoking was not allowed.

Stephen Mitchell is probably one of the best known of a few Scottish tobacco merchants who were to expand their businesses, moving from the low tech manufacture of pipe tobacco to highly mechanised cigarette manufacturing using modern machinery. Their companies were eventually to be consumed by growing conglomerates and, like other manufacturing enterprises, lost to Scotland.

Smith's 'Glasgow' Mixture.

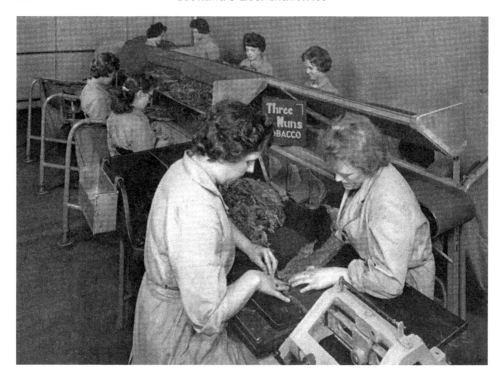

Producing Three Nuns – a popular J. & F. Bells/Mitchell & Sons brand.

Stephen Mitchell was not a well publicised man as very little is known about him and his lonely death from a fall in his retirement town of Moffat. Mitchell had been born in 1789 in Linlithgow, where his family had been involved in the tobacco business. In 1825, import legislation requiring the use of bonded warehouses in designated ports had taken his company to a base in Candleriggs and then to St Andrew's Square in Glasgow's Gallowgate area.

The company continued to flourish, being taken over by his brother and then his nephew, also Stephen. Stephen remained unmarried and retired to Floral Cottage in the spa town of Moffat. Unfortunately, he was found dead with head injuries, presumably through a fall on a walk to a local mineral well. He left an astonishing legacy, for not only had he made money from cigarette manufacture but he had invested in railways in Britain and in North America. His will provided bequests to charitable organisations and to the Unitarian Church in Glasgow. The largest, however, was the huge gift of £70,000 for the endowment of a large public library. This was gratefully accepted by the City Council and so was established perhaps this greatest public institution, one that provides lasting benefits to the city.

Mitchell's other legacy was, of course, the establishment of a cigarette manufacturing industry that combined with W. D. & H. O. Wills and others in 1901, to become the Imperial Tobacco Company.

Stephen Mitchell represented a tradition of tobacco trading and manufacturing in Scotland that had started with the 'Tobacco Lords' of the eighteenth century, who made fortunes in the trade between the New World and Great Britain and who are

Mitchell's famous 'Gold Flake'.

still remembered in thoroughfares in Glasgow's Merchant City such as Virginia, Glassford, Jamaica, Dunlop and Buchanan streets.

The Tobacco Lords were a product of the 1707 Treaty of Union that allowed trade between Scottish merchants and what had been exclusively English colonies. The stoppage to trade off the south-west coast of England during the French wars after 1735 gave an advantage to Scottish merchants and the position of the Clyde gave it a distance advantage when sailing ships took such a long time to cross the Atlantic. By 1760, with tobacco being transhipped from Glasgow to most areas in Europe, the town had outstripped London as the main port for tobacco in Great Britain, mostly because of the recognised entrepreneurship of the Glasgow merchant.

The Glasgow traders also undercut the Bristol merchants, who were otherwise focussed on the slave trade. Unfortunately, Scots traders also involved themselves, although to a lesser extent, in the notorious triangular trade including transportation of slaves from Africa to the Americas and then returning with tobacco, which was re-exported to Europe.

The wealth created by the tobacco merchants is well illustrated by the houses in which they lived, none so ostentatious as William Cunninghame's mansion in Royal Exchange Square, which is now the Gallery of Modern Art. Another is the Tobacco Merchant's House in Miller Street in Glasgow's Merchant City, one the last remaining mansions. Built for Robert Findlay, who died in 1802, it has been restored and is now home to the Scottish Civic Trust. The Lords were ostentatious in their black silk breeches and red jackets, sporting silver and ebony sticks. Given that Edinburgh was a magnet for nobles and courtiers, the Tobacco Lords were the nearest thing to aristocracy that Glasgow had and they intended to show it, irrespective of any Calvinistic roots.

Following the American Civil War, American merchants had become just as enterprising and were sending their produce directly to Europe, cutting out Glasgow traders. This trade was recovered in part as some customers were retrieved and Glasgow merchants continued their trading with all parts of the world, particularly in linen and cotton.

While the Tobacco Lords were busy trading in the commodity, others were buying it and converting it to a range of products including snuff, cigars and 'shag' for pipe smoking. In terms of domestic Scottish production, Mitchell's was probably one of the largest and best known names in Scottish tobacco and he and his likes established the cigarette manufacturing industry, which was to become a substantial employer in Scotland, particularly in Glasgow.

Imperial Tobacco came about as a vehicle to thwart the acquisitive interests of the American Tobacco Company (ATC), which had entered Great Britain with the ostentatious purchase of Ogden's, making it known that they were in the market for other companies.

Thirteen companies amalgamated while continuing to manufacture under their own names. Among these were Scottish companies Stephen Mitchell & Son, F. & J. Smith (Glasgow Mixture) and D. & J. MacDonald. They were then joined by J. & F. Bell (Three Nuns) in 1904.

Finlay and John Smith founded their company in 1858 and were based in George Street in Glasgow with a factory in nearby Albion Street, where they were employing 200 people in 1888 on snuff, cigars and pipe tobaccos. Smith's, like the others, continued to produce under their own name after the merger. Their George Street building is now part of the University of Strathclyde.

Like Mitchell's, D. & J. Macdonald was based in St Andrew's Square from 1840, subsequently moving to the Trongate, where they employed 150 workers using modern machinery.

The policy had been to merge but continue trading under the original names and the arrangement worked well for many years. However, by the end of 1980, the different companies had been integrated and the twenty-two constituent companies had been reduced to three; W. D. & H. O. Wills, John Player and Ogden's, which had come back from ATC as part of a non-competition deal.

In 1981, Imperial Tobacco continued their reorganisation as a result of a decline in the demand for tobacco products. Centralisation, rationalisation and efficiency were called for and they closed four factories, including the Wills cigarette factories in Glasgow and the Player's cigarette factory in Stirling in 1983. Rises in cigarette duty were also cited as a reason.

The Wills Factory had been based in Alexandra Parade and although designed pre-war in an Art Deco style, the factory opened in 1953 and, at its closure in 1982, was employing 600, manufacturing the Embassy and Lambert & Butler brands. It is now a business centre. A second, cigar factory, was opened in 1963 and closed in 1990.

Wills's closure was particularly felt in Stirling, where the main industries were and are tourism and finance. The factory, making Players and No. 6 brands, had been in existence for twenty years and its closure brought the end of 500 jobs, which had a huge impact on the economy of a town the size of Stirling. At the time of closure Wills's Scottish factories between them were making the astonishing figure of 160,000,000 cigarettes a week. This figure was supplemented by the volume of cigarettes manufactured by the Scottish Co-operative Wholesale Society (SCWS), which produced cigarettes on behalf of the Co-operative shops throughout Scotland. The manufacture, established in 1891, was seen as a democratic answer to both Imperial Tobacco and the American 'Tobacco Trust', whom they saw as putting tobacco companies out of business and driving up prices. By 1918, the factory was producing the enormous amount of 23,905,100 cigarettes per year as well as cut plug, shag and snuff.

Brands included Shieldhall Virginias, Kanata and Adana Turkish cigarettes and Rocky Mount cigarettes, which I clearly remember being sold in our local Co-operative store in Argyle Street in Glasgow. I will not confess to buying them myself at such an early age as I would have been then.

In 1959, when the Monopolies & Mergers Commission reported on the industry, the SCWS was reporting sales of £2,190,000, compared to £591,896,00 from Imperial Tobacco's fifteen factories. Imperial Tobacco had clearly established economies of scale and this continued with rationalisation. The Shieldhall factory remained in production until the early 1970s, when financial difficulties caused the merger of the SCWS and its English counterpart, the CWS.

The larger manufacturers of cigarettes and tobacco were concentrated in the West of Scotland, particularly in Glasgow, but there were also smaller producers. In 1864, there is a record of thirty-two producers, many of these combining retail with snuff, cigar and pipe smoking tobacco. John Duncan, for example, concentrated by 1888 on importing Havanas and making cigarettes. Their work rooms were on the top of

John Cotton Charter cigarettes.

An image from a cigarette card showing a model of the *Queen Mary* undergoing testing.

their building at 94 Buchanan Street. Their domestic trade was extensive and their main export market was Canada. The retail business, at least, was sold to Sinclair of Edinburgh in 1951.

There were a small number of producers in other areas. John Cotton, maker of Royal Edinburgh and Charter cigarettes, was established in Edinburgh in 1770 and made cigars, cigarettes and pipe tobacco. It was sold to Belfast-based Gallahers. Like some other brands such as Bell's Three Nuns, John Cotton continued as a brand of cigarillos in recent times. Their factory still exists as a business centre in Sunnyside in Edinburgh. Also in Edinburgh, John McKinnell's Dunedin Cigarette Factory in Powderhall produced Lorraine cigarettes and Clan tobacco.

In Dundee, the firm of Fairweather made the strangely named Tassie de Luxe cigarettes and Cut Golden Bar. In Perth, in 1911, Charles Rattray, who had left Fairweather's, set up his own factory and became known worldwide for tobacco such as Black Mallory and Jock's Mixture. Charles Rattray died in 1964 and his son, who succeeded him, retired in 1980. The recipes and brands were subsequently acquired by German company Kohlhase & Kopp, who still produce pipe tobaccos such as Rattray's 3 Noggins.

The acquisition and subsequent use of Scottish brand names is a common feature in the death of manufacturing industry. In many cases, this is not asset stripping but the natural conclusion when the value of a brand is contained in the name and little

John Cotton factory, Edinburgh.

Smith's Glasgow Mixture.

else and not in the means of production. The absence of cigarette manufacturing may be considered to be no loss at the moment but where it was the mainstay of an area, it was felt deeply. Lost too were the other inputs to cigarette manufacturing, including paper for the cigarettes and for packets as well as for inserts such as cards and coupons.

Cigarette cards were produced as a promotional tool and quickly became collectable, with companies issuing albums in which to collect their cards, which were issued in series covering many topics, from famous footballers to ships, aircraft and cars as well as flowers, first aid, air raid precautions and similar subjects.

Vehicle Manufacturing

The manufacture of powered vehicles in Scotland lasted less than a century but that century proved to be adventurous and innovative. However, enterprise and innovation often can't translate into success in the long term. There was an abundance of engineering skills in Scotland ready for the development of the internal combustion engine. Unfortunately, lack of management ability, lack of cost control and over-

Arrol-Johnston.

reaching ambition was the downfall of the fledgling vehicle companies. That is not to say that some of them were not extremely successful in their time and contributed substantially to the effort in both World Wars.

The manufacture of cars in Scotland started with those entrepreneurs like William Beardmore who were already involved in engineering and saw the motor car as the way ahead for transport. Their customers were generally the better off and enthusiastic motorist upgrading from horse and carriage. In fact, cars were actually very simple constructions and like the Arrol-Johnston, some makers simply continued to add coach bodies so that they looked like motorised coaches.

As industry, local government and the armed services moved from horse and carriage, the opportunities for providing motorised transport seemed endless. These early companies seized these opportunities and thrived at the beginning of the twentieth century, mostly due to their ability to turn their skills to the war effort through the mass manufacturing of lorries.

But, following the First World War, there was a tough time for car manufacturers because of a drop in orders, recession and competition. This was a time in which the lorry and car were very simple and copying was easy as long as a reliable engine was available.

The 1930s was a particularly difficult time in all areas of industry. Orders were few and far between during the Depression and car companies had difficulty in surviving, particularly those who had overstretched themselves by building lavish manufacturing plants. This period showed the lack of practical management skills, including marketing, business forecasting and budgeting. While there appeared to be funds available for investment, the good management of these funds appears in doubt.

Albion Motors was the only company to survive the 1930s until it was joined in modern times by the opening of the ill-fated Rootes Linwood plant, producing the Hillman Imp and other marques.

Albion Motors – 'Sure as the Sunrise'
I have particular memories of the Anderston district of Glasgow in the 1950s and 1960s as that was where I lived. One of these was the regular passing of grey-painted vehicles without their coachwork, only the chassis. Even the driver was unprotected as these skeletal vehicles headed eastwards along Argyle Street towards the City. My father explained to me that these chassis had come from the Albion works at Scotstoun. He would have been very familiar with these lorries as he was then a foreman motor mechanic with McIntosh's Removals in Argyle Street.

I don't remember having been told where they were heading although I eventually found out that some of them were heading for Walter Alexander's Coachworks to emerge as single or double-decker buses. Albion Motors is the best known name in car and lorry manufacture in Scotland and is to Scotstoun what John Brown's is to Clydebank, just up the road. However, while the Albion badge is still seen on the walls of the Scotstoun works, the days of manufacture of lorries and cars have long passed with the last lorry rolling off the production line in the 1970s. The Albion brand is now owned by American Axle & Manufacturing, a company which makes chassis and drive components. Only ghosts of the Albion drive down Argyle Street these days.

While it no longer makes vehicles, its 1899 founders, Thomas Blackwood Murray and Norman Osborne Fulton, would have been pleased to see their name still in existence over a century later. Murray and Fulton were previously involved in the production of another famous Scottish car, the Arrol-Johnston, but left the syndicate to form the Albion Motor Car Company. Albion was originally based at 169 Finnieston Street and their first cars were offered at £280 as 'suitable for the country house'.

Their first car was a 'dog-cart', used for shooting parties, with a compartment for dogs. This was later converted into a delivery van. John Murray, owner of the second car produced, actually drove it to London, covering 1,500 miles without mishap. Because of the lack of filling stations, petrol had to be bought in Glasgow and sent ahead. This car is now in the Royal Scottish Museum in Edinburgh.

The company moved to their Scotstoun works in 1903 and here car production continued until 1915, when competition and good sense made the company switch entirely to commercial vehicles, production of which had begun in 1909. This now included large numbers of 3-ton trucks destined for the War Office for service in France.

Albion was a successful brand, building up a solid following and a good reputation for quality. It was probably this that attracted a successful takeover bid from acquisitive Leyland Motors in 1951, which had a similar vehicle portfolio. At that time the main products were the Albion Chieftain, Reiver and Clydesdale trucks and the Viking bus. In 1968, the now renamed Leyland Motor Corporation merged with British Motor Holdings (including Jaguar, Daimler, Riley and Morris). This formed the behemoth British Leyland Motor Corporation (BLMC). Trucks and buses continued to be produced fully, then partly at the Scotstoun works until 1980 and these have been exported throughout the world.

BLMC and the Leyland Tractor – 'Bathgate no More'

With the formation of BLMC, the Scotstoun works remained open but in 1961 some of the production was moved to the new Leyland plant in Bathgate. The move to Bathgate was to signal a new phase in vehicle manufacture in Scotland, with the introduction of the Leyland tractor. Based on the Nuffield tractor, production continued until 1982, when the company was sold to the Nickerson Group and production subsequently moved to Gainsborough.

The new company had proved too difficult to be managed in the industrial relations and economic climate of the 1970s, particularly in that it was producing outdated cars, which were competing against themselves. Overmanning was rife as were labour disputes.

The problems resulted in Harold Wilson's Labour government bail-out of £2.4 billion to preserve jobs in Labour's industrial heartlands. Margaret Thatcher reluctantly continued to support the renamed BL Group but in 2005, now called MG Rover, it finally went into bankruptcy. Some of the marques continue to exist but the closure brought to an end production at Bathgate by 1985. Following the loss of

An advertisement for the Hillman Imp..

tractor manufacture, the plant had been concentrating on lorry assembly. The Albion name survived but was dropped when the company became Leyland (Glasgow). Albion Automotive emerged from a management buy-out in 1993. The existing owner took over Albion in 1998 and continues to produce transmission systems and chassis. So all is not lost in vehicle-related manufacturing.

Arrol-Johnston

And now, back to the Arrol-Johnston, which is considered by some to have been the very first vehicle manufactured in Great Britain and was so from 1896 to 1931. It was certainly the first in Scotland. George Johnston had been employed in locomotive manufacture in Glasgow and was involved in early unsuccessful experiments with steam-driven tramcars. He then turned his attention to the design of motor cars and manufacture was made possible when Johnston was joined by Fulton and Blackwood Murray, both of whom had engineering experience.

A syndicate was founded under the name of the Mo-Car Syndicate to fund the building of the car and, with major financing from Sir William Arrol, famous as the builder of the Forth Bridge, the Arrol-Johnston was born.

The company began its production at Camlachie, Glasgow, and then in Paisley before moving to a purpose-built factory at Heathall, Dumfries, said to be a replica of Henry Ford's Motel T factory in Michigan.

Similarly to Albion, their first production, in 1898, was a 'dog cart', with a 2 cylinder 12HP engine. This was a sturdy vehicle as it was produced, virtually unchanged, until 1907.

In the beginning, the company struggled and was helped out of its difficulties by William Beardmore, eventually bringing it in as a subsidiary of his company. The company did well with this foundation but the car market was extremely competitive. Despite a merger with Aster of Wembley in 1927, producing the Arrol-Aster, and rationalisation and concentration of production on one site, at Heathall, Dumfries, the company was unable to continue and ceased production in 1931.

One loss, as a result of the rationalization, was the Galloway, a subsidiary of Arrol-Johnston, whose cars were made in Tongland, Kirkcudbrightshire, from 1920 and then from 1923 at Heathall. The Galloway plant was an experiment in job creation for local women instigated by Dorothea Pullinger, daughter of the manager of Arrol-Johnston, T. C. Pullinger. Production was originally set up in a factory built for the manufacture of aircraft engines. However, with rationalisation, production moved to Heathall. Times had been tight and only a few hundred of the Galloway 10/20 cars were produced. At Heathall, the Galloway 12 replaced the 10/20 in 1925 but along with other marques was discontinued with closure in 1931.

During the short time as Arrol-Aster the company made the body for Sir Malcolm Campbell's car *Bluebird* in 1929 and an Arrol-Aster ran in the 1931 Le Mans 24 Hour Race. The Arrol-Johnston company was also to produce the very first off-road vehicle, for the Egyptian Government. They also produced one to travel on ice for Ernest Shackleton's South Pole expedition in 1908.

Walter Bergius and 'The Kelvin'

The start of the twentieth century was clearly a boom time for the fledgling automobile industry in Scotland, for another famous but short-lived car made its appearance in 1904 – 'The Kelvin', made by the Bergius Car & Engine Co.

Walter Bergius was an entrepreneur who quite appreciated the need to have a car with a reliable engine. The availability and patent issues surrounding the use of engines in the early days was problematic. Bergius' adoption of the word 'engine' in the company name turned out to be rather clever.

Bergius set up his company at 169 Finnieston Street in Glasgow, a hub for early vehicle production in Glasgow as 'The Albion' also started there. The company made fifteen cars between 1904 and 1906. In the early days of motorcar production, there was no such thing as a production car. Each vehicle was a development of the last. The Kelvin was no exception, with cylinders needing re-designed after the first outing. Future changes included redesigned bodies and the use of pneumatic tyres. The early designers were clearly learning from one another.

The Kelvin did prove its worth during a reliability trial in which it covered 1,000 miles over some of Scotland's most difficult hill roads. However, the development of the car was draining resources. As mentioned, it was the engine which was to come to the rescue when William Bergius, brother to Walter, suggested its use in a boat. A suitable launch, *The Kelvin*, was purchased and the engine installed. It was a great success and established the Kelvin as a marine engine. It was to become extremely successful as the British fishing fleet was installing engines. The production of cars was wisely abandoned, given the costs and competition, and development focused on the engine. The company moved to Dobbie's Loan in 1910 and was soon producing 700 engines a year. Further developments included the introduction of diesel engines. Walter Bergius died in 1949 and the company had to be sold to meet death duties. It has passed through a number of owners and the renamed Kelvin Diesels was finally purchased in 2000 by British Polar Engines, based in Helen Street in Glasgow.

Walter Bergius in The Kelvin, arriving in Pitlochry.

The Argyll

The competition from home and abroad was obviously fierce at the start of the twentieth century and your car had to be good to survive. The Argyll was to have a successful life until its demise in 1932. The Argyll had its origins in the Hozier Engineering Co., started by Alex Govan, in Bridgeton, in 1899 on behalf of the businessman William Smith, who already had substantial interests in Scottish industry. His first car, the Argyll Voiturette, was basically a copy of a Renault with a de Dion engine.

Govan was one of that great age of Glasgow engineers and entrepreneurs who studied at the West of Scotland College of Technology. He had had unsuccessful forays into bicycle manufacture which failed because of overproduction and competition, the same fate of some car companies. The Argyll itself had an on-off existence over its short lives.

The early success of the Argyll, said by some to be a product of its unique gearbox, brought it to a grand purpose-built factory in Alexandria opened by Lord Montague of Beaulieu in 1905. The factory, with its imposing sandstone and marble frontage, was never used to capacity. Just as soon as it was being built, the American economy was in decline and throughout Europe the demand for cars was falling even as competition was fierce. Govan had invested huge, some would say disproportionate, amounts on the new factory, including lavish staff facilities. His attempts at emulating American mass production techniques were in difficulty and in the middle of this Alex Govan died in 1907 of a brain clot. The company never recovered from its difficulties and was wound up voluntarily the following year.

Argyll Motorcar.

The company was resurrected in 1910 under the name Argyll Ltd. There were some successes in this existence with the 'Flying Fifteen' but a range of problems including patent litigation and bad management decisions along with the inherited problems of the huge factory and a too large range of vehicles led to shareholder lack of confidence and creditor concerns. These finally resulted in closure of the works in 1914. The liquidators took the decision that year to sell the factory to the Admiralty even while ambulances were being built for the War Office.

While there were clearly many dimensions to the closure of Argyll, it is clear that as well as bad management decisions there was very little thought given to the competition and what it was doing amd very little business forecasting and appreciation of cost control, which had created a lavish and unnecessary factory.

But all was not lost. While the liquidators had sold the Alexandria factory to the Admiralty, the company had still owned the old Bridgeton works and a bid for these was made by John Brimlow, who had been a service manager in the now dead company. It was he who restarted production in the original factory with the servicing of the 5,000-plus Argylls that had already been made. His intention was to eventually begin motor manufacture. To this intent, and with the backing of other ex-staff and directors, the Argyll Motor Company was formed.

Production in this phase actually lasted a reasonable time, but by 1928 the company was again in difficulty, returning mostly to servicing existing cars. The company finally closed in 1932. The closure of the Argyll company was probably inevitable given the competition from Europe, England and also from Scotland, mainly from Arrol-Johnston and Albion. However, while Arrol-Johnston hit the buffers, Albion had understood the need to move out of automobile manufacturing into commercial vehicle manufacturing. Argyll's late move into fire engines and ambulances was too late for survival.

You might imagine that with the emergence of the first municipal petrol vehicles, every town and parish would be clamouring for its first fire tenders and ambulances. The coming of the First World War brought huge demands for standard and therefore mass-produced lorries and vans, the kind of demand that Argyll was looking for but didn't see the opportunities.

Not so the Halley Industrial Motor Company, which saw openings in the commercial market at the start of the twentieth century.

Halley's Industrial Motors

The Halley Industrial Motor Company of 1906 had its origins in the Glasgow Motor Lorry Company, formed by George Halley in 1901, with one of its first and most popular productions being their fire engine. Originally based in Finnieston, it acquired premises at Yoker. Halley's introduction of its lorry body clearly came at the right time for municipalities and companies the length and breadth of Great Britain who were moving from horse-drawn wagons to motorised vehicles. Fire engines, ambulances and other municipal vehicles were clearly in demand and as the Great War approached there was a need for the army to be motorised. Halley answered this call and by 1914 was considered one of Great Britain's largest vehicle manufacturers.

It was probably by astute management that Halley survived during the tough trading decade that was the twenties, particularly when, in 1922, the Government was reported as having 'dumped' 18000 ex-services vehicle through the Slough Trading Company. This was to have the effect of swamping the market and putting British lorry

Halley 5 Ton Lorry.

manufacturers into jeopardy. Halley seem to have weathered this, possibly through sales of parts, more diversification into omnibuses, and street cleaning lorries.

A reconstruction and renaming of the debt-laden company as Halley Motors Ltd in 1928 allowed its continuance. It was in a stronger position in 1929 and in 1930, a controlling interest was taken by the North British Locomotive Company, in a new departure for them but in line with a general move by railway companies into motor transport. However, the company eventually succumbed to the Great Depression in 1935. North British would not repeat its injection of capital and it closed, with the Yoker works being taken over by Albion.

Halley vehicles exist in small numbers and are highly prized for restoration. Fine examples are the 1911 Leith fire engine and 1914 lorry in the Grampian Motor museum in Alford, which is one of the finest small museums in Scotland. And if you are in Alford you really must visit the Alford Heritage Centre, which gives an insight into the life of the ordinary working people of Donside and north-east Scotland and includes an amazing range of tractors. The name of Halley lives on in Halley Street, in Yoker, now mostly housing, and Halley Motors of Milngavie, which was founded by the son of George Halley.

William Beardmore and Company

For those who know of William Beardmore it will come as no surprise that his company was involved in vehicle manufacture. As one of Scotland's great industrial conglomerates, William Beardmore & Co. had involvement in most Scottish engineering industries including aviation and shipbuilding. Perhaps, though, their involvement in taxis would be the most surprising.

The company was founded by William Beardmore, later Lord Invernairn. The company was in existence between 1890 and 1930, employing 40,000 at its peak. Based originally at the Parkhead Forge, the company was initially involved in the manufacture of forgings for the marine industry, moving then into the production of armour plate and armaments. Diversification came with the purchase of the Robert Napier shipyard at Govan and then the building of naval shipyards at Dalmuir where aircraft carriers and Dreadnoughts were produced.

Involvement in vehicles had started as early as 1903 when Beardmore's had taken a controlling stake in the troubled Arrol-Johnston, which went out of business in 1931. During that time, Arrol-Johnston appeared to exist quite independently of Beardmore's other vehicle manufacturing enterprises. In 1917, Beardmore's also bought Alley & MacLennan's Sentinel wagon works, which had moved to Shrewsbury from Glasgow in 1915.

The Beardmore Motor Company went on to manufacture vehicles in factories at Anniesland, Coatbridge and Paisley. Their first car was a tourer which, with teething problems, was renamed the 12/30 and was produced from 1923. Their move into taxis was in 1919 with the Mark 1 Taxi that was produced in Paisley. The taxi and its variants proved to be sturdy vehicles, meeting strict requirements set by the Metropolitan Police.

Like many successful offshoot companies, their success is often affected by the success of their parents. Following the First World War and moving into the

Depression, Beardmore's ran out of steam as demand for its engineering products declined. In 1929, with the company in financial difficulties, William Beardmore was removed from the boardroom.

One casualty was the taxi, which was sold to the company directors. Production moved to Hendon, in London, where in various forms it had a rather longer life, surviving until 1966.

Beardmore had also ventured into motorbike production between 1921 and 1924 with the Precision. Road Rollers were also manufactured and Beardmore lorries made an ugly appearance in 1930, which I thought strange considering the difficulties they were in. They bought the rights to a French tractor unit that was produced in London but this part of the business was sold on as a going concern in 1932 with production continuing to 1937.

Madelvic Motor Carriage Company

With the coming of the internal combustion engine, there were many opportunities for the entrepreneur and industrialist. As long as you could obtain or make a petrol engine, the rest was in fact very easy. Lorries and cars were actually very simple constructions. Engineers and blacksmiths could make cars but they needed very different skills to take them to the market, where there was demand but where there was also competition.

One such company was the Madelvic Motor Carriage Company, founded by William Peck. His factory in Granton opened in 1898 to produce an electric-powered car with a fifth wheel producing the drive. There was not a great demand for the car although the company received orders from the Post Office for delivery vans to run between Edinburgh and Leith, the first motorised postal service in Scotland.

The vans were 18 cwt and powered by accumulators (early rechargeable batteries). Unfortunately, it looks like ambition and cost-overrun again reared its head and the company went into liquidation in 1899. But it was not all over. The Kingsburgh Motor Company took over briefly before collapsing, with the assets passing to Stirling Motor Carriages, who made buses from 1902 until 1905, some of which were exported to Australia. Stirling Motor Carriages, also trading as The Hamilton Carriage & Motor Car Works, was an old-established coachbuilder that bought Daimler chassis and applied their own coachwork. Stirling also has a claim to the first Scottish automobile produced.

It is thought that the site continued to host efforts to continue manufacturing lorries, buses and taxis but production finally ceased around 1915, with the factory being used to store torpedoes.

William Guthrie and The Glasgow Tractor

So far, it is clear that the manufacture of Scottish vehicles was down to a breed of entrepreneurs who had the skills to start an enterprise but not necessarily to see it through to mass production. This was the case with William Guthrie, whose first foray into vehicle manufacture was the manufacture of small cars produced by his DL Motor Manufacturing Co. These had a V-shaped radiator with 8, 10 and 12 HP models built as two seater, four seater and delivery vans.

Guthrie had been involved with the development of the Argyll car but appears to have left them to set up the Dalziel [renamed DL] Motor Manufacturing Co. in Motherwell. It seems that production of the car did not last long. Not many were made as Guthrie's attentions were turned to the manufacture of lorries for the War Office. Then, following the First World War, in 1919, Guthrie's attentions were on an agricultural tractor which he had been experimenting with.

Designed by Guthrie, the 27 HP 'Glasgow' was Scotland's only home-designed tractor, manufactured by the Wallace Farm Implements Co. of Glasgow. The design featured an unusual three-wheel configuration.

Wallace Farm Implements had been set up to manufacture the Glasgow. Managing directors of the company were William Guthrie and Duncan McNaughton Wallace, of a well-established agricultural company, John Wallace & Son. Included in the prospectus for the new company was the intention to purchase the National Projectile Factory at Cardonald, which had previously been used for the manufacture of munitions.

The period after the First World War was a boom time for agricultural production and John Wallace was obviously keen to apply the new developments in the internal combustion engine to agriculture. Production started at Cardonald with the ambition of making and selling 5,000 in the first year, but only a few hundred were ever made. The tractor seemed to be less popular at home than it was abroad with models being shipped to the Colonies, where some still survive today. It is thought that the machine failed because the company had little experience in agriculture. The all-important repeat order was not forthcoming so it looks as if it wasn't popular on the ground.

With a stock of unsold tractors, production ceased in 1924 and the company went into liquidation. It looks as if enterprising skills were not followed by marketing skills. It is also possible that in marketing they were not taking into account the growing competition from American tractors such as Fordson, John Deere, Case and International Harvester, which were all looking for new markets.

Another factor may have been that the agents for the Glasgow, the British Motor Trading Corporation, was in difficulties and was perhaps not the best vehicle for marketing a tractor. Possibly, like Argyll, ambitions prompting the purchase of oversized premises were unrealised.

Massey Harris

Another tractor to be built in Scotland was the Massey Harris. Based in Kilmarnock, Massey Harris, formed in 1891, was a Canadian company which was once the largest builder of tractors in the British Empire. Their continued success and expansion brought them to Kilmarnock and Manchester in 1949. At the beginning the factory was producing fifty tractors a week. In 1953, they merged with Ferguson, acquiring the 'Ferguson System' of hydraulic attachments.

The Massey Ferguson plant had a troubled industrial relations history but survived until its closure in 1980, at which time it was called Massey Harris Ferguson and was also producing a range of combine harvesters. The Massey Ferguson name had been used from 1958.

The 1980s was a difficult time for Massey Ferguson, given a decline in demand for agricultural products. As a result, they met some of the difficulties by closing factories. From Kilmarnock they moved production to Marquette in France, with whom production had previously been shared. There was some surprise at the time as industrial relations and quality at Marquette at the time were said to be worse than Kilmarnock. 1,500 jobs went with the closure in an area already devastated by closures, with more to follow.

The Stonefield – 'The Hardy Scot'

And while we are examining the history of the Scottish lorry, we mustn't forget the famous and ill-starred Stonefield, which, although it was an excellent vehicle, couldn't survive what was thought to be lack of short-term support and bungling at a government level. The Stonefield was the creation of Scottish entrepreneur James McKelvie. His idea was to produce a rugged all-terrain vehicle with a military and utility market in mind. He saw that there was a gap in the market above the smaller and lighter Land Rover. He was quite right, for it began to establish a demand from fire services and the military worldwide.

Production started in 1974 in Cumnock with an excellent all-terrain vehicle that passed military and fire service testing. Unfortunately, James McKelvie died in 1978 and the company was taken over by the Scottish Development Agency (SDA), which expanded production with a new factory capable of producing 2,000 vehicles a year. With the return of Margaret Thatcher's Conservative government in 1979, the SDA was forced to relinquish control of what was essentially a nationalised industry. This move created enormous uncertainty within the workforce as well as in the purchasing market. While orders were in the pipeline for what was an excellent product, through what was reported at the time as government bungling, a buyer could not be found and confidence in the company collapsed, causing its closure in July 1980.

This was all hugely political at the time as the factory was in an area of high unemployment. In the face of a huge campaign to keep the workforce going, the government was accused of rushing through a deal to pass the company over to Gomba Holdings. The government was roundly criticised by the Public Accounts Committee. The work was lost in any case when Gomba transferred existing production to an enterprise zone in Strood in Kent. The company finally closed in the early 1990s.

Rootes and the Hillman Imp – 'Linwood no More'

The revolutionary rear-engined Hillman Imp came about as Rootes' answer to the BMC Mini and the need for petrol-efficient cars following the 1956 Suez Crisis. Rootes was a well-established British car manufacturer based in Coventry. Their Hillman Minx had been a good seller but was recognised as a mid-range family car. Rootes wanted to compete in the smaller car market established by the Mini but also populated by the Riley Elf and the Wolseley Hornet.

Restrictions on the ability to expand their Liverpool plant brought them to Linwood, near Paisley, with a £10 million government grant to offset the huge loss of employment caused by the closure of shipbuilding and engineering works on the Clyde. The opening of the Rootes plant was accompanied by a sister plant, the Pressed Steel Company, which would supply panels to Linwood.

The Stonefield fire rescue tender.

The plant opened in 1963 and difficulties were experienced right away. There was naturally a lack of car-building skills in a workforce more used to riveting and plating. Rootes itself had little experience in building small cars, let alone one with the novel feature of an aluminium engine which was turned at 45 degrees to lower the centre of gravity. The aluminium castings made in Linwood had to be sent on a 600-mile round trip to England for finishing before being returned to the assembly line in Linwood.

Unfortunately too, the poor labour relations affecting other car factories were transmitted to Linwood and in 1964 there were thirty-one industrial disputes affecting production and only a third of the anticipated yearly output of 150,000 Imps was produced. A poor quality product in its first few years produced a possibly underserved reputation from which the car never recovered, even though it had done well in the British Saloon Car Championships, winning a third time in 1972. On the plus side it was a low-cost car but without the cachet of the Mini it was doomed not to have a long-term future. Ambition and huge factories were the downfall of the Argyll and other Scottish car ventures. It was the same for the Imp.

The investment in the Imp and in Linwood was the undoing of Rootes, which was taken over by Chrysler soon after the death of Lord Rootes, who had initiated an approach to the American company. While prices were reduced, sales were marginal and with less than 500,000 sold worldwide, production ceased in 1976. As part of Peugot Talbot, the plant remained open to produce the Hillman Avenger and the Sunbeam but closed in 1981. In all, 13,000 direct and indirect workers had been left jobless by the closures.

The first production Imp can be seen in the Glasgow Transport Museum.

The Glasgow Tractor.

Albion Claymore.

THE EXTRACTIVE INDUSTRIES

Coal – King of Scotland

Coal has been known about from at least the twelfth century but has only actually been used in any great quantity in the last 200 years. This may appear strange but when we think about the difficulties in extracting it, it might be reasonable to expect that where peat, wood or charcoal were more plentiful then that might be used instead. This was exactly the case with Scottish coal. Coal was certainly used for heating and cooking where it was available close to the surface, but in very local areas.

In this book you can read that very early industrial uses of coal were in salt panning and lime kilning, very local rural activities. It was only with the invention of the steam engine in the eighteenth century and the coming of the railways that coal came into its own.

But coal would not be enough to turn Scotland into an industrial power. There is a theory that Great Britain was where the Industrial Revolution started purely by accident. It may equally have happened in many other European countries. It just happened to be Great Britain. In Scotland, the enterprising landowners were in the fortunate position to take advantage of the fact that not only was there coal on their lands, but ironstone was available in the ground in Scotland. There may not have been vast quantities, but there was enough to kick-start the age of steam.

The earliest small-scale methods of extracting coal were in drift mines or in bell pits. The bell pits, named as, in cross section, they had the shape of bells, could only be used while they were small enough not to cave in. The word 'pit' would thereafter be retained for most other mining activities.

As mines developed, the technique of 'stoop and room' was used. A stoop is a pillar of coal and as the mine was enlarged, these were left in place to support the roof. You can imagine the danger posed by these methods.

As mining progressed, deeper and more dangerous shafts were dug. The mineshafts could only be supported by wooden shoring and the ladders and platforms used to reach the depths of the mine were also wooden. This all limited the extent to which coal could safely be extracted. Unfortunately, safety was not always at the forefront

Fife Coal Co.

of the landowner's mind, for the first commercial mines were developed by estate owners and they were still learning.

The early uses of coal included lime kilning and salt making and these were becoming profitable, and more so when it could be transported by sea and rail. But that was in the future. For coal extraction could only be local until the wood ran out, as it did, and the invention of iron and then of steel. It would also not happen until strange prejudices against it disappeared. It was looked upon with deep suspicion. Experimenting in London, the brewers and blacksmiths tried it but there were outcries, resulting in the King being petitioned, with laws being passed against it as 'an intolerable nuisance'. Ladies complained that coal smoke ruined the complexion and would not eat food cooked over coal. This would all change with the invention of the steam engine and the realisation that coal could be profitable. Someone writing in the sixteenth century recorded that 'the use of coal beginneth to grow from the forgo and into the kitchen and halle'. This is quoted in David Bremner's 1860 *Industries of Scotland*. He also says that 'coal was suddenly raised into importance with the invention of the steam engine: and since then it has been one of the most valuable agents in spreading civilisation, and in promoting the welfare of mankind'. It's an opinion I suppose.

The earliest written accounts are for the granting of rights to monks along the Firth of Forth to take fuel. This would be around 1200. From then to around 1500, the taking of coal was obviously increasing in importance, with some exports even though it was prohibited by the Crown. In the 1600s, we find the Privy Council setting prices for horse-loads of coal and allowing export licenses. This shows that coal mining was expanding and both Crown and landowners were beginning to establish a protected industry, albeit still primitive. In 1690, in the reign of William and Mary, this protection was extended, allowing only Royal Burghs to export certain commodities including coal, lime and salt.

One of the things preventing deep coal mining was flooding as there was no practical way of removing any quantity of water accumulating in or flooding mines. This was to change with Newcomen's invention of the steam engine, which was first used in Scotland for pumping water from mines. While James Watt is credited with the invention of the steam engine, he actually improved Newcomen's engine by the use of a separate condenser, widening the application beyond mines and speeding up the Industrial Revolution. The Newcomen engine produced steam, which was condensed by a stream of cold water, producing a vacuum in a chamber. It was this vacuum that caused a pressure difference, causing a piston to move, in turn moving a beam connected to a water pump.

The engine made a dramatic change to the amount of water that could be extracted. Around 1600, the amount of water manually pumped from mines could be as much as eighteen times the amount of coal taken. Newcomen's first engine pumped ten gallons per stroke from 150 feet at Dudley Castle, Staffordshire, in 1712. This was a breakthrough and was to change coal mining.

From 1745 until 1765, the increase in amounts of coal being exported to London from Scottish ports show the dramatic and continuing increases in productivity. From 2,400 tons in 1745 the increase was to 6,600 tons, an increase of 4,200 tons. The continuing development of the coal industry saw the disappearance of the stoop and room when the 'longwall' system was introduced in the 1870s. Rather than hold up the pit roofs with the wasteful stoops, timber pit props were introduced. The procedure started with miners cutting their own props before the start of each shift. This was the procedure at Grange Colliery at Bo'ness, where George Stewart realised the inefficiencies of the system. He went into partnership with Glasgow businessman James Love, starting up a large industry in Bo'ness, importing timber from Scandinavia and making the props on site. At one time there were 120 acres of timber storage in the area and by 1935, over 140,000 tons of pit props were being imported per year. Bo'ness, named 'Pitpropolis', had a declining pit prop boom as the trade eventually collapsed with the import of ready cut pit props and the import at other ports.

The other major improvement in work practice was the coal-cutting machine, developed first by James Baird as 'The Gartsherrie'. This was the first chain driven coal-cutting machine. It moved coal mining away from the purely manual to the mechanical. It was a prototype for many others over the next century and revolutionised coal mining. The Baird family was later to find very good use for their coal when they opened the Gartsherrie Iron Works, which was to employ thousands.

CAGE LOAD OF MEN

Just like a truck load of cattle,
Sixteen crushed on at a time,
The yawning abyss beneath them,
Awaiting the bottomer's chime,

To leave all the glories of nature,
And toil in the muck and the grime.
Hard-handed stalwarts of labour,
Nutured to grin and to bear,
Seldom a thought of the danger
That haunts every corner down there,
Praying to Christ it was shift change
But not in the language of prayer.

Extract – Joe Corrie miner 1894-1968

It used to be called 'King Coal', for, by the start of the twentieth century, we were reliant on it for industry, commerce and for the home. Gone were the days of suspicion and instead it was fueling domestic ranges, steam engines, steam trains, the shipping industry, foundries and steelworks. It was being turned into coal gas for lighting, heating and cooking. It had replaced water power in the mills. However, those who criticised it as a smelly and nasty in London when it was first introduced were proved to be right. For the cities and towns became shrouded in smog, a mixture of smoke and fog we called a 'pea souper', which I experienced often in Glasgow in the 1950s. This pollution was indeed to make life intolerable and eventually lead to the imposition of smokeless zones under the 1956 Clean Air Act.

The demand for coal increased up to and into the twentieth century, by which time we were also exporting a third of the output. There were 3,200 mines and, incredible to think now, they employed over one million people, or 10 per cent of the working population. In Scotland, in the early 1900s when the population was 4.5 million,

Old coal workings at Cowglen, Thornliebank, dug up at the start of the twentieth century.

there were around 150,000 people employed in the mines and 40 million tons of coal were being produced yearly.

Because of this, it became a powerful political issue. It was central to the British economy but those many workers began to ask questions about their working conditions and in particular the system of payments. The Tonypandy Riots in Rhondda in 1910 and 1911 were symptomatic of feelings towards the mine owners. This was an industrial dispute that got out of hand and resulted in Winston Churchill, the Home Secretary, sending troops to assist in quelling the riots. While the miners went back to work empty-handed, the issue of payments festered with, in 1912, the Miners Federation of Great Britain asking for national wage agreements and a minimum wage. These were refused by the mine owners and the disagreement led to a national strike. Given the strategic importance and the developing situation in Europe, the mines were taken into state control, a situation which lasted until 1921. On this occasion the miners were successful as the strike led to the Coal Mines (Minimum Wage) Act 1912.

Following the First World War, many export markets dried up and were never regained. A general slump affected industry and in 1926 the mine owners, who had taken back control, tried to increase profitability by increasing productivity while reducing wages. The inevitable fight back by the now powerful miners led to the 1926 General Strike in which many industrial unions participated, including railways, transport, dockers, printers and iron and steelworkers.

On return to work after nine days, the strike gained the workers very little, as they returned to lower wages and longer hours. Mines were being closed and miners thrown out of work. Unemployment was around 60 per cent in some mining areas. By the Second World War, employment in the industry had fallen to a third of its pre-strike 1.2 million. By the war, however, productivity had increased from 200 tons to 300 tons dug per miner.

With the coming of the war, many miners who had previously fought against the government were conscripted to fight in Europe. By 1943, 36,000 miners had left the industry before the government realised that they had made a mistake. They had conscripted highly experienced miners and as a result the supply of coal for the war and for domestic use had dropped dramatically. The Minister of Labour, Ernest Bevin, introduced a scheme to divert a percentage of conscripts, as well as volunteers, into the mines to replace those who had left. So, some young men who had been expected to find themselves fighting towards Berlin found themselves hewing coal in the mines. The 48,000 'Bevin Boys' were often discriminated against as avoiding war service and it was not until the 1990s that their contribution to the war effort was officially recognised. They continue to be represented by the Bevin Boys Association.

Just like the First World War, during the Second, the government took control of coal reserves. Following the war, Clement Atlee's Labour government fulfilled a long-held ambition to nationalise the industry, with the National Coal Board being formed in 1947. Two hundred companies were taken over, with the NCB employing 700,000 people, falling to 634,000 in 1960 after closures of uneconomic pits. The closures hit the Scottish coalfields particularly hard.

The continuing drop in demand continued to force the closure of collieries. Great Britain had been suffering from competition from coal mining subsidised in other countries and coal was beginning to be imported here. Open cast coal was already making inroads into Britain, mined at very much lower cost than traditional methods. Pressures piled on the industry from the growing use of nuclear power and then the introduction of natural gas, with many houses in Britain being converted to natural gas by the mid-1970s.

As the 1970s progressed there was increasing militancy, with the MFG being renamed the National Union of Mineworkers. The oil crisis of 1973 was helpful to the miners' cause. As oil prices quadrupled because of an oil embargo imposed by Arab countries, a 1974 strike was successful and credited with the downfall of the Conservative government of the time. During the late 1970s and 1980s, the industry continued to contract. In Scotland, in 1980, the industry had dropped to 20,000 employees producing seven million tons in just thirty mines, a tenth of the 1900 figure.

When pit closures were announced by the chair of the NCB, Ian McGregor, a local Yorkshire strike became national under the miners' leader, Arthur Scargill. The strike was to go down in history as Great Britain's worst ever. On one side, strikers were travelling en masse to pits to picket. On the other hand, busloads of police were also being transported in to protect blackleg workers who had been drafted in to break the strike. It was bloody and bitter and has left a legacy of mistrust in mining towns. The strike failed and the pit closures went on.

In 1987, the NCB was privatised and mostly English assets became UK Coal, now the biggest coal producer in the UK, owning both deep mines and open-cast. By the time of privatisation only fifteen productive pits remained open. Coal seams continued to be exhausted and this saw the closure of Wales' last deep mine in 2008. While deep coal is still mined at pits in the north and Midlands of England, coal mining in Scotland went into the hands of Mining Scotland and then Scottish Coal (Deep Mine) Limited.

The last pit in Scotland, owned by Scottish Coal, was Longannet, combining the Bogside, Solsgirth and Castlehill collieries into one huge complex with connecting tunnels. The output went to Longannet Power Station. Disastrously, but without loss of life, the Longannet mine flooded in March 2002 with millions of gallons of water inundating the mine. There was no possibility of pumping out the water and Scottish Coal went into receivership. The reason for the influx is not known but presumed to be a collapse of the rock strata or failure of a dam that was protecting the mine from old mine workings. Ironically, with record production figures, the Longannet mine had had good prospects and was considered a blueprint for the future of modern deep mining.

Open cast mining still continues in Scotland with mines operated by the Scottish Resources Group. The open-cast mines in Scotland produce over 50 per cent of the output of Britain's open cast mines. 95 per cent of the coal produced goes for electricity production and will be critical to energy production for years to come, particularly as coal is now being imported to supplement home production. So coal in Scotland is not completely lost, just smaller, but just as important as it always was.

Before we leave mining, perhaps we should say something about those who have risked their lives down Scotland's mines in search of black gold. Even from the very beginning the industry was dirty and dangerous and in the front line were women and children until legislation changed working practices. From the time of going down a mine, all kinds of dangers would be present. There were accidents from failure of equipment, particularly cages (lifts), fire damp (mostly methane), explosion, flood and roof falls.

The dangers in the pit were well known and at one time an expected 'collateral damage'. In records from 1866, David Bremner shows the dangers. In all areas of Scotland, in 472 collieries with 41,246 miners and 12 million tons of coal raised, there were seventy-seven lives lost. They also recorded the fact that for each life lost, 161,000 tons of coal were raised. A chilling statistic!

While every death is a disaster, there were some major, multiple deaths which continue to be remembered with due reverence. The second largest, remembered by a statue in Hamilton, was the disaster at Udston Colliery on 28 May 1887, when seventy-three colliers were killed by a fire damp explosion. Among these was William Bates, forty-one, of East Kilbride who was married with seven children. As often happens in small communities, a number of people from the same family were killed. William Boyce was killed along with three brothers as well as a brother-in-law. The deaths were denounced by the Secretary of the Scottish Miners' Federation, Keir Hardie, as murder.

The Udston quarry was a small pit with 200 men and boys working in three seams of coal up to 1,000 feet underground. The fire and explosion is thought to have been caused by unauthorised shot-firing. Having started shift at 6 a.m. and three hours in, a fire and explosion ripped through the mine during a breakfast break. It is said that the sound of the explosion could be heard through 135 foot of solid coal in the nearby Greenfield colliery.

On 18 September 1959, at Auchengeich Colliery, Lanarkshire, forty-seven miners died while travelling on bogies towards the coalface. A faulty fan for air purification caused a fire and the resulting smoke enveloped the men, who had been stuck in the road (passage). There was only one survivor of the disaster. This was one of the worst mining disasters in the twentieth century. There were forty-one widows and seventy-six fatherless children.

It was a hugely dangerous occupation and between 1870 and 1880 about 2,700 men and boys were killed in the UK's mines. This finally resulted in a Royal Commission, one result of which was the setting up of mines rescue stations in the Coal Mines Act of 1911.

These mining deaths are not forgotten. While the pits are now gone and replaced with housing estates and shopping malls, in virtually every town and village in the mining areas you will find memorials to both the existence of the colliery and the people who worked and died there. The Scottish Mining website also contains details of the deaths in all the Scottish collieries.

If you would like to see how a colliery worked then you can visit the Scottish Mining Museum which is based in the former Lady Victoria Colliery. The Lady Victoria, opened in 1895, was said to be the first 'super-pit' of its time and worked until 1981. It is considered to be one of the best preserved Victorian collieries in Europe. By visiting it you can see how coal mining developed in Scotland as well as seeing a fine example of a colliery winding engine.

A colliers' row in Cowdenbeath.

Montgomeryfield Pit, Dreghorn.

Carved in Stone – Scotland's Granite Story

It was in 1974 that I first stood on the edge of what was then Europe's largest man-made hole, the Rubislaw Quarry in Aberdeen. Here, beside the 'Blondin', the wire that stretched over the 400-feet wide, 450-feet deep quarry and was used to hoist stone up from the bottom, I wondered at the scale of the quarrying operations that had once been carried out there.

At that time, most of the dizzying depths of the quarry could be seen. The quarry, opened in 1741 and closed in 1971, has gradually being filling with water, the cost of pumping being one of the final reasons for closure. Now the quarry is virtually full but there are plans afoot to drain some of it and use it for leisure purposes.

I had been taken there by George (Dodd) Watt, who wanted to show me what real stonework was. 'Now loon', he said. 'Hauf o' Aiberdeen has come oot o' that hole. Thon great wire was for taking the men up as well as the stone. They would walk doon in the morning but were allowed to take the bucket up at the end of their shift.' We could see the remains of the precarious gangway snaking down into the deep hole.

Dodd was a labourer who I had met while working on the new Market Building on Aberdeen's Union Street. It may have given him a living but he was indignant that concrete was being used on this new building while virtually the rest of Aberdeen's long main street was built of the silver granite from Rubislaw. I suppose I made the happy mistake of asking him to expand on it, which he was pleased to do, at length. It turned out that he, his father, uncles and several cousins had all worked in the huge granite quarrying and building workforce in and around Aberdeen, at one time numbering 25,000 before its demise in the 1930s.

Rubislaw quarry.

As we looked over the quarry, Dodd explained.

That wire there we called the 'Blondin' aifter thon famous tight-rope walker. The hole got that narrow at the bottom that taking the stone up was difficult so John Fyffe came up with this system. There was a bucket attached to a trolley and that would go out to the centre and then down on the wire. John Fyffe was from Monymusk. He went on to become the world's biggest producer of granite.

Dodd went on to explain to me that the stone from this quarry has gone into London's Waterloo Bridge, provided foundations for Middlesbrough's famous Transporter Bridge and graced churches and municipal and commercial buildings worldwide.

The export of granite from Aberdeen started about 1764, one of the first customers being London contractors for the laying of pavements. What was first of all a primitive process with hand tools was mechanised around 1795, mainly as the result of an order for huge stones for the Portsmouth Docks. There followed orders for the Bell Rock lighthouse, London's Waterloo and London bridges as well as locally for Aberdeen's Union Bridge and Union Street. The export trade had taken off and in 1817 alone, 22,170 tons arrived in London.

In any town and city in Britain, and many beyond in the British Empire, you might walk in and out of churches and cathedrals or municipal or commercial buildings

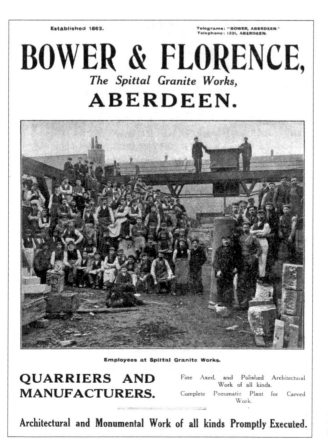

Bower & Florence, Spittal Granite Works

built or faced with granite. You might walk on streets edged with it. You might drink out of municipal fountains made of it or read inscriptions on statues and plaques made of it. Finally, you may also stroll around the graveyard where fantastic constructions of Aberdeen Granite commemorate the dead.

Of course, explained Dodd:

> It wasn't just the stanes that were sent awa'. My own uncle Robbie went to Sydney to build the granite columns for the Sydney Harbour Bridge. Their first idea was to work the granite in Aberdeen and ship it to Sydney but they found good granite in Moruya and the workers were exported rather than the stane. He spent seven years there till the steel started to go up. I also had great uncles that went to Barre in Vermont in the USA to muckle quarries over there. My mother and father used to get postcards from them.

It was talking to people like Dodd, fiercely proud of their industrial roots, that made me think that a book like this would be a tribute to them. My further research found that while the 'Silver city with the golden sands' will be forever associated with granite production because of its proliferation of granite buildings, quarries and works, nevertheless there were other quarries in Scotland.

From Boddam near Peterhead came red and blue granites which are often combined with Aberdeen silver granite and grace many buildings, fountains and monuments including the India Office, Australia House and Covent Garden. Also from the same source were the original fountains in Trafalgar Square, which were built by McDonald Leslie in Aberdeen. Apparently, the Square was redesigned in 1939 and the fountains were sent to the Commonwealth, one to Confederation Park in Ottowa and the other to Regina in Saskatchewan. The quarry closed to commercial extraction of blocks in June 1956, although aggregate is still extracted.

From Dalbeattie in Galloway went silver-grey stones for docks in Liverpool and Swansea as well as for lighthouses. In its polished form it was used for London buildings and it was also used extensively for local building. Galloway granite, where it is still accessible, is mostly used for aggregate although some is still extracted for monumental and architectural purposes.

And under the tarmac of thousands of roads throughout Great Britain and beyond can be found granite setts of varying hues. Now covered over, they can only be seen when exposed by roadworks. Many of these, certainly in Scotland, would have come from Tormore Quarry, on the Ross of Mull, where the reddish brown stone was also used on Glasgow University and the Holburn Viaduct in London. The quarry was said to have produced the largest granite blocks in Great Britain, sixteen metres long. Blocks of five metres were shipped to the USA. These large blocks were also used for lighthouse construction, Skerryvore included.

Just as the paper industry produced those who excelled in the manufacture of papermaking machinery to improve the process, so it was that there were equivalents in the granite industry. Alexander MacDonald was a quarrymaster in Aberdeen and he invented the first steam-driven polishing machine. He also introduced steam-driven lathes and cutting machines and drove the industry into mechanisation. The

Sydney Harbour Bridge.

Tormore jetty, at the quarry at Fionphort on the Ross of Mull.

ability to cut finer slabs meant that thin facings could be produced rather than just blocks and this expanded the market.

It was Alexander MacDonald who produced the very first polished granite memorial, which was erected in the Kensal Green Cemetery in 1832. It created a vogue as well as a demand for MacDonald's, which supplied the growing funeral trade for many years. The sarcophagus at Frogmore containing the remains of Queen Victoria and Prince Albert, made from a single flawless block of Aberdeen granite, must have signalled the pinnacle of Alexander MacDonald's career in a Great Britain obsessed with death and funerals.

Another enterprising company was J. Abernethy & Co., of Ferryhill Foundry, which was the largest producer of granite working machinery in the world. This included lathes and cranes, with some of these produced for export to Moruya for work on the Sydney Harbour Bridge. These possibly went with the large numbers of families who departed Aberdeenshire to work granite for the great bridge. Apparently, one of their lathes produced granite columns for many of Sydney's public buildings from the 1880s and was still in use in the 1960s, turning columns up to 21 feet long.

But the export of granite making machinery was not a one-way process as granite producers were happy to import tools from the United States, including the new technology of pneumatic tools from Vermont in 1866. Another machine to be imported was the still-used Jenny Lind polisher, named after the great Swedish singer. Apparently, the hum from the polishing head was redolent of her dulcet tones.

But back to Dodd, who was among the large group of curling fanatics in Aberdeen. 'Ye know,' he said, 'that you can't fault Aberdeen granite for monuments but for a proper stane ye would have to go to Ailsa Craig. Those are bonny stanes. An ye can still get them tae. Though curlings nae whit it ance wis. Wi all this health and safety you cannae get on to the ice. Ah weel at least we have a fine rink in Aiberdeen'.

Dodd's love of curling of course led me on a trail to find a bit more about the stanes, I mean stones. It is well known that Scotland is the home of golf but less well known as the home of curling and, therefore, the home of the curling stone. Curling stones traditionally come from Ailsa Craig, that tough little island off the Ayrshire coast. This very particular granite, Ailsite, has properties extremely suitable for curling stones as it can take the substantial knocks as they bang against one another.

Kay's of Mauchline, in Ayrshire, has exclusive rights to the Ailsa Craig stone and has been producing stones since 1851, albeit in lesser numbers because of lower demand. The quarry is virtually dormant now and the island is a nature reserve.

The end of the granite industry has many parallels with other Scottish industries and there is no single reason for its demise although trade embargos imposed by the United States on imported goods following the Great Depression in the early 1930s protected developing American industries while causing collapse in other countries. This had an effect on granite exports to the United States.

While granite is extracted for architectural and memorial purposes on a small scale, large scale extraction of building or 'dimension stone' as it is now called has all but ceased. Developments in concrete building and paving materials have come a long way, as has brick technology. Tarmac has replaced granite setts. Thankfully there is little need now for the scale of granite memorials once required after the last two

An engraving of Rubislaw Quarry from *The Illustrated London News*.

Curling in Ontario, Canada, 1909 – possibly using imported Scottish stones although by that time they were producing their own.

world wars and, in any case, many of these are now imported from as far away as China. Well, why not, as we once sent it worldwide too?

Architectural tastes too have changed and while granite is in vogue for iconic buildings like the new Scottish Parliament building, this does not constitute an industry. Mostly it is crushed as aggregate for roads and decorative purposes. And while I think Dodd has long retired from his reluctant work with concrete, he still enjoys throwing the stane on the Aberdeen Curling Rink playing 'The Roaring Game'.

In Aberdeen you can get a good insight into the history of granite extraction and building on Aberdeen's Granite Trail run by the Aberdeen Heritage Trust: www.aberdeencity.gov.uk. The Future Museum in Kilmarnock also has a range of exhibits featuring quarrying in the South West of Scotland; www.futuremuseum.co.uk.

Scotland's Treasure Chest – The Mining of Lead, Gold, Silver and Zinc

I remember my father telling me that the source of the River Clyde was in the Leadhills. Years later I was to learn that this is the familiar name for the Lowther Hills in the Southern Uplands and that Leadhills is actually a village.

The lead industry in Scotland dates from Roman times. It was an important metal and was used by them for pipes, aqueducts, gutters and for coffins. Mining seems to have been carried out in fits and starts in the eighteenth and nineteenth centuries and lasted at Leadhills until 1928. The industry peaked there in 1810 when around 1,400 tons was being produced annually. Much of this was being exported to Holland and Belgium for the production of lead-glazed pottery and tiles. Leadhills, at 395 metres above sea level, is the second highest village in Scotland after nearby Wanlockhead, both located at this high altitude because of the mining activity. It was in Leadhills that miners clubbed together in 1741 to form Scotland's first subscription library.

Wanlockhead, 'God's Treasure House', was joined to Leadhills by the Leadhills & Wanlockhead Branch Railway, which ran from 1901 until 1939 to take the lead to the central belt of Scotland. Mining for lead, zinc, copper and silver was carried out here but declined in the twentieth century, finally ending in the 1950s. It is clear that there were financial difficulties here around 1921, for after eight months on strike, the workers at the mine returned to work on 50 per cent of their previous pay.

While the Lowther Hills are most well known for lead mining, there were nevertheless many other, mainly minor, mining areas in Scotland. Lead was mined at Creetown in Galloway by the Craigtown Mining Co. When a new military road

Highest inhabited village in Scotland, Leadhills

Leadhills.

was being built from 1763 from Gatehouse of Fleet to Creetown, a seam of lead was uncovered and this prompted landowner Patrick Heron and merchant William Carruthers to exploit the seam. It seems to have taken some time to get started, with additional partners joining in. Mining took place between 1770 and 1790 but was getting increasingly more difficult. On top of this, the price of lead in Great Britain collapsed around 1815 at the end of the Napoleonic Wars when Spanish lead mining resumed.

There are remains of lead mines above Tyndrum. It is known that these have been mined sporadically for over 600 years, at one time providing King James I with silver. In 1730, Sir Robert Clifton took a broad lease for mining on the Breadalbane estate. He discovered lead and worked the Tyndrum mine commercially. Unfortunately, he was jailed for bad debts. No wonder he had to give up his lease early. A company called the Mine Adventurers of England took over the lease and later the Scots Mining Co., which from 1768 to 1791 worked the mine and smelted the ore. Gold and silver were also mined.

On the island of Islay, lead and silver mines may date from medieval times and were certainly worked between the seventeenth and nineteenth centuries in mines including ones at Gartness, Ballygrant, Woodend and Robolls. These seem to have been abandoned around 1880 but there is a report that during the period 1862 to 1880, 1,426 tons of lead were produced along with 18,424 ounces of silver.

In Strontian, Lochaber, the opening of a galena, or lead sulphide, mine in 1725 by Sir Alexander Murray and the road builder General Wade led to another interesting discovery. While the lead was used, among other things for bullets for the Napoleonic Wars, the discovery of Strontium led to other possibilities and for a new element to be named after this little village. Strontium became extremely important in the production of sugar from sugar beet, in which it was used in the crystallisation process. The mine itself lasted only a short time but at its peak around 1730 it was employing around 600 men extracting lead, zinc and silver. From then it went into decline, only being worked sporadically during the nineteenth and early twentieth centuries.

There is a record from the late 1800s showing that Great Britain was actually ahead of Spain in the production of lead. In 1868 Great Britain produced 71,000 tons while Spain produced 67,000 tons. This was to change as British companies moved into Spain to exploit the mining, which had hitherto been carried out in very inefficient and underfunded operations.

It is highly unlikely that, in modern times, any lead mines in Great Britain would have been profitable other than during interruptions to supply from Spain, where lead and other minerals had been mined from Roman times. The lead from Spain was abundant and far cheaper and easier to mine than the relatively small amounts found in Scotland. In fact, British companies were instrumental in the development of the Spanish mines.

The English-owned Linares Lead Mining Co. had been formed in 1852, followed by the Fortuna Co. in 1854. These were managed by staff brought from England. The lead being exported to Great Britain inevitably reduced the prices of home-produced lead. The Spanish mines were rich in metal and labour prices were extremely low.

Also taking advantage of these conditions was the Scottish Tharsis Sulphur & Copper Works, with a factory in Glasgow's Garngad.

Charles Tennant had built the St Rollox Chemical Works on the banks of the Monkland Canal in 1799. The huge factory, employing 500, produced bleaching powder in a process patented by Tennant. In 1866, Tennant bought the Tharsis copper mines in Andalucia, where eventually 2,000 workers were employed. Many of the managers and engineers were Scottish and formed a unique community. The product of these mines was dispatched to Glasgow, to the copper works also built in 1866. By 1872, Tharsis had acquired seven metal processing companies in Great Britain.

Nearby, the Rio Tinto mines was taken over in 1873 by Scottish businessman Hugh Matheson and partners. With profits from Jardine Matheson's opium trade he established the Rio Tinto Group, which was to become one of the world's biggest mining and metal companies. These companies and others were to have a marked effect on the lead mining industry in Great Britain, which went into decline and eventually ended.

But back to Wanlockhead, where it wasn't just lead that was found. Gold was also mined here, and at 22.8 carats, some of it was the world's purest and found its way into some of the Scottish Crown Jewels (the Honours of Scotland), held in Edinburgh Castle. James IV took an interest in gold mining in the area. He opened mines at Crawford and it was from here that gold ended up in the Scottish Crown that was remodelled by James V in 1540. Gold coins minted in Edinburgh for both King James V and for Mary Queen of Scots also came from the area. The Crawford Moor Mine was certainly being worked on James's behalf by Sir James Pettigrew as Treasury accounts record payments to him and his workers.

Historical Notes on the Occurrence of Gold in the South of Scotland, written by Andrew Dudgeon around 1870, records that in 1593 gold, silver and lead mines in Crawford Moor and Glenconnar were given by James V to Thomas Foulis, goldsmith in Edinburgh, for twenty-one years in consideration of the great sums due to him 'and his dearest spouse'.

A French account of the mining in the reign of James V stated that gold was separated by sand from washing and that at a time 300 men were employed over several summers in this process. The search for gold did seem to be very active in James V's reign, with generous grants provided. Very little seems to have been done in response to this in other areas of Scotland and in the Crawford Moor area it appears never to have been profitable. While there are reports of gold being found, this was generally isolated nuggets or grains and there was no great evidence of gold in veins and in any quantity.

There was one mysterious report regarding an Englishman, George Bowes, who was given permission to search for gold. At Wanlockhead, he discovered 'a small vein which had much gold upon it'. He swore the miners to secrecy and having worked on the vein carried the product away to England after closing up and hiding the shaft. The vein appears never to have been rediscovered so maybe there is scope for another gold rush? You can certainly still pan for gold and small amounts are found. In fact, in 1992, Wanlockhead hosted the World Gold Panning championships and hosts the British and Scottish Gold Panning Championships.

There was a small gold rush in Kildonan in Sutherland when gold was discovered in the River Helmsdale on the estate of the Duke of Sutherland in 1868. The first find was a small nugget found by Robert Nelson Gilchrist. Gilchrist was from Kildonan but had spent seventeen years in the Australian goldfields. With his experience and permission from the Duke he prospected a wide area, discovering gold in a number of places, particularly in the Suisgill and Kildonan Burns.

The news of this filtered out and, catching the attention of the *Illustrated London News*, a gold rush was on. Soon, along the glen, a shanty town akin to the Californian Gold Rush had sprung up. But it was a short-lived rush. The Duke was concerned about the effects of the panning on his tenant farmers, as well as on the salmon fishing and deerstalking. While he was originally pleased, giving the discoverer of 'Sutherland's Gold', Gilchrist, a gold watch, as time wore on and tourists were flocking to see the workings he became less enchanted.

Because of the success of those left panning, the price offered for the gold dropped. The panners were working long hours for very little profit and while they seemed happy to do this, he was not inclined to open up the area for more prospecting. Added to this, with the herring season opening many of those panning went back to the fisheries, leaving around fifty still working. While the Sutherland estate was taking in license fees from the panners, he was about to lose more from the loss of income from hunting, shooting and fishing, an important industry in the Highlands. It had been relatively recently, in 1852, that Queen Victoria had bought the Balmoral Estate and deerstalking and buying country estates and shooting lodges had become increasingly popular. This had become a major source of income, not to be spoiled by the meagre income from panning licenses. His agents made the announcement and the gold rush was over on 30 December 1869.

That did not mean that gold was worked out for now, for purely recreational purposes, you can visit Helmsdale and pan for gold in the Kildonan Burn. You can still find gold in flakes and sometimes little nuggets. But don't look to dig up a fortune. In fact, it is recorded that there are around 100 sources of alluvial gold in rivers and burns in Scotland, so a persistent person might earn a little.

On the other hand, while gold panning may be only for entertainment, the chances are that Scotland may in future be a gold exporter. For in 2011, a plan was approved to re-open and develop a gold mine at Cononish near Tyndrum. Scotgold plans to extract over £50 million in gold and silver from the mine. The current high price of the metals has recently made the project viable. The scarcity of Scottish gold also increases the value.

The mine is based in the Loch Lomond National Park and detailed measures have been taken to ensure the environmental damage is minimised. Around fifty jobs will be created over a ten-year period when the area round the mine will be returned to its natural state. The mine had previously been opened in the 1980s but low gold prices made it uneconomical to work.

If you would like to know more about the history of lead mining, you can visit the Scottish Lead Mining Museum in Wanlockhead. You can take a trip underground and visit the miners' cottages to see how they lived as well as visiting the subscription library.

Limestone Quarrying and Kilning

The countryside used to be a very busy place. Travelling through Ayrshire, Lanarkshire, the Lothians and Fife this might surprise you as outside of towns and villages, it can now be very quiet. This disguises the fact that at one time farms and estates were more populated than they are now. Farming was a very labour intensive industry involving large numbers of staff in activities including seeding, ploughing and harvesting. This would have involved stablemen to look after the large numbers of horses which were needed. There were staff working in dairies, and during the harvest large numbers of people would come from the cities and towns to work in the fields, picking potatoes or soft fruits. Grain would be milled in local mills and animals would be butchered in local abattoirs.

The countryside was also industrious for while we now are used to factories in industrial estates, many of our traditional industries started in the heart of the country. Bricks and tiles were produced on site from clay quarries. Pits were sunk for coal wherever it might be found and, as in the Bathgate area, shale oil pits and refineries sprung up.

Over a period of time, these occupations became industrial and moved to larger plants or disappeared. The farms became mechanised and less people were needed as there were no horses to be looked after. Cows were being milked by machine with milk being collected by tanker. What was a busy and noisy landscape became still. What has also disappeared from the central belt is the noisy, smoky, smelly lime kiln, which once was a farm industry. Now you might pass these, sometimes huge, structures with only a vague notion as to their importance to the Industrial

The Old Lime Kiln, River Ayr Walk.

Revolution and to agriculture. Their disappearance is probably a very simple lesson on how the transition from farm to factory production happened.

Limestone has been quarried and mined in Scotland for centuries. Its use in agriculture was one of the first and it is still used today to improve crops. They may not have known the chemistry but early farmers knew that it worked. Lime neutralises acidic soils as well as providing calcium as a nutrient. This makes the soil healthier and therefore more productive. By burning the limestone they were able to produce quicklime which, in a powder form, is spread on the fields.

In building it had a number of very important uses and was one of the earliest known mortars. To make a mortar, it is mixed with sand and water. However, it was gradually replaced as ordinary Portland Cement (OPC) was produced. While OPC is still used considerably in new building it has been realised that, when it comes to restoration of older buildings, lime mortar is superior given that it doesn't shrink and is extremely durable. Lime mortar has had a bit of a rebirth as it is normally a requirement in the conservation of older structures.

In papermaking, which was a large industry in Scotland, it was used as a paper-bleaching agent and for reducing acidity, therefore prolonging life. It was also used in carpet backing, where it was a filler and strengthener.

In iron and steel making it is used as a flux to remove impurities from the molten mix, where it forms the slag, which is then removed. In dust form it was also used in coal mines as a damper on coal dust to dilute it and prevent explosions.

As a limewash, or whitewash, it was used extensively as a decorative surface on house walls and in cellars as a wall surface. I remember it being used extensively in pub cellars to improve light. It was also seen in farm dairies and other food preparation and storage areas as it was mildly antiseptic. It was used on glass roofs of factories and glasshouses to reduce sunlight. Some older readers may also remember that whitewash was used often for lettering on shop windows. Applied with a brush, it was a way to advertise today's produce and prices.

The production of quicklime was a very energy-intensive process and kilning it was one of the first industrial uses of coal; pits were dug or mined in order to feed the local lime kilns as they were built. For example, the Boddin Point lime kiln near Montrose, which is very similar in design to most others, was built by landowner Robert Scott. This was a time of land improvement in the eighteenth century during which innovations such as drainage and new field systems were introduced. The lime kiln there was built in 1750 to produce quicklime to reduce acidity in the soils on the estate. Ships would disembark coal from Fife to fire the kiln, which had three shafts. Ships would take the quicklime away for distribution around the coast of Scotland. Unfortunately, this example of a lime kiln is not in a good state as it is heading into the sea through erosion of the coastline.

A limekiln is basically a large furnace with an opening at the top. Loading gangs would bring limestone chunks from the quarry in carts. These would be layered in the furnace with coal (or peat where it was available) and then it would be set alight. The fire would burn slowly upwards and once it was out the kiln would be left to cool for two to three days. The quicklime that had accumulated at the base would be raked out by an unloading gang. The operation typically took about a week.

James Reid & Co., limestone merchants – loading Caledonian Railway wagons.

East Lomond lime kiln.

It was a dangerous occupation. Re-charging the furnace on top of the burning lime meant that the burners were working in a fiery, malodorous and poisonous atmosphere. At the bottom, where the lime would emerge, was no less dangerous. Quicklime is caustic when combined with water so the workers had to be extremely careful to prevent this. It is unlikely that they would have worked only in dry weather so the discharge holes of the kilns may have been protected in some way.

While single kilns are very common, there are kilns of a more industrial nature such as at Charleston in Fife, where there are the remains of fourteen built by Charles Bruce, the Fifth Earl of Elgin. These eventually produced about a third of all the lime used in Scotland, no doubt putting smaller kilns out of business. The kilning of lime at Charleston gradually ran down from 1930s and finally ended in 1956. The huge kilns are now under the protection of the National Trust for Scotland and here you can get some idea of the scale of the operation. Charleston is a planned industrial village next to Limekilns, which, ironically, was a very much smaller producer.

So it can be seen that in agricultural and industrial Scotland lime had extensive uses and again that was probably its downfall. For as the uses increased, particularly in the iron and steel industry, the industrialists got involved and began producing lime at their own works or in a large commercial enterprise. In addition, the opening of the railways meant that cheaper lime from the larger kilns could be imported. The use of OPC and paints also reduced the demand in the building trades. In many cases local demand other than for agriculture was dropping. In any case, quarries were worked out and mining the rock increased costs. In 1850, there were fifty limestone mines in Lanarkshire alone but by 1950, a full hundred years later, there were none. A wide range of circumstances had conspired to close them.

The kilns in Scotland were found mostly in the midland valley from Ayrshire through to the Lothians and Fife. Here, there were adequate deposits of a range of limestones which were quarried at the spot where the kiln was built. In the Lomond Hills, for example, East Lomond Limekiln and quarry is a good example of a lime kiln surrounded by abandoned workings. As you walk round the heritage trail here you will walk on the white chalky limestone rubble left behind.

If you want to know a bit more about how lime is produced and how it is used in building, you might want to visit the Scottish Lime Centre Trust, also in Charlestown. This promotes the knowledge and traditional skills required for the conservation, repair and maintenance of historic buildings. It has a visitor exhibition showing the social and economic history of limeworking.

As seems to be the case with many commodities, a great deal of quicklime now comes from China, which exports ten times more than the next biggest exporter. However, there is still a demand for agricultural lime containing calcium and this is provided in crushed form from a number of quarries in Scotland. Leith's operate a number of these, one being Lugton Quarry. Lugton Lime, founded by James Reid & Co., has been involved with lime spreading throughout Scotland for most of the twentieth century. The lime was manufactured by a milling process at Lugton after extraction from the quarries at Hesshillhead and Treane, both of which are located at Beith in Ayrshire.

Salt of the Scottish Earth – The Scottish Salt Industry

Knowing of Prestonpans, I had always vaguely imagined that salt was produced there in the same way that it is in some warmer countries, that is by evaporation in large pools bordering the sea. Well, I was quite wrong as I was to discover that, in fact, while evaporation in that way may have been carried out at one time, salt making wasn't just as easy as that. We simply don't get the quantity of solar heat that it takes to evaporate large quantities of seawater.

Salt has been used throughout history for cooking and for preservation and once was a valuable commodity, used at times as wages. 'To be worth your salt' means that you are good at your job, a saying that comes from the Latin word 'salarium'. Roman soldiers were partly paid in salt or given an allowance to so do.

Salt, for commercial purposes, was produced by boiling sea water in large pans over coal fires and this is one reason that they are found close to the sea and close to coal mines and, along with lime kilning, one of the early industrial uses of coal. In fact, both industries were interlocked, with mine and estate owners investing in pans to supplement income. Coal dross, which was otherwise unprofitable, was an ideal fuel for the fires, which would be kept burning continuously. This was called panwood, probably evidence that wood was also once used.

The pans were probably not a standard size but there is a record that they could be 18 feet long by 9 feet wide and 1½ feet deep. The pans were originally made from lead and presumably smaller. When wrought iron became available, that was used.

It took 100 tons of water and fifty tons of coal to produce three tons of salt. The burning coal embers would be evenly raked underneath the pans to spread the heat

JAFFA ROCKS AND SALT PANS.

Joppa Salt Works.

until all or most of the water was boiled away, leaving the salt crystals. These would be raked from the side of the pan and placed in wooden boxes or wicker baskets at the side of the pan to drain. It was then moved to a 'girnel' or storehouse for drying and packing.

It seems that my suppositions were not entirely wrong as 'bucket pots' were intermediate pools on the shore where seawater was collected to allow solids to drop to the bottom and where a small amount of evaporation would take place depending on the weather.

It was a smelly and dirty process. In some cases, bullock's blood was used to purify the salt. As the mixture was boiled, the blood and dirt rose to the top and was skimmed off. In 1815, William Chambers, of the Chambers publishing house and future Lord Provost of Edinburgh, described the process in Joppa, where his father was the manger of the salt works and possibly lived in the last remaining building associated with the works, the manager's house:

> A smokey, malodorous place, consisting of a group of sooty buildings situated on the sea-shore half way between Portobello and Musselburgh.

Alex Nisbet & Son owned the salt pans at Prestonpans and at Pinkie and took over the Joppa works in the nineteenth century. This was one of the founding companies of the Scottish Salt Co., which was formed in 1889. Salt was produced at Joppa until 1953 and the retiral of the last salter.

Salt was a very expensive product and it was worth the bother to mine coal to produce it. Salt was used for preserving food and if you have already read about the Scottish herring industry then you will know how important salt was to that industry as the gutted herring was salted, packed in barrels and dispatched throughout Great Britain and Europe. Salt in the seventeenth century was Scotland's third largest export.

In Prestonpans, where a mural describes the process, there were around forty pans at the height of production. Salt was made from the early 1100s. In earlier years, the reigning king or queen retained the rights to many industrial activities such as glassmaking and salt manufacture. In the twelfth century, King David gave the first Royal Charter to Prestonpans to produce salt. In 1900, there was only one surviving sea salt plant and this closed in 1959. The Scottish Screen Archive holds a short film showing the operation of the salt works in 1956. Salters are seen removing salt from the edge of the steaming vats and placing it into trolleys. Also seen is a motor trolley moving sewage pipes, showing that at the time salt was being produced for salt-glazing of clay sewage pipes. This would be another reason for the demise of the salt works as plastic and steel pipes began to replace clay pipes for water and drainage. Apparently, the process was very environmentally unfriendly as it produced a lot of air pollution. What with the steam and the fumes, it must really have been a very unfriendly place to work. Mr Chambers seems to have been right.

The main centre of salt panning was along both shores of the Firth of Forth, which at one time produced 95 per cent of Scotland's salt. The Prestonpans area was responsible for around 29 per cent. Besides Prestonpans and Joppa, there were numerous other pans, testifying to the importance of the industry.

At Kennetpans some remains can still be seen, thanks probably to the fact that it is part of a bird sanctuary. In Grangepans, now part of Bo'ness, salt was produced until around 1890. There were also large pans at Wemyss, and Methill. In St Monans, in Fife, a restored windmill remains from the salt mill there. This was established in 1771 by the Newark Coal & Salt Co. Coal was extracted from a nearby colliery and transported to the salt pans that were housed in nine buildings. Rather than manually lift water or use steam engines, the windmill was used. The salt works employed twenty men and the colliery thirty-six. Salt was produced here into the early 1800s but seems to have ceased before the end of salt duty in 1823.

Brora, in Sutherland, with an expected distillery and wool mill and an unexpected coal mine, was a very industrial town. Here, Lady Jean Gordon, Countess of Sutherland, set up salt pans in 1598 using coal from the local mine. Lady Jean's 'Old Salt House' had two large buildings on the Back Beach next to the Winter Port. These pans were replaced and salt panning restarted in 1746 but ended in 1777. A third attempt was started in the nineteenth century and in 1818, 400 tons of salt were being produced annually and had a ready market in the herring fisheries.

There were also salt pans on the West Coast and it may not come as a surprise to learn that Saltcoats is called after one of it's earliest industries. Maryburgh, on the St Nicholas Golf Course in Prestwick, was built around 1760 and is said to be one of the best remaining salt works in Scotland.

Sea water is free and this was a major advantage to the Scottish salt industry. However, the coal, labour and maintenance are not. The economics of any industry dictate that the organisation that can lower these costs may be the winner. This could be achieved by making the process more efficient and in some cases, where it could be afforded, steam engines were employed to pump the sea water into the pans. This saved on the laborious process of manually handling the water using buckets. Over time productivity was improved but the product had impurities. This could be improved by a slower process but at the cost of reduced quantity. Unfortunately, any lowering of costs still could not compete with Cheshire salt. Cheshire, in the north-west of England, has been mining and panning salt since the seventeenth century. Here, extraction of salt became an industrial enterprise and, inevitably, would make inroads into the Scottish sea salt industry. To give some idea of the competition, Salt Union Ltd quarries rock salt from 150 metres below ground and are currently producing 1 million tonnes of rock salt a year for de-icing of roads.

British Salt, owned by Tata (owner of our Dalzell and Clydebridge steelworks), produce salt from a process also used in earlier days. Water is forced down bore holes and a brine solution comes back up which is evaporated and purified to produce pure salt.

In fact, the demise of the Scottish salt industry was purely an economic one. Before 1823 there had been a tax on salt imposed in the time of Mary Queen of Scots. Being less than the duty imposed in England, Scottish salt was in an advantageous position, being exported (and often smuggled) to England and Europe. That is, until the duty was repealed in 1825, when the advantage was lost and coastal saltworks started closing.

The end of the Napoleonic War saw pressure on the government to repeal the salt tax. This was coming from the industrialists and inventors who were beginning to use salt for the production of alkalis. Unfortunately for the Scottish salt industry, this repeal produced an expansion of the salt mining industry to meet the needs of the growing chemical industries. This expansion was almost entirely based in Cheshire and smaller salt companies, including those in Scotland, were unable to join in this burgeoning business.

The English manufacturers were not having it all their own way. As often happens, other countries were developing their own salt industries. Overproduction and competition forced the industry to combine. In England and Wales, the Salt Union and the United Alkali Co. were formed in 1888 and 1890. In Scotland, in 1889, the Scottish Salt Co. was set up with similar objectives, to protect the industry. The Scottish Salt Co. existed until the closure of the last works in 1959.

Ironically, instrumental in the removal of the salt tax was Charles Tennant of the famous Scottish chemical company based at St Rollox. Salt was an important raw material in the manufacture of chemicals. The lowering in the price of salt made a big difference to these chemicals, which were hugely important to the Industrial Revolution.

The arts are deeply indebted to Mr Tennant for other benefits, particularly for his exertions in removing the duty on salt. This he ultimately succeeded in accomplishing, after a struggle of many years with the kelp proprietors. Few legislative enactments have been so beneficial to the country, as well attested by the rapid increase of alkali manufactories. The manufacture of Sulphuric Acid, and of alkali from salt, was also greatly improved at St Rollox, and first conducted there on a scale commensurate with their national importance. The manufacturing interests of this country possess an advantage in the extraordinary cheapness of these and other chemical products, which they owe in a great degree to Mr Tennant's scientific talents and activity as a manufacturer. – From an 1839 obituary

With the repeal of salt duty in 1823 and the import of cheap rock salt from England and abroad, there was nowhere to go. The salt industry collapsed and the last salt pan closed at Prestonpans in 1959, a persistent works that lasted after most others had closed. This had been because they had diversified into other products while the quality of the rock salt had improved.

We know that the television chef can promote hitherto little known or used food ingredients. This has certainly been the case with rock salt which, in grinders, is now extremely popular and has replaced the traditional salt cellar on many dining tables and kitchens.

Hebrides Sea Salt, based in Lewis in the Western Isles, is responding to this expanding market. They process around 2 tonnes of sea water per day to produce 100 packets of salt. They hope to increase this to 2,000 packs per day. The seawater is evaporated in shallow pans before being gently heated in ovens to complete the process. this is presently sold online and in independent retailers. A nice return to a very traditional Scottish rural industry.

James (Paraffin) Young and the Scottish Shale Oil Industry

For those of you who are interested in Scottish industrial history and life, you would get a pleasant surprise on visiting Australia. For in that country you will find countless examples of the engineering products of Scotland. In Sydney Maritime Museum is the HMAS *Onslow*, a submarine built at Scott's on the Clyde; the inside is bristling with labels from many Scottish engineering companies including periscopes from Barr & Stroud, where I served my apprenticeship.

There are public fountains and thousands of examples of cast iron 'lacework' balconies produced by or based on designs from Walter MacFarlane's Saracen Foundry.

In Queensland, in the rain forests near Daintree, I came across an ancient and abandoned complete sawmill whose centrepiece was a Lister engine complete with a large oil tank. On this tank was a label with a list of recommended oils, one of which was 'Scotch Oil'. We are very familiar with Scotch whisky but this was a new one on me and I was intrigued enough to investigate further.

While I was vaguely aware of the role of Paraffin Young in the development of the oil industry in Scotland, I had always thought that he was from Fife. It turns out that he was from the Drygate in Glasgow and had originally been apprenticed as a joiner to his father, John. His mother was Jean Wilson, who married John in 1809. Some say that he was also an undertaker. This may well have been the case as very often those who made the coffins also helped bury the dead.

Like many ambitious men of the time in Glasgow, James attended night classes at Anderson's University (the Andersonian). Here he was influenced by famous lecturer Thomas Graham. During his time here he started a lifelong friendship with David Livingstone and was to fund an unsuccessful search for him.

Deans Crude Oil Works.

In 1831, Young was appointed as Graham's assistant and went with him when Graham moved to University College, London, helping him with his researches. In 1839, he moved as manager to Irishman James Muspratt's chemical works at Newton Le Willows, Merseyside, then on to Charles Tennant's works in Manchester. During this time, he investigated potato blight for the Manchester Literary and Philosophical Society, and suggested the use of dilute sulphuric acid in treating the tubers as a means of stopping the disease.

At the Andersonian he had befriended Lyon Playfair, who wrote to him in 1847 telling him about a spring of oil at Alfreton in Derbyshire. This belonged to Playfair's brother in-law. He though that Young might be able to turn it into a profitable venture. So, Young, with Edward Meldrum, bought the rights and started making oils for lights and lubrication. The spring began to fail but during the three years till 1850 an old friend of his from the Andersonian days, Hugh Bartholomew, manager of the Glasgow Gas Works, wrote to him about 'cannel' coal, which had for a long time been used by the people around Bathgate and Armadale as a fuel.

Young had been experimenting with the distillation of paraffin from coal using slow distillation and succeeded in this with cannel coal. He took out a patent for the production of oils and paraffin wax. Young and Meldrum then entered a partnership with William Binney, opening in Bathgate the world's first oil works in 1850, using cannel coal.

As the supplies of cannel coal were running out, Young bought up the mineral rights to vast areas of West Lothian. He had discovered that shale was oil bearing and while not as rich in oil as coal from his Bathgate mine, if mined in quantity it would be profitable; and it was.

In 1865 the partnership ended and the works were bought by Young, who set up

Pumpherston Refinery.

Young's Paraffin Light & Mineral Oil Co. He opened the world's largest oil works in Addiewell, taking shale from seven pits and employing 13,000.

Young's first patents had run out in 1864, creating competition, and soon there were around 100 separate extraction and processing companies with a total workforce approaching 45,000. At its peak, up to three million tons of coal and shale were extracted each year. There was not enough labour in the area so workers came from other areas in Scotland, from Ireland, from Cornwall, and from Wales.

By the time Young retired, his company had continued to expand with the sale of paraffin and paraffin lamps. Through licensing of his patents, Young's products and manufacturing process travelled the globe and thus gave rise to 'Scotch Oil'.

The end for shale oil was in sight as, in 1859, liquid petroleum was discovered in the United States and was found to be much cheaper than Young's shale oil. However, that industry was in its infancy and was far from being as efficient as the West Lothian works. These works had successfully established substantial ranges of products, which included detergent, paint, petrol and diesel, bricks, petroleum jelly, wax and wax candles, town gas, ammonium sulphate fertiliser and sulphuric acid.

The output reached a peak in 1913 and up to 1925 there were twenty-five shale mines in operation, but as the new oilfields in Persia began to export there was a gradual decline. In 1920, there had been a merger of the remaining oil companies, including Young's, to form Scottish Oils, which was to go on to be part of the Anglo-Persian Oil Company that ultimately was to become British Petroleum (BP) in 1954.

With the coming of the Second World War, there was new investment in shale oil production in the face of threats to imported oil. There was a new crude oil works at Westwood near West Calder, new pits were sunk and others modernised. Following the war, the older works were closed until production finally ceased in 1962 when a preferential tax on home-produced oil stopped. The last shale pit was at Westwood, West Calder. The Pumpherston refinery continued until 1993, having being used for the production of detergents.

However, oil refining was not dead in Scotland as, in 1924, the Grangemouth Refinery was opened by Scottish Oils, which had taken over Young's around 1920. By this time Scottish Oils was owned by the government-backed Anglo-Persian Oil Company. The refinery was a direct descendent of the shale oil industry, using the experience and processes invented in Scotland, but was built to refine oil from Persia.

Grangemouth is Scotland's only refinery and was clearly in the right place to take advantage of the discovery of North Sea Oil in 1974. The huge refinery is now run by Ineos and has around 2,500 direct and indirect employees.

But there may be a return of shale oil. It has been recognised that oils extracted from shale may be a viable proposition given the advances in technology and the diminishing product from the Gulf and from the North Sea. Scottish companies already have an interest in that process, which is called 'fracking'.

Fracking is hydraulic fracturing using pressurised fluids injected into veins in rock. This releases shale and other gases and substances. There are environmental concerns although supporters point to the hitherto unaccessible massive amounts of hydrocarbons that this process can release. It is estimated that 300 million tonnes of oil shale remain in the Scottish oilfields but only time will tell whether this can be extracted at a cost which protects the environment.

And the Scottish oil industry moves on, no doubt on the back of the pioneering work in West Lothian. With the discovery of oil in the North Sea in 1970, the Scottish oil industry was back in the big time, particularly with the discovery of the Forties and Brent oilfields. It is estimated that the oil industry in its largest sense employs 150,000 workers in 2,000 companies. These include those highly skilled and experienced engineers who take their skills worldwide, just like Young's 'Scotch Oil'.

The extraction of shale for oil was every bit as dangerous as what we would call normal coal mines and this was demonstrated with a horrendous accident at the Burngrange Pits in West Calder when fifteen men were killed. On 10 January 1947 there were fifty-three miners underground when firedamp was ignited by an open acetylene lamp. This set off a succession of fires and explosions although most of the casualties were overcome by fumes. The firefighting continued for four days, assisted by firemen from the new National Fire Service who had volunteered even though they had not been trained in mine rescue. David Brown, who was an overman, was awarded the Edward Medal for his courage in repeated attempts to save the men. James McArthur also received a commendation. The reporter A. M. Bryan:

> As expected, those engaged in the rescue and recovery operations upheld the high traditions established by the men in the mining industry in these activities. Calamity is indeed man's true touchstone. I should like to record my tribute to the excellent work done by all concerned under very difficult and trying conditions over the long period from the occurrence of the explosion to the recovery of the bodies of the unfortunate victims. It was unfortunate that none of the trapped men was rescued alive, but that was in no way the fault of the representatives of officials and workmen, the National Fire Service, the Mines Rescue Brigades or H.M. Inspectors who took part in the operations.

A Young's Paraffin Oil tanker on an Albion chassis from Scotstoun.

Astonishingly, the enquiry into the disaster found that there had been no breaches of statutory regulations. However, it made some long lasting recommendations including the setting up of a divisional fire fighting service for the National Coal Board as well as a Mines Rescue Service. This had been the second major accident in the shale industry, the first being at Starlaw Pit where seven men had burned to death in 1870.

Before we leave James Young we should just mention that in 1872 he also discovered the use of quicklime to neutralise acidic bilge in ships. This significantly prevented rust in iron hulls. He worked with Professor George Forbes to accurately measure the speed of light. Being a great friend to David Livingstone, he financed some of his expeditions as well as an unsuccessful search operation by Lieutenant Grandy when Livingston was missing. After Livingstone's death he supported his family and contributed to the anti-slavery movement.

He also paid for statues to be erected in George Square of his chums, Thomas Graham and David Livingstone. While he paid for statues for others it is strange that he has never been immortalised in bronze. However, he has a far bigger memorial. I said that as a by-product he helped to save the whale. Again, quite unconsciously, he has left us some stunning wildlife habitats in the bings composed of red blaes, which is what is left over after oil is extracted. It was only later in the process that it was found that the used shale could be utilised as an ingredient in the manufacture of bricks.

Where these hills still exist they have become habitats for a range of species. Forty species of bird have been recorded on one bing alone. I said' 'where they still exist'. This is because the red blaes has some value. It was used substantially in motorway construction so a lot of them have been levelled. They were also used at one time as surface for football pitches and produced lots of skint knees.

James Young died in May 1833 and is buried at Inverkip. The James Young Halls at the University of Strathclyde bear his name, as does the James Young High School in Livingston. If you fancy a pint there is also a pub in Bathgate with his name. But above all, there is a marvellous museum dedicated to the shale oil industry in Scotland at the Almond Valley Heritage Centre in Livingston.

Putting the Roof on Scotland – The Story of Slate

If you were to go to some high point in Glasgow, Edinburgh or indeed most city, town and village in Scotland and look over the rooftops, you might spend some time guessing at the number of roofing slates. There must be millions and millions. Then think that these have all come from somewhere in Scotland. Then you would get some idea of the slate industry that there once was.

Prior to the eighteenth century, it was perfectly natural for buildings to be roofed with thatch, heather, grass, flagstones or indeed any available material that was or could be made impervious to the weather. However, with the growth of the town and the city and the need for a bit more fireproofing, particularly on the tenement buildings that were going up, there was a general move towards slate. Slate had been used for centuries in the areas where it could be easily worked or to where it could be easily carried. With the introduction of the steamship and of the railways, heavy building materials could be transported long distances by sea and by land. The slate industry was born.

Scottish slate is found in a rough belt which runs across the country and includes the Slate Islands, Ballachulish, Luss, Aberfoyle and Huntly. At one time there were around eighty quarries in operation, thirty of these commercial.

The Slate Islands are in the Inner Hebrides, north of Oban, and comprise Seil, Torsa, Shuna, Luing, Lunga, Easdale and Belnahua. On these islands, slate quarrying started around 1630 and by 1900 they were producing 8 million slates a year. In fact, one little island in Easdale Sound, Eilean-a-beithich (Island of the Birches) completely disappeared as quarrying took it below sea level when it was flooded in 1881. The quarrying had gone so deep that only a rocky buttress kept out the sea; this was washed away in a storm. 240 men and boys lost their jobs.

On Easdale there were once 500 people working up to seven quarries. The slate from here was exported as far as Nova Scotia and in Scotland it roofed Glasgow Cathedral. Between 1840 and 1860, Easdale was exporting between 7 million and 9 million slates a year. All of these having to go by sea, it was not uncommon to see up to twelve vessels waiting in the sound to load.

Mining here finished in the 1950s and the population dropped to only four people. However, it is now a lively community, having been repopulated, including by relatives of some of the original inhabitants. Here there is also a museum operated by the Scottish Slate Islands Trust which tells the story of the 'Islands which roofed the world'.

In Macduff, slate was quarried in the Slate Hills and one of the most important was Foudland, where production started around 1700. By 1850, 2 million slates

Ballachulish Slate Quarries.

were being produced in a year. Here, at 1,500 feet above sea level, workers split the slates by hand while sitting on the ground, protected from inclement weather by little slate-and-timber bothies. Not surprisingly, the quarries would close down for the winter.

Most of this slate would be going to the north-east, including to Balmoral Castle, from Foudland, but as in modern times, economies of scale and price outweigh local supply. As the railways opened up, slate from elsewhere in Scotland made its way to the north-east and the quarries in the Macduff slate formation closed. The purplish Macduff slate has proved to be extremely durable, with slate still on roofs after 100 years. Macduff is one of those areas which has been investigated with a view to re-opening slate workings.

Ballachulish is probably the best-known Scottish slate quarry, certainly to builders and architects in Glasgow, being the source of much of Glasgow's roofs. Ballachulish slate is easily worked and durable. By 1900, 15 million slates a year were being produced from quarries on the shore of Loch Leven, the largest being East Larroch. Like all other quarries, the decline which set in ended in 1955 with closure. Investigations on re-opening have centred on the Khartoum Quarry, which produces a grey-black slate.

Bremner, writing in his *Industries of Scotland* in 1869, describes the work at Ballachulish:

The men who work in the quarry are divided into 'crews' of five, six, or seven. Each crew choose a certain part of the rock face on one of the levels, and make a kind of bargain with their employer to work that particular spot for a year, receiving a sum of money agreed upon for every thousand slates made by them, so that their wages depend upon the diligence with which they work as well as upon the quality of the rock they may select. The slates are divided into four classes—viz., 'Duchess', 'Countess', 'sizable', and 'undersized'. The first mentioned are the largest, being twenty-four inches long by twelve broad; while the 'Countess' slates are twenty by ten inches. The other two classes are smaller. Each crew makes the four kinds, should the quality of the rock allow it, and receives a different sum per thousand for each sort. In working, some of the crew stay always in the quarry and blast the rock face, while the others are out upon the rubbish bank splitting up the blocks furnished by their comrades. The Ballachulish quarriers are said to be the best blasters of rock in Scotland. Slung up the face of the perpendicular rock on a kind of chair attached to a rope fixed at the summit of the level, the worker hammers away at a sharpened iron rod known as a 'jumper'. When he has finished the 'bore', a charge of gunpowder is inserted, and fired with a slow match. So well is everything arranged, that in the memory of the present generation only one man has been killed by a blast, and in that exceptional case it was entirely the man's own fault. After the charge is expended, the workman climbs up the rope, which he fixes round his leg in a peculiar manner, and placing his feet against the perpendicular face of the rock, loosens with a crowbar the masses of stone that have been shattered by the explosion, and sends them crashing down the steep.

Aberfoyle was once the third-largest slate quarry in Scotland, producing 80 tons a year around 1800. In 1900 it was producing 1.4 million slates. It is said that slate from here went into the billiard tables on the *Queen Mary*.

As demand grew, quarrymen and their families moved in 1850 from Ballachulish and the Western Isles to work in Aberfoyle. This necessitated the building of a village by the Aberfoyle Slate Company. This became known as the Aberfoyle Cottaries, only one of which is still in existence; Hill Cottage, which was the first house built at the quarry and in which William MacKenzie, the quarry foreman, lived. Prior to that the quarrymen had lived in wooden bunkhouses. Also built was a school and a church and a co-operative store. Again demand dropped, with the lack of cargo closing the railway in 1951 and the quarry following soon after.

The slate industry in Scotland ended in the 1950s, mostly because of the introduction of new materials such as the concrete 'Marley' tile. The closure of the quarries in a very short period of time raised the price of slates and cheaper alternatives continued to sell well, particularly as techniques and materials developed and manufactured tiles became available in a range of colours and styles. This was also before planning controls were in place to prevent unsuitable building styles and finishes.

However, tastes are changing back and there is a general move towards more natural and environmentally friendly building materials. This has been spurred on by the conservation movement, which often insists on restored and new buildings in a conservation area being roofed with traditional materials similar or identical to neighbouring properties.

This, perversely, has had a negative effect on existing buildings, with abandoned (and some not so abandoned) buildings being robbed for their slates. With the demand rising, slate is being imported but it is recognised that it is inferior to Ballachulish and other Scottish slate for roofing.

As a result, Historic Scotland are now investigating the re-opening of certain quarries to restart operations. It does seem strange that there is not a Scottish source of traditional roofing material and no doubt it will not be long before there is at least one source. Meanwhile, 'Scottish' slate is being imported from China.

However, you can experience a new slate sensation. A few years ago I was invited to a reception at Edinburgh Castle and was extremely surprised to be served my buffet on what seemed to be a roofing slate without the fixing hole. Indeed it was a slate, for there is a strange modern trend to serve dishes on slates and a wee industry has sprung up around this. A number of Scottish companies are now serving a wide range of domestic Scottish slate products, including serving plates, place-mats and coasters. So you really can have a drink 'on the slate'.

Ballachulish station, with the short line to the quarry visible on the extreme right.

A Permian sandstone quarry at Locharbriggs, Dumfries.

THE TEXTILE INDUSTRIES

King Cotton in Scotland

The growth of the cotton industry in Scotland is no different to the tale of many other industries, that is, rural and home-based until the merchant entrepreneurs saw profit in industrialising the processes and meeting increased demands during the Industrial Revolution. In many places in Scotland spinning and weaving had been carried out at home, in the same way that tweed is still woven today in the Western Isles as an industry, and elsewhere as a craft.

Cotton was obtained from wherever it was available cheaply. Supplies from America were interrupted by the American War of Independence but, following this, Glasgow's tobacco lords, who had lost their monopoly on the American tobacco output, invested heavily in cotton and sugar.

The adventurism of the British East India Company policies also enforced the exportation of raw cotton to Britain for processing and then its return to India and elsewhere for sale. In British mills the cotton, also sometimes imported from Egypt, fed the growing mechanisation of the industry.

In many cases the manufacture of cotton had supplanted the making of linen, which had been one of Scotland's main industries in the eighteenth century. However, cotton was cheaper and easier to spin and the mills converted. Cotton and linen manufacture co-existed for a time and was even combined in a material called fustian. Eventually most manufacturers changed. In Dundee and the east this move was towards jute, while in the Glasgow and surrounding areas the change was towards cotton.

The imported cotton is spun into yarn before being woven into soft, naturally whitish material, which is still the world's most popular natural textile. On importation, the downy cotton is taken to the mills where it is first cleaned and combed by carding machines into 'slivers', ropes of material which are then pulled and twisted into smaller and smaller strands. The spinning machines further turn this into finer threads. At this point the process has been identical to that in Paisley's great thread mills, but in the weaving mills the thread goes into the production of cotton fabric.

Glasgow was a major weaving centre, with thousands of people involved in manufacture. These were mostly centred in Calton and my own home area, Anderston, which has, or had, streets named after the industry, for instance Heddle

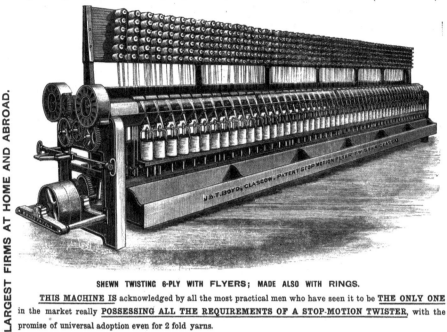

BOYD'S PATENT STOP-MOTION TWISTER (Class O).

REFERENCES MAY BE MADE TO LARGEST FIRMS AT HOME AND ABROAD.

SHEWN TWISTING 6-PLY WITH FLYERS; MADE ALSO WITH RINGS.

THIS MACHINE IS acknowledged by all the most practical men who have seen it to be **THE ONLY ONE** in the market really **POSSESSING ALL THE REQUIREMENTS OF A STOP-MOTION TWISTER**, with the promise of universal adoption even for 2 fold yarns.

DESCRIPTION AND ADVANTAGES.

Stop-motion reliable.

More perfect twist.
No bunch knots.
No bad twist at piecings.
No singles. No Waste.

Cheaper labour.
Labour saved.

No stoppage for doffing.
Great increase in speed of spindles.

Parts all made interchangeable,
and to standard gauges.

Lubrication.

Space saved.

Each Spindle is provided with a RELIABLE STOP MOTION, which, when any one end of a set of threads being twisted together fails or breaks, *instantly* stops the *individual spindle* and *feed roller*, so that it is impossible for either to move further (leaving a *perfectly twisted thread* between the feed roller and spindle, and the *broken end* ready to be pieced in the single *behind the feed roller).* A neat piecing in the single strand and the proper amount of twist where a piecing is made are ensured, whilst bunch knots, singles, doubles, and waste are avoided.

A cheaper and less experienced class of workers may be employed, and even with these a much larger turn-off secured. No time is lost stooping down, stopping spindles, seeking end on bobbin, and bringing same up through the feed rollers. In the case of parallel bobbins, each bobbin is doffed when filled, saving the necessity of stopping of the frame for doffing. A speed of 2,000 to 8,000 per minute, even with slack twist, may be attained, according to size of bobbins.

The construction is simple. The parts, considering the work done, are few. They are all interchangeable, and accurately finished to standard gauges.

Oiling is arranged for in the most approved manner. All working parts are well covered in from dust

The width of a frame having spindles on both sides is only *32 inches*, exclusive of boxes.

J. & T. BOYD,

SHETTLESTON IRON WORKS,

GLASGOW, N.B.

From an 1883 trade magazine: 'A cheaper and less-experienced class of workers may be employed'

Place. (A heddle was an integral part of the loom). Houldsworth Street was named after Henry Houldsworth from Nottingham, who came to manage a cotton mill but moved into iron. His Cheapside Street factory was successful in making cotton-spinning machinery, the first maker in Scotland.

However, with the advent of the first water-powered machines, particularly Arkwright's 1768 water frame, mills were set up where there was an adequate flow of powerful water. Rivers in Glasgow were already host to any number of other types of mill, including grain, flint and paper, so the industry moved out of the city towards powerful water wherever it could be found. It was the steam engine which was to allow mills to move away from river banks, but in the meantime that was where they were established. For example, mills existed at New Lanark, Balfron, Stanley, Blantyre, Deans and Catrine.

I first discovered New Lanark around 1984. While I had known a bit about Robert Owen and the history of the Co-operative movement, I was unaware of the mills opposite the amazing Falls of Clyde, where the river hesitates on its journey from the Lead Hills before continuing its journey through Lanarkshire and Glasgow to the Firth of Clyde and the Atlantic.

Here, where the power of the river could be harnessed, Robert Owen in 1785 founded his model mills and community in order to prove that industrialists could be fair-minded people. When I visited the mill it was in a state of disrepair and at the very beginnings of a restoration funded by the government using unemployed people on the Community Programme. The mill lade was empty prior to rebuilding and the mills were empty. I was informed that they had been previously been used by a scrap metal company and that the metal was piled high within each floor of the great mills.

Since that time, the mills have undergone a monumental improvement programme, culminating in the award of UNESCO World Heritage Site status in 2001. New Lanark now boasts not only a mill visitor centre but a hotel and conference centre and is a mecca for co-operators worldwide.

New Lanark was originally planned by David Dale, Glasgow merchant, and Richard Arkwright, the engineer credited with inventing the spinning or water frame, as well as being recognised as the originator of the modern factory system. Arkwright left the project and Dale was left to built the mills on a site leased from Robert McQueen, Lord Braxfield, of Lanark.

As the mills progressed, Dale also invested in the workers by building a model community comprising a village, church, shop and school. On completion, it was one of the largest industrial communities in Scotland. By 1793 it employed over 1,100 people. Many of these were children from Glasgow and other orphanages. David Dale was considered an enlightened industrial pioneer who understood his responsibility to care for his young workforce. He housed them and they were well fed.

Robert Owen was the son-in-law of David Dale. As manager and part-owner, Robert Owen took over the Lanark Twist Co., the new name for the mills, in 1799, with Owen continuing his care of the workforce by setting up a nursery and a welfare system to supplement the school, which taught music and dance.

The mills seemed to continue successfully and in 1881 they were taken over by Henry Birkmyre and Robert Galbraith Sommerville. This signalled a new direction for the mills when Birkmyre introduced patent net looms to weave fishing nets from the cotton spun at the mill. When the Gourock Ropeworks took over in 1903 the mills were making cloth. The company had a number of subsidiaries, including Thomson Black & Co. of Shettleston. Because of its range of specialised products, the mills weathered the economic ravages of the 1920s and in 1970 the Gourock Ropeworks Ltd became part of Bridon Ropes, with the Port Glasgow Works closing in 1976.

I was surprised to learn during my visit that the mills were in continuous production until 1968, when they were taken over by Metal Extractions Ltd. The workers' tenements had previously been transferred to a housing association, but the mill buildings were in terminal decay. Following their listing as Category A historic buildings and as an Outstanding Conservation Area, the New Lanark Conservation Trust was formed in 1974. New Lanark is now a bustling industrial museum and living village, surviving as a testament to the beginnings of Scotland's industrial era.

One of the village streets in New Lanark is Caithness Row, which has a strange place in the history of Scottish emigration, as reported by the *Statistical Account of Scotland*. Apparently the name came about as a result of the misfortunes of the ship

In a cotton mill.

Fortune, which had set sail from Skye in 1791 for Maryland. It lost its masts in a storm and ran for shelter to Greenock. David Dale heard of the would-be emigrants' plight and offered them the option of staying to work for him, with houses provided. He also built a further 200 houses for Highland emigrants, after which Caithness Row was named when it was completed in 1793.

At Catrine, on the River Ayr, architecturally splendid mills were built in 1747, but following a fire in 1963 they were demolished in 1967. David Dale again had a hand in these mills, along with Claude Alexander of Ballochmyle. They were subsequently bought in 1801 by James Finlay, who expanded them. The mills continued with production to the extent of a new mill being built in 1950 but declined into the 1960s.

Incidentally, the 'Lions of Catrine' were the two waterwheels added in 1828. These powered the mills and were said to be the biggest in the world, becoming a tourist attraction. They were powered by the River Ayr, which fell 15 feet at the spot. Made of cast iron, they were dismantled in the 1940s for scrap.

In Balfron, Stirlingshire, Robert Dunmore built the Ballindalloch Cotton Mills to use the powerful waters of the River Endrick. The mill opened in 1789. Within a couple of years the small village had expanded, with the building of a planned village to house 1,000 workers and street-names still named after the works, such as Cotton Street, Weaver Street and Spinner Street. The works were described in 1844:

> Ballindalloch Cotton Works, situate in the Parish of Balfron, and the county of Stirling, 19 miles distant from Glasgow, containing 10,752 mule spindles, of which 1,248 are self-acting (Smith & Orr's patent), with the necessary preparation, driven by a waterwheel 28 feet diameter, calculated to be equal to 35 horse-power, with a steam engine to assist in dry seasons of 16 horse-power, the supply of water being obtained from the River Endrick and from a reservoir covering 30 imperial acres … The total extent of land, including site of works, dwelling houses, &c., is about 77 imperial acres …

The other remaining memorial to the Scottish cotton industry is the Stanley Mills in Perthshire, now preserved as a visitor centre.

At Stanley, the conditions were right for the establishment of a mill. As ever, there was a landowner – John Murray, Duke of Atholl – who was keen to profit from the flow of the River Tay and established a cotton mill there with local MP George Dempster. Again Richard Arkwright was involved in the process, and Bell Mill was opened in 1787, with 350 people employed there within ten years. We can see in this book how the Napoleonic Wars caused problems for companies who depended on imports of raw materials or exports of finished products. This was also the case with cotton. On top of this, the new East Mill at Stanley, which had been completed in the 1790s, burned down in 1799. George Dempster lost a fortune.

The mills were bought by James Craig of Glasgow in 1801, along with the Glasgow businessman David Dale, who had set up New Lanark in 1786. In 1813 the business failed again but was re-opened in 1823 by Buchanan & Co. of Glasgow, and by 1831 they were employing around 890 people, of whom 540 were women and 500 were under eighteen.

We are familiar with the term 'dark satanic mills'. This term could not be said to apply to the cotton industry in Scotland, for the mill owners in Scotland generally seem to have been more inclined to treat their workers with respect, at least in the comparative terms of the time. The Stanley Mills being above Perth, 'Gateway to the Highlands', they attracted workers from as far away as Caithness, some of these undoubtedly escaping the Highland Clearances. No doubt many of the mill owners made a great deal of money from their workers, but they did appreciate the need to attract and keep the workforce, to the extent of providing 'model' villages, schools and shops. They also provided employment for those displaced by the clearances and for foundling children in workhouses.

One of the things which was absent from a perfect set-up when the mill was established was an easy transport link. The cotton was imported to Glasgow but was being brought to Stanley by cart. When the railway came in 1848 it proved a boon, shortening the transport time from days to hours. (The Scottish Midland Junction Railway linked Perth to the Aberdeen Railway at Forfar. The stretch between Perth and Stanley still remains as part of the main rail route from Perth to Inverness.)

In 1876, Perth businessman Colonel Frank Stewart Sandeman bought the mills, improving them and diversifying the products. The mills and the estate bought with them seem to have been profitable at the time as Sandeman is recorded as having deposited £240 with the Bank of Scotland in June 1876. At that time the weekly wage bill was between £107 and £172 and a dairy maid on the estate farm was earning 14*d* a week.

The mills had been some of the longest-living of Scottish cotton mills and were in almost continuous use, but were inevitably declining over time. They found productive work during both World Wars, producing webbing for the services, but following the Second World War they continued their decline. In 1936 they were employing around 350 people, but by 1965 this was down to around 180 and continued falling through the 1970s. They finally closed in 1989. After a period of dereliction, they were taken over by Historic Scotland in 1995 and are now a wonderful visitor centre showing life in a cotton mill in the nineteenth century.

The Golden Fibre – The Story of Jute in Scotland

O, dear me, the mill is running fast
And we poor shifters canna get nae rest
Shifting bobbins coarse and fine
They fairly make you work for your ten and nine
'Jute Mill Song' – Mary Brooksbank

Jute, known as the Golden Fibre, is a plant which has been used for centuries, spun on simple wheels to make clothes, ropes, twine and sacking. It is cheap, strong and second only to cotton in importance. It is grown on the Indian subcontinent and in China, Thailand and Brazil, but it was from the Indian subcontinent that Scotland's first jute arrived.

Jute – The Golden Fibre.

Bengal and Bangladesh were and still are the largest producers of raw jute, very little of which now comes to Great Britain. It was very different in the days of the British Empire. During the time of the British occupation, or 'Raj' from 1848 to 1947, the raw jute was exported to Britain for processing and created a huge industry in Dundee and the surrounding area.

Spinning and weaving flax was already a trade carried out in Dundee when the first bales of jute were unloaded in Dundee in 1820. The British East India Company had distributed samples of the raw plant to promote interest as they saw it as a possible profitable enterprise. However there was little interest from weavers or mill owners until eventually, after a second attempt, a champion of the fibre, Dundee merchant Thomas Neish, persuaded the local manufacturers to have another go at weaving the material. This time the experiments worked. There was a recession in the trade for hemp bags in 1831. This, combined with a failure in the Russian flax crop in 1834, as well as the fear of war with Russia in 1838, persuaded the Dundee manufacturers and traders that trying out jute again would not be such a bad thing.

It was in 1840 that the industry fully took off, pioneered by Dundee merchant and shipowner Thomas Davidson, who was the first to import raw jute directly from India to Dundee. On 26 April 1840, the barque *Selma* discharged its cargo, marking the start of Dundee as a free port. Up till 1840 the port of London had a monopoly over the import of tea, sugar, jute, hemp and other raw materials from India. Davidson visited London and, armed with the statistics on imports, managed to persuade the government of Dundee's case. He won them over and Dundee was declared a free port for goods from East India, marking the beginning of the jute industry and the rise of 'Juteopolis', Dundee, as the centre of the world's jute industry. The *Selma* brought 1,026 bales of jute. This could be contrasted with the figure 100 years later in 1940 when 1 million 400-pound bales were disembarked.

Instrumental to the success of the industry was the whale. The raw jute plant was woody and difficult to weave, with the first attempts eventually being sold as doormats. It took some experimentation to convert the flax mills to processing jute, but it was discovered that when treated with light whale oil, the fibre became manageable and so started a chain which linked whales to jute, jute to linoleum and saw exports throughout the world, marking Dundee as one of Scotland's busiest ports.

Softening and batching is the start of the process at which the coarse, raw plant is treated with a mixture of oil and water which penetrates the fibres and makes

Distillers Company Limited yeast bag.

them workable. (The whale oil was eventually replaced by mineral oil.) There were eight other processes, including carding, where the material is teased out into loose fibres. After spinning, the threads produced are spooled, ready for weaving into the very recognisable cloth, before passing to the calendering machine, which rolls and smooths the material.

In the history of the making of the United States of America, there are few more iconic images than the sight of the wagon train making its way over the great plains and mountains of the New World. Just like the Turkey red bandanas from the Vale of Leven, jute contributed to the pioneering of the West, not just as covers for wagons, but also as the basis for tents, ropes, boot lining, sailcloth, floor coverings, meat wrapping, horse blankets, wicks, explosive fuses, deck chairs and a host of other purposes including, of course, sackcloth and the sack. No wonder it was called 'the fabric of a thousand uses'.

I would wonder whether those people labouring away in the noise, stoor and the stink of the jute mills could appreciate that their finished products would be travelling the globe, carrying the produce and manufactures of Scotland to the British Empire and elsewhere.

For the mills were unpleasant places in which to work. Before any health and safety laws were in place, most mills and factories were dangerous and dirty. The

Jute mills and factories in Arbroath.

dust in the mills was everywhere, as were the grease and oil fumes. The continuous, ear-shattering roar of the mills would eventually affect the hearing.

Women were the mainstay of the mills, supplemented by children, some under ten, whose size meant that they could be under the machines, cleaning and picking up material. It was inevitable that there would be deaths and disease. They called it 'mill fever', when bronchitis was brought on by exposure to the dust and the fumes.

The industry was enormous and at its peak around 1870, 50,000 people were employed in sixty mills in Dundee alone. Many of these were Irish, Italian and Polish immigrants escaping the famine and poverty of their homelands. The industry also expanded beyond Dundee to include Blairgowrie, Forfar, Arbroath and other east coast towns.

Of the mill owners of Dundee, there are some who stand out and exemplify the industrialists and sometimes the benefactors of the city. If you were to visit a concert in the Caird Hall in the centre of the city then you would get some idea of the contribution.

Sir James Key Caird was the son of the founder of Caird (Dundee) in 1832 and based in the Ashton Works. Following his father, he developed the business as the demand for jute products increased worldwide. He invested in modern machinery and took over the Craigie Works in 1905. Caird had a good reputation, with his workforce numbering 2,000 at its peak. He understood, more than most industrialists, the effects of working conditions. Besides the gift of the Caird Hall, he endowed Dundee Royal Infirmary with funds to research and treat cancer, a 'mysterious disease' at the time. He also funded Ernest Shackleton's Antarctic expedition of 1914–16.

Baxter Park in Dundee is named after the Baxter family. Between 1840 and 1890 they ran Baxter's Mill in Princess Street, known as the Dens Works. Baxter Brothers became part of Low & Bonar in 1924 and continued to trade under their own name until 1978.

In Lochee, once a separate village but eventually part of Dundee, James Cox established a linen business around 1700. The company had 300 weavers in 1760 and by the fourth generation of the family, in 1815, they were producing the first broad hessian. This 45-inch-wide cloth was a new product for the Manchester market and was welcomed.

In 1864 the Camperdown Works was built, reputed then to be the largest factory in the world, employing over 5,000. The company also gave Dundee one of its historic landmarks, Cox's Stack. Still standing, it is a Grade A listed building and the best surviving example of an industrial chimney in Scotland. The 25-acre Lochee Park was donated by the Cox brothers to the city in 1890.

While there were benefactors, as ever, many of the mill owners and industrialists had no particular loyalty to the workforce in Dundee, Arbroath and other mill areas. It made sense to them to invest their money where the labour cost was even cheaper; that is, back in the Indian subcontinent, the source of the raw material.

This movement began with Margaret Donnelly, who was first to set up a jute mill in Calcutta in 1855. By 1900, Dundee had lost its status as the world's largest jute town, being overtaken by Calcutta, which, by 1930, was producing 70 per cent of the world's jute products. The mills there thrived, built and managed by Dundonian engineers and managers. In fact the process was assisted by the fact that textile students came from Calcutta to study at Dundee Technical College, an early indication of the potential for the education industry in Scotland.

A Home by the Hooghly by Eugenie Fraser describes the lives of the 'Jutewallahs' in Calcutta. These were the Scots from Dundee, Forfar and Arbroath who made their homes along the banks of the Hooghly, living in compounds and preserving their Scottish but very comfortable way of life to the extent that they attended yearly St Andrew's Day dinners and Burns Suppers. By 1890 there were 3,000 working in Calcutta, where there is also a Scottish cemetery. The Scots were not seen as empire-builders like the British Army or civil service. Neither were they products of the public schools. They were proud professional engineers and managers and worked well with their Indian colleagues. Many of these managers and engineers remained in India well into the 1960s and some beyond. Their links with India, as well as the links of many other Scots in India and Pakistan, are preserved by Caledonian Societies in both countries.

The Dundee mills had a slow wind-down as there was still a demand for jute products in Great Britain, particularly for base for carpets and linoleum. It would also be some time before the Indian subcontinent penetrated the markets held by Britain. This would come in time as many of the Indian jute mills were British-owned and had access to the vehicles and markets of Empire.

By 1900, Calcutta had overtaken Dundee as the world's biggest single jute manufacturer. The writing was on the wall for the Scottish jute industry. However, the Dundee mills were modernised, working conditions improved and high levels of production continued through two World Wars and well into the 1960s.

The end eventually came as synthetic materials developed. Materials such as nylon, rayon, acrylic fibres and particularly polypropylene began to replace traditional materials in carpets, packaging, ropes and twine and virtually every known use of jute. While some firms survived the changes, gradually the great mills closed down, some becoming warehouses, some remaining in a state of dereliction until better times in Dundee have seen them converted into flats and offices.

Following the exit of the British from India in 1947, the end was also in sight for the Scottish jute barons in India. They had set up the industry but it was time to go home. Most of the industry there was passed on to local businesspeople and the industry continues to thrive, developing products for fashion and industry where natural fibres are more in demand. Natural jute, for example, is used extensively in preventing soil erosion. A new, environmentally friendly food-grade shopping bag has been produced and is being exported globally. While it may not see the end of the plastic bag, it is nevertheless making a contribution. One of the world's largest companies and the owner of our last remaining steel mills in Scotland, Tata of India, has very recently offered for sale an entire flat-pack house made of jute and destined for India's destitute and homeless. The possibilities do seem endless.

There is also a movement towards natural burials and a Dundee company has answered the call by selling natural jute coffins! We have earlier looked at the linoleum industry and Forbo, previously Nairn's of Kirkcaldy, still produces original linoleum made from completely natural products, including a hessian base.

If you would like to get some sense of what it might be like inside a jute mill then you can visit Dundee's marvellous Verdant Mill. Built for David Lindsay in 1833, the mill at one time employed 500 people. The site was derelict in 1991 when the Dundee Heritage Trust took it over, taking six years to convert it to its original state and opening it in 1996 as one of Dundee's great visitor centres.

Again, like many of the industries that we have visited, there are survivors. In the amalgamation and rationalisation of companies, some have embraced the challenges of new materials, new techniques and new processes to emerge as world-class and sometimes international companies. One such company is Low & Bonar which opened a jute-weaving factory in 1912, soon expanding into North America and Africa. From jute weaving it progressed into backings for tufted carpets and bag manufacture, becoming listed on the stock exchange in 1947.

Low & Bonar was one of the companies to manage the changes, diversifying into power transformers and plastic packaging. Further developments included the production of polypropylene yarn. Finally moving out of jute by the end of the 1970s, the company acquired flooring and packaging companies. Packaging, plastics and flooring were divested more recently, with the company concentrating on its place as a materials business. This includes non-woven carpet tiles, building products, artificial grass, awnings and other coated products.

And Dundee itself is thriving. Proud of its industrial history, it has emerged from the gloom of poverty and dereliction as a new and innovative city, Scotland's fourth-largest. With two universities, it is now a centre for the biomedical sciences and technology and is recognised for its digital media and entertainments business and education, particularly in computer games and other interactive media. It is also known as the 'City of Discovery', home as it is to Robert Falcon Scott's Dundee-built RRS *Discovery*. The *Discovery* is the focus of Discovery Point, which marks Dundee's scientific and maritime endeavours.

The Scottish Thread Industry

If you have mills and factories making linen, cotton, woollens, canvas, shoes, sails and most of the fabrics needed by industry and commerce, then you would need something to hold this all together. If you had a huge industry producing sewing machines of all shapes and sizes then you would surely need threads of all shapes and sizes for the machines. This is exactly what was produced in Coats's thread mill in Paisley. Here, in a huge monument to the Industrial Revolution still prominent in Paisley's landscape, were produced threads which went throughout the world.

It was my Auntie Polly who explained Coats's to me. She lived in Glasgow's Nitshill and it was as easy then to go shopping in Paisley as it was Glasgow's city centre. As a wee boy I was shopping with her. 'What's that building, auntie?'

'That's Coats's, Michael. I know some lassies that work long hours there at the mills making thread that goes all over. I'll show you some when we get back.' And from the drawers of her Singer sewing machine she came out with a range of bobbins, not just from Coats's but also from other Scottish manufacturers like Clark, Kerr and Cochran, all of Paisley. From that day I was able to play with the bobbins as well as empty out huge biscuit tins of buttons and hooks of every shape, size and colour. She was a great dressmaker. Looking back at Coats's takes me back to Paisley,

Coats's Abbey Mill, Paisley.

more famous I suppose for the Paisley pattern but whose growth was just as much a product of the thread industry as it was of shawls.

The thread industry started with James and Patrick Clark's silk thread business in Paisley. Paisley weavers had been imitating shawls from the Kashmir, and producing them at a fraction of the cost. However, Napoleon's blockade of Great Britain stopped the import of the raw silk needed for making the shawls. Patrick Clark's invention of twisted cotton threads suitable for the shawls overcame this problem. They opened the first cotton thread mill on the River Cart in 1812. Other members of the Clark family had been involved in the thread business and, over a period of time and amalgamations, the firm of Clark & Co. appeared and in 1880 the great Anchor Mills was employing over 3,500, producing 15 tons of goods a day. One of the companies merging with Clark's was Peter Kerr of Underwood Mill in Paisley, which had the distinction of having installed, in 1799, the first James Watt steam engine in Scotland.

Perhaps one of the greatest innovations was the development of a six-cord soft thread, which was the first thread suitable for use in the new sewing machine. Before the invention of the sewing machine in 1846 by Elias Howe, thread was usually made of three cords, useful for hand sewing but wiry, uneven and not strong enough for machines. This thread revolutionised the sewing industry, and therefore Clark called it 'Our New Thread'. This became known as O.N.T, the famous trademark for the Clark Thread Company product.

Meanwhile, James Coats had entered the weaving trade in 1802 and went on to open a cotton mill at Ferguslie, Paisley to make thread. Retiring in 1830, the company became J. & P. Coats after his sons James and Peter. The company continued to expand, with the building of new premises such as the imposing No. 1 Spinning Mill.

Clark & Co. was Coats' biggest rivals. Their continual expansion saw the acquisition of mills in Newark, New Jersey and the opening of international markets, particularly in Russia. London Stock Exchange listing was achieved in 1890. Much of

Testing ONT spool cotton.

this expansion was in the United States, where Clark began manufacturing in Newark, New Jersey. Coats followed five years later, manufacturing in Pawtucket, Rhode Island. The two companies eventually came to dominate the cotton thread market there.

Clark had built the great Anchor Mill in Paisley while Coats built the Abbey Mill, both as impressive as one another. Clark's Anchor Mill was closed in the 1980s but was saved from demolition, preserved and is now host to apartments and businesses.

John Paton had founded a mill in Alloa in the 1770s, producing yarn for knitting materials. Johnstone's Mill was acquired by Paton in 1896 and in its ninety years of existence became a major supplier of laces to Great Britain's considerable boot-and-shoe industry. All kinds of chords, tapes and braids were also made. The company merged with James Baldwin of Halifax in 1920. Both Clark's and Coats's separate businesses were successful and long-lived and saw a merger in 1952. A further merger with Paton's and Baldwin's in 1961 created Coats Patons. Coats plc was formed when the Guinness Peat Group took over in 2003.

Thread and the related industries were behind Paisley's growth and at its peak in the 1930s J. & P. Coats alone employed 28,000 in the Anchor and Ferguslie Mills. Although the companies diversified into the new synthetic fibres, imports from mills in India and Brazil were having an impact. The Second World War had a major effect on demand as well as supply, as did the change of ownership of some mills. By the 1980s thread production had stopped in Paisley. All of this had an effect on the supported industries, which produced mill machinery and other supplies.

Coats still has its own brand and still dominates the thread market. It very generously maintains a branch office in its original Abbey Mill in Paisley, which is now a business centre.

Selection of Scottish-made threads.

For completeness we should also say that there were other mills, including the Crofthead Mill in Neilston, founded by James Orr & Sons but purchased by R. F. & J. Alexander in 1859. The company was quite long-lived and went into partnership with Tootal Broadhurst Lee, with the company retaining its name. The Crofthead Mill finally closed in 1992, making a large number of people redundant.

One survivor in the thread business is W. & J. Knox of Kilbirnie. Established in 1778, they have adapted to business conditions and supply yarns for carpet and nets for the marine industry as well as sporting and military purposes.

Coats, Clarks and others have also to be remembered, not only for the lasting legacy of the huge mill buildings but for their benefaction. In common with many other Scottish industrialists like Carnegie, Mitchell and Lipton, they left a lasting legacy in the form of public works, donations and buildings.

If you take a walk through Paisley you will pass by and be able to enter many of the buildings donated by the Coatses and by the Clarks. These include the 1871 Museum and Library donated by Peter Coats, as well as the Coats Observatory. George Clark gave £20,000 for the erection of the town hall.

J. & P. Coats also left a legacy to education in the Needlework Development Scheme. This created a loan scheme for schools, of historical and modern embroideries, in order to promote embroidery as art. The scheme started in 1934 and was organised by the art schools of Aberdeen, Dundee, Edinburgh and Glasgow. The textiles were available to domestic science and training colleges, women's institutions, art schools and schools. At the outbreak of the Second World War, the 900 embroideries were dispersed among the original art schools and the scheme ceased. However, in 1944, Glasgow School of Art was instrumental in restarting the scheme, which lasted until 1961 when funding was withdrawn. However, the scheme had met its aims, having acquired a unique collection of 3,000 articles. These were dispersed among fourteen museums and educational institutions in Great Britain, including the National Museums of Scotland.

Patons, Johnstone.

If you would like a wee insight into the lost world of thread making then the Paisley Thread Mill Museum is a wonderful attraction for anyone with an interest in our industrial heritage. The museum is run by volunteers, many of whom worked in the mills.

The Sma' Shot Cottages, also in Paisley, transport you back to the life of mill workers in the 1700s and 1800s.

The sma' shot, by the way, was a cotton thread which bound all the colourful weft threads into the warps of Paisley shawls. The sma' shot could not be seen in the finished shawl, so the manufacturers would not pay for the thread. This was at a time when many employers would charge for the raw materials or tools needed for the process.

By the middle of the century the weavers were fed up with the employers and took strike action. In 1856, after a long and bitter dispute, the workers won their case and the employees were paid for the hidden thread.

The Cowboy Connection – Turkey Red

On the River Leven, just above Dumbarton, is the site of the manor house where Robert the Bruce spent his last years quietly fishing and hawking. The river in his time, as now, was wide and fast-flowing, taking water from Loch Lomond to the Clyde. It was this clean, fast water which was to be the main reason for the growth of one of Scotland's most interesting and least-known industries, outside the Vale of Leven at least. And just like Robert the Bruce's manor house, there is virtually nothing left to see of this great industry which stretched the length of the River Leven, with dyeworks on either side. This is the story of Turkey red.

The manufacture of Turkey red was a huge and important industry, employing thousands, with exports not only of bandanas to the Americas but sarongs to Asia and saris and shawls to India. As with many industries, it was subject to the march of time, foreign competition, foreign government protection and development of new

Iconic western art – Texas cowboy by English illustrator Stanley L. Wood (1866-1928).

processes. The industry lasted barely 150 years but its story parallels the fate of many of the industries in Scotland.

Prior to the production of Turkey red dye in Scotland, textiles were either plain cottons or linens. Any patterns in the cloth had to be weaved in with wool or cotton threads which were pre-dyed, much in the same way as Harris Tweed is still produced on hand looms. The natural dyes that were used simply would not take to finished fabrics.

This was all to change with the introduction of Turkey red. The name of the dye derives from Turkey, where the process appears to have been used in earlier days. It was also called Adrianople red, Adrianople being in what is modern Turkey. While the name implies that only the colour red was produced, in fact, by the process of bleaching out the red, a wide variety of vibrant colours were possible.

Turkey red is derived from the compound alizarin, obtained from the root of the madder plant. This vegetable dye has been in use since prehistoric times. However, its composition and production had been a guarded secret, compounded by a highly complicated manufacturing process that involved multiple stages and ingredients.

In much the same way as spices, cloth was an extremely important trading commodity. Natural earth colours like brown were less expensive than bright colours and red was particularly valued and valuable. This is why deep reds are often associated with royalty. Turkey red was a particularly vibrant colour which was durable, colour-fast and extremely attractive, but the method of making it was elusive.

It was George Mackintosh, father of Charles Mackintosh, inventor of the waterproof coat, who introduced the Turkey red dyeing process to Scotland in 1785. Along with David Dale of New Lanark fame, he persuaded a Frenchman, Pierre Jacques Papillon, a chemist from Rouen, to come to Scotland and explain the long and complicated process. This, along with secrecy and protectionism of the formula, had prevented a wider knowledge of how the dye was made.

The process involves what is called a 'mordant', which allows the dye to penetrate the fibres of the cloth without being washed away by water. There were successive processes involving a wide range of ingredients, including alum, bull's blood and manure. This process was called animalising and must have been extremely smelly. There were multiple steps to the process, this being one:

> The cotton is dyed in parcels of 10lb at once for which take two gallons and a half of ox blood and mix in the copper with 112 gallons of milk, warm water, which are to be well-stirred. Then add 25 lb of Turkey madder and stir the whole well together. Having beforehand put the 10lb of cotton on sticks, dip it into the light and move and turn it constantly one hour, during which gradually increase the heat so that the liquor may begin to boil at the end of the hour. Then sink the cotton and boil it gently one hour longer and lastly, wash and dry it...

The first foray into the manufacture of the product was at Dalmarnock (then called Barrowfield). In 1805, Mackintosh and Dale sold their factory on to Henry Monteith & Co., whose 'Great Bandana Gallery' is described in the *Glasgow Mechanics'*

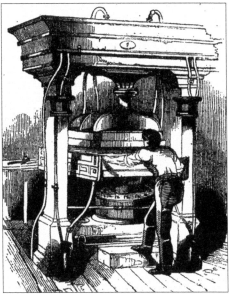

Two images taken from an article on dyeing in *The Penny Magazine of the Society for the Diffusion of Useful Knowledge*, 1844. *Above left:* Wringing out yarn. *Above right:* A bandana press.

Magazine of 1824. Monteith already had textile factories at Blantyre and in Bridgeton. His new Dalmarnock factory had sixteen presses, able to produce 1,600 pieces of 12 yards' length every ten hours. The *Mechanics' Magazine* said of Monteith's,

> Their factory deserves to be studied as a school of practical science ... the gallery consists of sixteen of these engines, beautifully constructed, placed in one range in sub-divisions of four, the space between each set serving as passages to admit workers. To each is attached a pair of patterns in lead. When operated the two patterns close on one another very nicely, by means of guide pins at the corners ... by this arrangement of presses, 1600 pieces, consisting of 12 yards each, that is, 19,200 yards are converted into bandanas in the space of ten hours, by the labour of four workmen.

The start of Turkey red in the Vale of Leven can be attributed to another well-known Glaswegian, William Stirling, who originally operated bleach fields at Dawsholm on the River Kelvin but moved from there in 1770 to the Vale, where he was able to acquire a bigger pool of labour as well as using the clean waters flowing into Loch Lomond. It was here in 1816 that he extended his bleach works and introduced Turkey red.

John Orr Ewing was another to become involved in the industry in the Vale, leasing Croftingea in 1835. His brother Archibald was then funded by John to get involved and he leased the Levenbank works, then buying Milton in 1860 and Dillichip in 1866.

By the 1860s, William Stirling & Sons and the Orr Ewings between them were employing 6,000 workers, producing 10,000 pieces of cloth per day. The Turkey red and calico industries in the Vale caused the population there to rise from less than 200 to almost 20,000 by 1891, many of these being emigrants from Ireland and the West Highlands.

The growing populations settled mostly in the growing villages of Alexandria, Renton, Jamestown and Bonhill. In these villages can be see the houses built for the workers and the managers, as well as public parks gifted by the companies to the communities.

In all there were around fifteen Turkey red companies in the Vale in the 1880s, but time was running out. German scientists, in 1868, had discovered an artificial alizarin and, having a monopoly on this, prices rose steeply in the 1880s for British producers, the biggest being in the Vale. In addition, in the 1890s India had begun to impose import tariffs on imported dyed yarns to protect its own textile industry.

In 1897, steps were taken to meet these challenges through merger and acquisition. The United Turkey Red Company (UTRC) was formed, joining the firms of John Orr Ewing, Archibald Orr Ewing and William Stirling. Alexander Reid & Sons of Milngavie was acquired in 1900.

These companies were managed as separate entities but were amalgamated, resulting in a violent strike in 1911, this being at a time when many west of Scotland industrialists were introducing 'Scientific Management'. Reaction to increased workloads and reduced wages caused a lot of unrest, and at the nearby Singer's sewing machine factory, almost the whole workforce of 11,000 struck.

But the end was in sight for Turkey red. The UTRC had continued to develop in the west of Scotland and became increasingly mechanised. However, while they had the technical knowledge and monopoly on manufacturing Turkey red, the UTRC board was resistant to diversifying into synthetic dyes. The inability to compete with companies using the new dyes put an end to the industry. A reorganisation in the 1920s did not help. Although fabrics continued to be printed, the company was taken over by the Calico Printers Association, which closed the Alexandria works, known locally as 'The Craft', in 1960. 250 years of textile industry in the Vale were at an end.

Interestingly, the Calico Printers Association was eventually to become Tootal Ltd which, through merger, became Coats Viyella, the successor company of J. & P. Coats, cotton thread manufacturers of Paisley.

As for the man who introduced Turkey red to Scotland, Pierre Papillon, he wasn't getting on well with George Mackintosh and went into business on his account in 1787. He built a dyehouse and a tenement in Brunswick Street. He left the business to be run by his two sons, who unfortunately ruined the business, putting him into destitution at his death, leaving his widow in poverty. If it could be any consolation, a Bridgeton street, Papillon Street, was named after him. It was subsequently changed to French Street.

There is very little to see of the industry now in the Vale of Leven. Behind the rusting gates of Alexandria's UTRC factory can be seen remaining buildings, now part of a warehouse complex. There are no other substantial remains except here and there some girders on the pathway which once linked the dyeworks by rail. That path is now part of the Turkey Red Heritage Trail, which takes you from Dumbarton

Bridge to Balloch along the River Leven. Along the way are boards explaining where this great industry existed at Dalquhurn, Cordale, Milton, Dillichip, Levenbank, Croftingea and Alexandria. The villages of Renton and Alexandria are only steps away from the heritage trail.

The Turkey red industry is gone but that other, older industry still continues as anglers join the ghost of Robert the Bruce, fishing the banks of the River Leven.

You can find out a bit more about it on the Balloch and Haldane Community Council website; www.ballochhaldanecc.org.uk.

New Lanark in the late 1960s. Note the roofless condition of the mill on the right.

SCOTLAND AND THE SEA

Scotland's Lost Fisheries

The Silver Harvest – Scotland's Herring Industry
The herring has been important for centuries in the Scottish diet and was once purely caught as a domestic food to provide a cheap source of essential nutrition. The herring is a pelagic fish, that is those that live in the upper layers of the sea. It is related to the mackerel and the pilchard. The herring is still caught and still has an extremely important place in Scotland's economy.

The small, open, early boats were sailing craft until reliable inexpensive engines became available and one of these, the Kelvin engine from Glasgow, became extremely important in making the seas more accessible. The modern boats, with their technologically advanced searching and netting, are far superior to those small craft which plied the North Sea in the heyday of the hunt for herring.

At one time there were around 30,000 boats involved in the search for the 'silver darlings' off Britain's east coast and in the Irish Sea. The Scottish fishing industry flourished like no other, becoming the largest in Europe. Much of this had been promoted by a bounty of £3 per ton given by the Government to herring boats over 60 tons. This was to encourage what had been an inefficient trade, as well as providing a training ground for prospective recruits to the Navy.

Herring was and is a delicacy in many European countries and Scotland was well-placed, with many east coast harbours, to take advantage of the bounties and meet the needs of a growing market for the fish on the Continent and in Russia.

The quick preservation of herring is necessary because, being fatty, it rots quickly. This gave rise to a huge industry in salt-cured herring, which was packed in barrels for export to the markets in Germany and Eastern Europe. In 1907, at the height of the boom, 2.5 million barrels of fish were exported. Besides the need for salt, this also required the manufacture of huge quantities of barrels and boxes. Just as important was the production of kippers by the smoking of herring, which was evident in the hundreds of typical smokehouses in fishing towns and villages along the East Coast and islands of Scotland.

While the hunt for the herring was originally seasonal, it was extended substantially by what was a huge travelling factory of fish curers, packers and porters who followed the fishing fleet as it moved. Instrumental in this were the Scotch fisher

Herring gutters, Wick harbour.

Herring boats in the harbour, Wick.

Wick Fishing Season: a group of fishermen and wives gutting herring in Wick.

lassies from every fishing port in Scotland, who travelled the length and breadth of Scotland and as far south as Lowestoft, Great Yarmouth and Grimsby to gut the fish as it was landed.

As with many other industries, war had an enormous and lasting effect. The herring fisheries had proved to be an excellent training ground for the Royal Navy in the First World War, with many of the fishermen recruited to the war effort as well as their craft, which had been requisitioned for the Navy. After the war, the requisitioned boats returned to an already declining industry. The Russian and German markets for herring had collapsed and too many boats were chasing the same amount of fish. Many had to be laid up.

As often happens, war allows competitors to enter the market and this was the case with the herring fisheries, which saw big challenges from Iceland, Norway and Germany, which used to be a market rather than a catcher. Not only that, but tastes at home were changing. Herring was increasingly seen as a poor person's fish.

To counter the continuing fall in demand and the crisis facing the industry, the Scottish Herring Producer's Association was founded in 1932. That year saw a desperate situation in the industry and the new association was seen as a way to consolidate and represent the needs and views of everyone within the industry. An early success was arranging for an export deal of 100,000 barrels of cured herring to Russia.

The Second World War naturally disrupted the industry again, and after hostilities were over much of the fishing concentrated on the white fish market, with most of the fishing fleet being renewed with assistance from the government. But the number of boats at sea continued to fall as technological advancements meant bigger nets, more efficient catching and more time at sea. Improved living standards on the Continent

The trial trip of an Aberdeen trawler.

Herring gutters at Stronsay, Orkney, await the return of the boats.

A fisherwife awaits the return of her husband's boat, Cullen Bay, *c.* 1905.

Preparing for the Lewis herring fishing at Cullen, Banff, *c.* 1905.

and changes in diet, with less emphasis on the traditional herring, also played its part. The number of people involved in the industry fell dramatically and never again reached the point when every fishing port in Scotland was as crammed with fishing boats as the barrel was crammed with herring.

While the industry is a lot smaller and herring is still important, mackerel is now the main catch in pelagic fisheries. It is a secure industry and still an important one and the Scottish fleet is still at the forefront of pelagic fishing. Modern methods and modern equipment mean that today's boats can catch as much as the earlier fleet, but they are limited by quotas to preserve fish stocks.

The Scottish Merchant Fleet

> Dirty British coaster with a salt-caked smoke stack,
> Butting through the Channel in the mad March days,
> With a cargo of Tyne coal,
> Road-rails, pig-lead,
> Firewood, iron-ware, and cheap tin trays.
> John Masefield, 'Cargoes'

There can hardly be any school pupil of my generation who was not required to recite by heart John Masefield's 'Cargoes'. It represented all that Britain held dear as

SS *Perth* of the Dundee, Perth & London Shipping Company.

a maritime nation and the Scot's need for adventure in the far-flung corners of the Empire and the Commonwealth.

One of literature's great stereotypes is the Scottish ship's engineer, solid and reliable, protective of his machinery and with fierce loyalty to his captain and his ship. It was no surprise to discover Scottie at the engines of the USS *Enterprise* telling Captain Kirk that 'Ah cannae get any mair oot o' this engine Captain or she'll blow up.'

This remarkable stereotype exists but it was true that you would find Scottish mariners in every corner of the globe serving on Scottish ships. We not only built the ships but also owned them, managed them and provided the crews, many of them Scots with their famous engineering skills.

Modern folk who travel around Scotland and beyond might complain about the traffic hold-ups, about train breakdowns and delays and about cancelled flights. If they lived over 100 years ago then the biggest complaint would have been the state of the roads, in that there were no roads to speak of. When Queen Victoria ascended the throne in 1837 there were still very few railways in Scotland, and those that existed were mainly for the transportation of goods and raw materials such as coal from the coalfields of Fife and Lanarkshire.

Before the railways, local travel was on poor roads and by horse or by stagecoach. For longer distances or speed, sea was the only option. People from the north of Scotland who wanted to travel to Edinburgh would do it by sea as it was the quickest method. This same would be true of travel between Edinburgh and London.

This gave opportunities to Scotland's entrepreneurs, who were ever-ready to seize on a profitable venture. They established a great merchant fleet that plied the waters round our shores just as if they were today's motorways. The seas were teeming with

The London & Edinburgh Shipping Company Limited.

boats of all sizes, trading from port to port, carrying any and every cargo. There were many, many companies and rather than try to catalogue them I have chosen a few as illustrations.

Typical of the coastal trade was the London & Edinburgh Shipping Company, based in Leith. The company, set up around 1809, carried a wide variety of cargo and it was the company's clipper *Isabella* that made history in Scotland by being the first ship to bring into any port, apart from London, the first import of tea. This was in 1833, following the end of an importation monopoly held by the East India Company. The tea was destined for Andrew Melrose & Company, set up in 1812 and still going strong as a brand of Typhoo.

Just before the First World War, a first-class ticket to London from Edinburgh on the 'First class steam ships', the *Malvina*, the *Marmion*, the *Iona* or the *Morna*, would have cost you 22 shillings with provisions from the steward 'on moderate terms'. The 1,244-ton *Malvina* was sunk by German submarine *U-104* on 3 August 1918, about a mile from Flamborough Head. Fourteen souls were lost. The submarine was believed to have been destroyed by depth charges from an armed yacht.

In the 1930s, the company was running a passenger and cargo service three times a week between Leith and the Hermitage Steam Wharf in London, using the steamships *Royal Fusilier*, *Royal Archer* and the *Royal Scot*.

Built in Dundee in 1924, the *Royal Fusilier* was advertised as 'the newest and finest steamer on the coast'. It offered electric light, hot and cold baths(!) and had a music room. With the growth of the railways, the passenger trade between Leith and London declined and stopped altogether during the war years. Following the Second World War the company went into decline and liquidation followed in 1964.

On the other hand, the Dundee, Perth & London Shipping Company is a fine example of the Scottish company that has adapted to circumstances and continues to thrive. The DP&L was formed in 1826 as the result of an amalgamation of two rivals on the important Dundee-to-London routes.

Thirteen of the company's twenty-three ships were employed on the London route, while others traded to Glasgow via the Forth and Clyde Canal and onwards to Liverpool. Steamship operations started in 1830 with the wooden paddle tug *Sir William Wallace*, with two more, the *Dundee* and the *Perth*, in 1833 from Robert Napier's Glasgow shipyard.

The company continued successfully and during the Great War many of the ships were requisitioned as armed boarding or escort vessels. The *Dundee* saw distinguished action in March 1917 when she intercepted a steamer off the Norwegian coast. This was the German raider *Leopard*, masquerading as a neutral Norwegian vessel. *Dundee* engaged *Leopard* and kept her at bay until she was sunk by HMS *Achilles*.

Following the war the company again built up its shipping routes, acquiring the Dundee & Newcastle Shipping Company and the Kirkcaldy Steamship Company. Routes to Lisbon, Antwerp, Seville and Barcelona were opened.

In the 1920s trade was stable, and with nine ships in 1926, much of the cargo was locally produced goods such as D. C. Thompson's magazines, Keiller's jams, Valentine's postcards and stationery, paper from Guardbridge paper mill, jute and linoleum, seed potatoes and cased whisky. By return, Danish bacon and eggs were carried back to Kirkcaldy.

The Second World War again brought instability, but the company contributed substantially to the effort, including pipeline operations on Project Pluto, a pipeline laid across the Channel following the D-Day landings. Only one ship was lost during those times, the *Gowrie*, which was bombed by two German aircraft east of Stonehaven. The crew survived but the ship later sank.

Following the war, ships of the DP&L, like other owners, faced increasing competition from road and rail. Their new vessels *Lunan* and *London* sailed successfully for many years, as did ships on new routes carrying back esparto grass from Libya for the paper industry, iron ore from North Africa, timber from Archangel and sugar from Jamaica.

But the coastal trade was becoming increasingly difficult. Coal-carrying was diminishing and passenger travel was in decline. By the beginning of 1963, there were four coastal vessels left and in 1967, after 140 years of ship owning, the flag came down on the last ship, the *Kingennie*, in 1967.

However, it was not the end for DP&L, which diversified into shipping agency work and now, as part of Cortachy Holdings Group, has interests in property, travel agencies, industrial supply and recruitment.

The company is still based in its lovely building in East Dock Street, Dundee and from their boardroom comes the image of the SS *Perth*, built by the Caledon Shipbuilding Company in 1915, the fifth vessel to carry the name. The SS *Perth* saw service in both wars, in 1941 saving the sixty-man crew of the *Somerset*, which had been struck by a bomb. Over four years of service she escorted sixty convoys and rescued 455 survivors.

The Clyde has a special place in Scottish maritime history. It was Henry Bell of Helensburgh who, in 1812, built the *Comet* and started the first passenger service between Glasgow and Greenock. On either bank of the Clyde grew communities who needed serving and this gave rise to the famous puffers immortalised in Neil Munro's

Para Handy tales. This was the beginning of the Caledonian MacBrayne services, still plying their trade and connecting the Western Isles to the mainland.

And to the Clyde from Ireland came the thousands of 'navvies' to build our railways, dig our canals and, like my grandfather, work in our steelworks. The ferries between Scotland and Ireland are legendary and continue to operate, although they are now much more modern than the Burns & Laird *Laird's Loch* on which I sailed from the Broomielaw to Ireland in 1960. The *Laird's Loch* belonged to the Burns & Laird Lines Ltd, which was an example of the ferry companies that were set up for passenger and cargo throughout Great Britain, with services to our islands and to the Continent.

In 1821, James and George Burns introduced a passenger steamer service between Glasgow and Ayr and later expanded this to Liverpool and Belfast. George Burns was the co-founder, along with Samuel Cunard and David McIver, of the company which became the famous Cunard Steam Ship Company. John Burns, George's son, became the chairman of the Cunard Line and 1st Baron Inverclyde. The Cunard Line prospered under his chairmanship and then that of his son, George A. Burns.

Cunard was very quick to start replacing wooden paddle steamers with iron steamers and adopting screw steamers, its first being the *China* in 1862. Its first steel vessel was the *Servia*, which was second in size only to the *Great Eastern*. Built by J. & G. Thomson of Glasgow in 1881, she was the first steel ship to have a Royal Mail contract and was therefore named the RMS *Servia*.

Burns & Laird was formed shortly after G. & J. Burns and the Laird Line were acquired by Coast Lines in 1920. Coast Lines was itself taken over by P&O in 1971 and by the middle of the decade most of the individual liveries had disappeared. P&O continue to provide services to Ireland and to the Continent.

From 1921, the Aberdeen Steam Navigation Company operated between Aberdeen and London, continuing until 1945 when it was taken over by the Tyne-Tees Steam Shipping Company, part of Coast Lines. Passenger services lasted until 1948 and cargo until 1962, when competition from rail and road finally closed the line.

There were those entrepreneurs who went beyond serving our own shores to join us to the Americas and to the British Empire. This great merchant enterprise was to last up to the Second World War, when disruption, competition and cost were to bring the beginning of the end both of the operation of liners and then of cargo steamers.

It was Scottish entrepreneurs like George and John Burns who grew this great merchant fleet. Another of these, perhaps the greatest name in Scottish shipping as well as Scottish art and culture, was Sir William Burrell, born in 1861 into a shipping family. William and his brother took over the running of the firm from their father. They were astute in ordering modern ships at low cost when the market was in a slump and then selling these on at profit when the market picked up. This made them very rich and this allowed William Burrell to indulge his passion for collecting art and antiques.

The company had started in William's grandfather George's time, plying trade along the Forth and Clyde Canal. With the purchase of a share in a steamship in 1866, their business expanded worldwide, acquiring six more steamers by 1875. Two of these were prefixed 'Strath-', which was used throughout the company's existence.

Typical of William Burrell & Sons' ships was the unfortunate but history-making *Strathclyde*. The *Strathclyde* was built in 1871 by Blackwood & Gordon of Port Glasgow. Captained by J. D. Eaton, she was on her way from London to Bombay via the Suez Canal, carrying seventy crew and passengers.

Leaving Dover on 17 February 1876, just over 2 miles from the coast the German steamer *Franconia* overtook her and a collision ensued. The *Strathclyde* sunk quickly. Thirty-eight were drowned, including thirteen in a lifeboat that had been swamped by heavy seas. A trial of the German master was held at the Central Criminal Court in London and he was found guilty of manslaughter. An appeal found that he was not covered by English law and was released. This event led to Great Britain adopting the law of International Territorial Waters, which other countries already used.

After years of successful trading, the brothers again used the rise in the market value of ships, now caused by the outbreak of the First World War, to sell. Between 1913 and 1916 almost the entire fleet was sold, including vessels which were still on the stocks. William Burrell invested the proceeds and embarked on his passion for collecting.

In 1944, Burrell gave away almost all of his art collection to the City of Glasgow along with a bequest of £250,000 to house it. Burrell insisted on a site which would be near to the city but not subject to the pollution therein. The difficulties in finding such a site meant that the full collection was not displayed until 1970 in its beautiful setting in Pollok Country Park. Burrell was knighted in 1927 for services to art and the city. He died in 1958 and is buried in Largs.

The Gow and McGregor families had come together in the 1850s in the business of cargo handling. Alan Gow had ordered a sailing ship, the *Estrella de Chile*, for use on the Glasgow and Liverpool, Cape Horn and Chile route. He started the use of the title 'Glen' on his second ship, the *Glenavon*, by which time a formal partnership existed between Gow and McGregor. The Glen Line was formed by them in 1910. They were entrepreneurial in building ships for the China tea trade, using the Suez Canal, which opened in 1869. As the tea trade was based in London, the business was moved there.

In 1911, Elder Dempster & Co. acquired the Glen Line but it was sold to Alfred Holt's Blue Funnel Line in 1935. By 1978, all Glen Line ships had been sold.

Donaldson Brothers was founded in 1855 and its first wooden sailing ship sailed from the Clyde to Brazil and the River Plate in Argentina in 1858. This was followed by routes to Montreal and Quebec. By 1900, Donaldsons were using twelve cargo steamers on their transatlantic routes, including an important contract for newsprint from Newfoundland to England and passengers for Canada.

The Merchant Shipping Acts required that, from 1825, the ownership of any vessel must be divided into sixty-four shares, with any 'transactions', i.e. changes in ownership, being recorded in Customs Houses. The Donaldson Line moved from this system to incorporation as a company in 1913.

Both the Donaldson Line and the Anchor Line operated passenger services to Canada and in 1916 the Anchor Line took an interest in the company, setting up Anchor-Donaldson Limited.

With the liquidation of the Anchor Line in 1935, the Donaldsons acquired much of it and formed the Donaldson Atlantic line. The company had also started a service

TSS *Athenia*, main deck.

to the American Pacific coast in 1924, and while these services were resumed after the war, the ships and service were sold in 1954 to the Blue Star Line. While a service to the Great Lakes started in 1957, the end was near. Containerisation was said to have played a role in the line's demise when it went into liquidation in 1967 and the ships were sold.

Like many other shipping companies, the wars took a terrible toll on the ships and crew of the Donaldson Line. The *Argalia* and the *Athenia* (1) were torpedoed in 1917 off the coast of Ireland. Fifteen lives were lost on the *Athenia*. In the Second World War, the *Athenia* (2) went down in history as the first British ship to be lost to enemy action, on 3 September 1939, with the loss of around 120 lives. Twenty-eight of the dead were American citizens and this gave rise to German fears that the USA would enter the war. The captain, Fritz-Julius Lemp, admitted to having sunk the ship in error and it was said to have been hushed up by Hitler. It also gave rise to conspiracy theories that the ship had actually hit a British mine and Germany was being blamed.

The *Athenia* had been built at Fairfield Shipyards in Govan for the Anchor-Donaldson route to Canada. Around twenty other ships from the line were lost to torpedoes or bombs. This is testimony to the sacrifice of the crew and passengers of those merchantmen who braved the rigours of wartime seas.

The Aberdeen Line was set up by George Thompson. His first trade was in timber from Canada, eventually running twelve sailing vessels to South America, the West Indies, the Mediterranean, the Pacific and Australia. The company came under the control of the White Star and Shaw, Savill and Albion Lines in 1905. The Aberdeen title was dropped in 1938 and the last ship was scrapped in 1957, when the company disappeared.

Another well-remembered name is the Ben Line, which had its origins in William and Alexander Thomson's business of importing marble, for which the *Carrara* was built. Alexander retired and William Thomson & Co. of Leith was formed, trading to the Far East, the Baltic and the Mediterranean. The company became Ben Line Steamers in 1919. The company survived long after many other Scottish shipping companies, possibly because it entered the world of containerisation through joining a consortium of companies, Associated Container Transportation, as well as one with Ellerman Lines, becoming Ben Line Containers in 1970. It diversified into the oil industry, becoming one of Britain's largest drill contractors.

With the decline in British shipping, the Ben Line began to get rid of ships and by 1996 owned only one drill ship. Now the company exists as an agency working in shipping in the Far East, still with an office in the Bonnington Bond in Leith.

George Gibson & Co. Ltd was also established in Leith in 1797, trading with the Continent and, reflecting that town's connection with the wine and spirits trade, with Lisbon and Oporto. By 1956, according to the Leith Dock Commission, the fleet comprised thirteen motor vessels and two on charter. It also provided stevedoring and shipping agency services. By December 2007, the last ships owned by George Gibson, the *Sigas Ettrick* and the *Sigas Lanrick*, were sold.

The company, like many others in shipping and in Scottish industry in general, had been swallowed up in mergers and acquisitions. While there are some remaining ship owning companies, containerisation probably signalled the end of the great era of

Scottish merchant enterprise. There was little need for our small-scale vessels when the world wanted bulk-transport and containerisation.

Not only did our enterprising merchants and seafarers penetrate the farthest reaches of the globe; when they got there they also stayed and developed industries. Typical of this was Paddy Henderson. P. Henderson & Co. was a Glasgow company formed in 1829 which exported coal and imported marble. When Patrick died in 1841, the business was taken over by his brother George, a sea-captain. James Galbraith joined as a partner and was instrumental in expanding the business. They started a service to Bombay and Australia and then New Zealand for emigrants and Royal Mail.

One of Galbraith's contributions was the Irrawaddy Flotilla Company, which operated passenger and cargo services on the great Irrawaddy River in Burma. It was set up to begin with on a contract to carry troops but moved to general cargoes and lasted from 1865 until the late 1940s. The IFC ran the largest riverboat system in the world with, at its peak in 1920, 600 vessels carrying 900 million passengers a year.

The paddle steamers used by the company were made in Scotland and were dismantled and then shipped to Burma for re-assembly. The manager of the fleet, John Morton, saw the threat if the Japanese got hold of the boats when they invaded Burma. He was ordered to scuttle all of the 600 vessels, seriously hampering the movement of the Japanese on the river.

John Morton wrote in his diary of 28 April 1942 that, 'Mandalay was evacuated yesterday, the IF the last to go. We are being chased out quicker now than was expected and I have orders for more sinkings here at Kyaukmyaung. There are over 200 of our fleet sunk at Mandalay. Imagine how I felt drilling holes in their bottoms with a Bren gun.' John Morton received the CBE and was later killed when the MV *Henry Stanley* was torpedoed and sank in December 1942.

From the *London Gazette* of November 1942, on the award of his CBE:

John Morton, lately Manager, The Irrawaddy Flotilla Company, Burma. Throughout the Burma campaign Mr. Morton toured the country by air, rail, river and road in order to keep in touch with the staff of his widely distributed organisation. It was in no small measure due to his personality, powers of organisation, ability and leadership that the essential needs of the army were met as regards the transportation of men and materials by river, and tens of thousands of civilian lives were saved.

In 1948, following the cessation of hostilities, the company became the Government Inland Water Transport Board.

Apparently the paddle steamers inspired Rudyard Kipling's poem, 'The Road to Mandalay':

Come you back to Mandalay
Where the old Flotilla lay:
Can't you 'ear their paddles chunkin' from Rangoon to Mandalay?
On the road to Mandalay,
Where the flyin' fishes play,
An' the dawn comes up like thunder outer China
'crost the Bay!

The Irrawaddy Flotilla Company paddle steamers on the Irrawaddy.

The British & Burmese Steam Navigation Co. was set up to run liners to Burma. Expansion and new capital was required, so the Albion Shipping Company was set up, with P. Henderson & Co. managing. These were sold to the Elder Dempster Line in 1952. Henderson continued to operate to Burma. The company was acquired by the Ocean Steamship Co. in 1965. However, the Arab–Israeli Six-Day War closed the Suez Canal and the Burma trade ceased. Henderson's last ship was sold in 1972, and their ship owning days were over.

You can see that there were a great many factors in why Scottish merchant shipping declined, and containerisation is only one of these. There was a boom in shipbuilding after the Second World War, when sunk and damaged ships had to be replaced. But a number of developments weighed against the continued success of a home merchant fleet. With the improvement in our road systems and the introduction of motorways, there was less need for coastal cargo boats. The huge expansion in air passenger and freight travel also took passengers away from the liners and cargo away from the steamers.

But one of the major factors is that Scotland is no longer a manufacturing country. So much of our industrial output in the past went on boats owned by Scottish lines and built in Scottish yards. The buildings in Glasgow's Merchant City, in Dundee, Aberdeen and in Greenock are a 'Who's Who' of the Scottish Merchant Marine. Here, from the Atlantic Chambers, the Baltic Chambers, from Pacific Quay and Atlantic Quay, products were sent round the world.

Railway engines went to South Africa and we received cotton from the Indian subcontinent. Sugar-refining equipment was sent and sugar received in return. Our coal and our steel went out by ship, as did locomotives and boilers, bridges, cranes, machinery for power stations, for gasworks and for mills. Jute came into Dundee and left as linoleum. Granite went from Aberdeen and marble came from Italy. Rags and esparto grass came into Leith and left as paper and board. When products leave now, they leave in container ships or bulk carriers and normally from ports in England.

If you would like to see a slice of our maritime heritage then the Trinity House Maritime Museum in Leith, run by Historic Scotland, houses a wonderful collection of treasures from Leith's seafaring past. For centuries it has been the home of the Incorporation of Masters and Mariners, who looked after the welfare of those at sea.

The Maritime Museum in Aberdeen is a wonderful modern repository of all things maritime connected with Aberdeen and beyond, including whaling and the oil industry.

Above right: The Glen Line

Above left: Donaldson Line

The Aberdeen Line.

Henderson Line 'Passing Ailsa Craig', *c.* 1938.

The Carron Line's *Avon* on a company-issued postcard, *c.* 1910.

The P&O vessel *Medina*, newly built and ready to serve as a royal yacht, seen here at Greenock.

The SS *Highlander* of the Aberdeen, Newcastle & Hull Steam Co. Ltd.

Advertisements for the Aberdeen & Commonwealth Line.

A passenger list for the Allan line, 1913.

Benvalla, of Leith's Ben Line, is seen here under the Forth Bridge.

The Scottish Whaling Fleet

In eighteen hundred and twenty-three
On March the thirteenth day,
we hoisted our colours to the top of the mast
And for Greenland bore away, brave boys
And for Greenland bore away.

The lookout in the crosstrees stood
With spyglass in his hand;
There's a whale, there's a whale
There's whalefish he cried
And she blows at every span, brave boys
She blows at every span

So go the words of the traditional 'Greenland Whale Fisheries'. Whaling has produced a folklore for what was a hard and a filthy occupation requiring months and years away at sea, usually in the Antarctic oceans.

While there is a debate about whether it was the Dutch or the Basques who started whaling, many others were not long to follow, with Scottish ports Dundee, Leith, Peterhead, Aberdeen and Montrose all involved in the industry to various degrees.

In our own waters, whales were first processed at land stations. There were at one time four such stations in Shetland. The method was the original and primitive one of using boats to drive the whales ashore, where they would be caught, cut up and processed. Between the years 1903 and 1914, when the British government

Bottle-nosed whales driven ashore in the Shetlands.

suspended whaling because of the war, a total of 4,900 whales were caught by the four companies operating the stations.

But it was the Industrial Revolution which was to encourage the commercial exploitation of the whale and to pursue it into far oceans and to near extinction. Our schoolbooks in the 1950s were still full of stories about the splendour and challenge of the hunt and I don't suppose we gave a thought to the rights and wrongs of hunting the whale.

And the need for the whale in oiling the wheels of the Industrial Revolution was seen very early in Dundee, which was to become a great whaling port based on the supply of the fine whale oil necessary for the jute industry. This industry did not really take off until the discovery that jute was more easily worked if it was softened first by light oil, and whale oil was perfect for the job.

Dundee was not only a whaling port but famed for building whalers. It was Alexander Stephen who, in 1857, built the first steam whaler, the *Tay*, for the Dundee fleet. They also built Scott's *Discovery* for his first Antarctic expedition. He also used the last whaler to be built in Dundee, the *Terra Nova*, for his second expedition, in 1910.

In 1788, Peterhead's first whaler, the *Robert*, set sail, which was to mark Peterhead's beginning as one of Europe's great whaling ports. In 1893, with the return of the last boat, the *Windward*, with blubber from only one whale, the great days of Peterhead were at an end; the only memories being the graving dock, Blubber Box Quay and the streets named after the great ships and their captains, like Hope Street, Captain Gray Place and Geary Place.

In Peterhead you can see the very hard evidence of both the whaling and the granite industry; a dry dock for the building of Greenland whalers, which was built through a levy on the whale oil landed at the port.

Whaling was a dangerous and a dirty business and was best suited to the energies of young men. It was, in the main, unskilled but extremely hard work and one in which the living conditions were basic, or worse.

> Aye there's men who flense the blubber and there's men who work the saws,
> For many skills are needed doon among the ice and snows,
> And the cooker men are clever getting oil wi' steaming heat,
> But the lads who swing a blubber hook are canny lads to meet.
>
> Oh it's sailing oot o' Scotland and it's heading south we go
> To the cold Antarctic oceans where the Blue and Fin whale blow
> And the first time is adventure and you're feeling kind of glad
> That you're sailing on a factory ship to be a Blubber Lad.
>
> Harry Robertson

The Bounty Act of 1749 was to create a huge upsurge in whaling, causing the opening of many ports and the building of a great whaling fleet. The Act, which lasted until 1824, provided for, among other things, an incentive for the building of ships of 40 shillings per ton for all ships over 200 tons.

The Act gave rise to many new whale products, making use of the oil for lighting houses and streets, this before the advent of the production of coal gas. By the beginning of the 1800s it was also used for lubricating the new machinery of the Industrial Revolution, and there was a dramatic increase in the number of whaling ports operating in order to support the demand for whale products. Besides oil, the whale provided products such as ambergris for use as a fixative in perfume and baleen, the bony plates from the whale's mouth, which were used in such things as collar-stiffeners and corsets.

The company most associated in Scotland with the whaling industry was Christian Salvesen, which was formed by Norwegian Christian Salvesen in Leith in 1872. Christian was from a family of merchant shipowners. His early days were in shipping and forwarding and he started a steamship line to Stavanger in 1886. It was in the early 1900s that they commenced whaling in the Arctic and then the Antarctic, establishing a base on South Georgia that they called Leith Harbour, after the home port.

The company developed into factory ships, with the *Southern Harvester* and *Southern Venturer* serviced by a fleet of whale-catchers. Salvesen finally came out of whaling in 1963 to reinvent itself as an international transport and logistics company, becoming public in 1985.

As whales are a finite resource and were being overfished then, it was inevitable that the days of the whaler would be numbered. There was less use too for products from the whale. Whale oil was replaced with mineral oil for softening jute. Plastics

Salvesen whaler in the South Atlantic.

The harbour, Leith.

began to replace whalebone for corsets. Most of all, petroleum and petroleum by-products made whale oil redundant, with the only remaining reason for hunting being for whale meat, which is still looked on as a delicacy in some areas. In some countries such as the Faroes and in Northern Canada and Greenland, whales are still hunted and eaten. There are ongoing debates about the future of whale hunting, with some countries wanting to lift the International Whaling Commission moratorium on commercial whaling. However, Scotland, one of the great whaling nations, is no longer involved.

If you want a flavour of the hunt for the whale you can do no better than listen to the songs and stories of Harry Robertson. Harry was a Scot who emigrated to Australia in 1952 and who worked in the whaling industry in its dying days. His songs record the noise and bustle of the industry, its culture and its life.

> We laboured seven days a week, with cold hands and frozen feet.
> Bitter days and lonely nights making grog and having fights
> Salt fish and whalemeat sausage, fresh penguin eggs a treat
> And we trudged along to work each day through icy winds and sleet.
> Harry Robertson; 'The Wee Dark Engine Room'

Salvesen's *Sevilla* was once a passenger ship of the Hamburg Amerika Line.

A whaling factory ship operating in the Ross Sea, off the coast of Antarctica.

Landing a whale, Harris, *c.* 1910.

The whaling station at Harris, *c.* 1910.

Scottish Shipbreaking and the Man Who Bought a Navy

Often, on the train from the North on my way to Edinburgh over the Forth Bridge, I would pass Inverkeithing. There, I would see ships being broken up over time at the harbour. I hadn't given a great deal of thought to it. While we proudly acclaim the history of shipbuilding in Scotland, I was surprised to discover the heritage we also have in ship breaking. It shouldn't have been a surprise, I suppose, given the maritime and shipbuilding heritage combined with the entrepreneurial spirit of the Scot.

Nowhere was this demonstrated more dramatically than at Scapa Flow, that Orcadian water which was Britain's major naval base during two world wars. It is where the great *Royal Oak* lies, having been sunk by a German U-boat on 14 October 1939. It is now a war grave, protecting the memory of the 1,234 who died as a result of the attack.

It was also where the German High Seas Fleet was interred following the end of the First World War. Negotiations were underway to decide the fate of the ships. However, Admiral Ludwig von Reuter decided to pre-empt any decision by scuttling the seventy-four vessels. While the guard ships of the Royal Navy managed to beach some of the craft, fifty-two of the great warships sank.

While von Reuter was feted as a hero in his homeland, the issue disposed of a problem that the British had in dealing with the ships. While some countries were laying claim to them by way of reparations, the United States was resisting this. Britain simply wanted to get them disposed of. And that's what happened when, on a pre-arranged signal, the sea cocks of the entire fleet were opened and the ships began to sink. The sight would have been amazing, as it was to a party of Orkney schoolchildren watching from a small launch.

The raising and salvaging of the German fleet at Scapa was an inconceivable thought to the Admiralty at the time. In any case, there was little need as, following the end of the war, there was plenty of scrap metal and the cost of salvage was out of the question. However, as time progressed scrap increased in value and the local population was complaining about the hazards to shipping.

It was Ernest Cox who was to achieve the unachievable: the raising of the cruisers and battleships in order to break them up. Given the cost of building a ship, his initial purchase of twenty-six destroyers for £250 seems like a bargain. Maybe it was, but Cox made little from the salvage operations, although he did well with scrap iron.

Cox was an electrical engineer from Wolverhampton who moved to Hamilton and married into a steelworks family. His success in engineering and munitions contracts saw him also enter the scrap metal business as scrap was becoming an essential ingredient in the steel furnace. The use of steel, including scrap, had been pioneered by shipbuilders Denny Brothers of Dumbarton and was increasingly taken up by others, therefore creating a market.

A shortage of contracts in 1924 is said to have prompted Cox to look at the idea of the salvaging the Scapa Flow wrecks.

He owned a German dry dock previously used for testing submarines. Rather than break this up for scrap, he hit on the idea of modifying it to raise ships. He split it in half and installed heavy winches. While other salvage companies had looked at the wrecks and walked away, convinced they would lose money on a job which couldn't be done anyway, he persisted. He met many difficulties. He had no experience to draw on but he persevered, eventually raising twenty-four of the twenty-six destroyers over a period of a year and a half. This gives the wrong impression of the speed of lifting. Whereas the first to come up took months, the very last to come up were doing so in a matter of weeks. The last to come up emerged in three days. Cox had learned from experience.

One of the methods he used successfully was pumping compressed air into the hulls once they had been patched up by divers. This had previously been done in 1919 to raise the *Leonardo da Vinci*, the 24,000-ton Italian battleship which had blown up and sank in the Bay of Taranto in 1916. This was the method he used for lifting SMS *Moltke*, a 25,400-ton battlecruiser. It was the last to sink in Scapa Flow in 1919 and one of the last to rise again, in 1930.

Can you possibly imagine the difficulties faced by divers as they worked in the murky depths to seal off hatches, pipes, portholes and vent in the overturned ships? Besides being covered in seaweed, there was also 10 years of rust to contend with.

One of the methods of gaining access to the ships was by attaching airlocks to the upturned hulls. While the ships were being raised by compressed air, the airlocks enabled workers to enter the ships to seal up pipes and other apertures without the need for divers.

One visitor to the lifting of SMS *Kaiser* described entry to the hull:

The door was swung upwards into place and held until the air pressure shut it securely. Another valve was turned and pandemonium broke loose. It seemed that

Work being carried out on the *Hindenburg* using airlocks with the aid of the tug *Sidonian*.

all the railway engines in the world were letting off steam at once. The interior of the lock grew thick as a London fog as the compressed air gushed into it from the interior of the ship. I swallowed hard to keep the pressure adjusted. Meanwhile I watched the needle of the pressure dial swing round till the shrieking noise subsided and I knew the ordeal was over and the ordeal was over and that the pressure inside the lock was the same as the sunken *Kaiser*.

With a huge harvest of ships in his net, Ernest Cox had had enough of Scapa Flow and left to pursue his scrap iron business. He passed on his remaining interests in his business to the Alloa Shipbreaking Company.

Many of the ships raised at Scapa Flow by Cox were bought by the Alloa Shipbreaking Company, their chief salvage officer on site being Mr T. Mackenzie, who worked hand in hand with Cox in the raising of the ships. The company was formed in 1922 and changed its name in 1929 to Metal Industries Ltd. Besides a base at Scapa Flow, it operated in Faslane and Rosyth as well as in nearby Charlestown. Metal Industries became a very successful conglomerate, with 12,000 employees and twenty-four subsidiaries in 1961. In 1967 it became part of Thorn Electrical Industries.

The Faslane operation of Metal Industries was based where the submarine lifts and jetties for the Trident missile submarines are now. Many famous warships were scrapped at Faslane, including the aircraft carrier HMS *Indomitable* in 1955.

The feat must have taken a toll on Cox and perhaps that's why he left behind some of the largest ships at enormous depths. However, Mackenzie decided he could do it and by use of airlocks up to 100 feet long he succeeded in raising the 28,000-ton *Bayern*, the *Konig Albert* and the battleship *Kaiserin*.

Along the coast from Rosyth and Bo'ness where the great German battleships were being torn apart, at Thomas W. Ward's yard in Inverkeithing those British ships which had defended the Empire and sent the German fleet to Scapa Flow were also being scrapped. Thomas 'Tommy' Ward was a scrap metal merchant based in Sheffield and became adept at dismantling ships, opening a specialist department in 1894 and becoming the largest supplier of scrap metal to the steel industry. He started breaker's yards throughout the country and one of these was in Inverkeithing. His company lasted until 1980, when it was taken over by Rio Tinto.

Among the great names succumbing to Tommy's cutters was HMS *Dreadnought*. In 1914 *Dreadnought* was the flagship of the 4th Battle Squadron, based at Scapa Flow. She saw little action during the war except for the sinking of a submarine. She was in reserve at Rosyth in 1919 and put up for sale in 1920, being bought by Tommy Ward for scrapping in his new yard at Inverkeithing. Putting his yard at Inverkeithing was an astute move, as any ships he bought would simply have to be towed a short distance, and he probably knew that following the war ships would be decommissioned. Inverkeithing also had good rail and sea links for the transport of the scrap steel to steelworks.

Many other warships met their end at Inverkeithing, among them the famous HMS *Mars*, moored for many years on the Tay and used as a training ship. Launched in 1848 as a ship of the line, she was a supply ship during the Crimean War and was converted to screw propulsion and subsequently served in the Mediterranean. In 1869, she was moored in the Tay, where she became home to many homeless and destitute boys from Dundee and throughout Scotland. They learned seamanship, carpentry, tailoring and metalwork. The story of the ship and her boys is told in Gordon Douglas' book *We'll send ye tae the Mars*. The ship was broken up in 1929.

But it was not just naval vessels which were broken up at Inverkeithing. The yard also saw the end of merchant vessels big and small, including some famous liners. The RMS *Olympic* was the sister ship of the ill-fated *Titanic* and lead ship of the White Star Line's three Olympic Class liners, the third being *Britannic*. Launched from Harland & Wolff's Belfast yard in 1910, she was once the world's biggest liner. She was a highly successful ship, nicknamed 'Old Reliable' for her role as a troopship during the First World War.

In the 1930s the White Star Line merged with Cunard at the behest of HM Government. This allowed government funds to be released for the completion of the RMS *Queen Mary*, stuck on the stocks at John Brown's Clydebank yard. While the *Olympic* had had a modernising refit, it was still unprofitable. The *Queen Mary* and the RMS *Queen Elizabeth* were to take on the transatlantic business so the older liners were laid up. The *Olympic* was partly disassembled in Jarrow before her hull was finally taken to Inverkeithing for final breaking. Other ships included the RMS *Empress of Australia* and Cunard's *Mauretania*.

The first *Mauretania* had previously been broken up just round the coast in the dry dock at Rosyth. Cunard's *Mauretania*, built by Swan Hunter & Wigham Richardson at Newcastle, took the Blue Riband for the fastest transatlantic crossing in 1909 and held it for twenty years.

Ship breaking is still occasionally carried out at Inverkeithing, but under the ownership of RM Supplies Limited.

There were other shipbreakers in Scotland. In Port Glasgow, the great French liner *L'Atlantique* was a tourist attraction as she was taken apart by Smith & Houston of Glasgow. *L'Atlantique* caught fire near Guernsey and consequently, while still afloat, was a total loss. In 1936 she was sold for scrap and taken to Port Glasgow for scrapping. Smith & Houston scrapped many ships of all sizes, including the aircraft carrier *Persius* in 1958.

In Bo'ness, Forth Shipbreaking was opened in 1905 by P. & W. MacLellan of Glasgow, who ceased trading in 1979.

In Troon, the West of Scotland Ship Breakers Ltd was a substantial enterprise employing up to 200 men which lasted around eighty years until 1983, breaking up several hundred British naval and other ships. The company had been taken over by Arnott, Young & Co. in 1938 and joined their other yards at Cairnryan and Dalmuir, previously William Beardmore's shipyard. Ship breaking was once the main industry in Cairnryan and it seems to have specialised in the breaking up of aircraft carriers, including HMS *Eagle* and HMS *Ark Royal*.

In Scotland, if shipbuilding was such a huge industry and ship breaking large by any standards, why are ships now only scrapped occasionally? The answer to that inevitably lies in the cost of the process. While people like Tommy Ward turned the industry into one of mass destruction, the fact is that it is a very labour intensive industry. Modern-day legislation on health and safety and the environment also make it a much more careful process than it might have been earlier. Ships may be full of asbestos, a scourge to those who built them. They may have been painted with toxic lead paint and they may contain oils and fuels, all toxic and dangerous to anyone going near them with cutting equipment.

Unfortunately, the developing world is where ships are now broken up, sometimes simply on the beach to where they have been towed. It is estimated that of the several hundred ships due for scrapping each year, 85 per cent meet their ends in India, China, Turkey, Bangladesh or Pakistan. These countries have low wages and less strict environmental controls than developed countries. Accidents are endemic, as in many cases basic protective equipment is not provided. Falls and asphyxiation are common.

In response to the many concerns, the European Union took steps in 2012 to ensure that European Union-flagged ships are broken up in compliance with the standards set down in the Hong Kong International Convention for the Safe and Environmentally Sound Recycling of Ships, 2009. This includes the obligation to recycle ships in safe and sound facilities and to include strict environmental provisions.

There are present estimates of the industry reaching the need to break up 2,000 ships a year from the present few hundred. This is mainly due to the current overcapacity in world fleets. In storage, ships rust and become out of date. There comes a time when the costs of breaking up are less than the costs of storage, crewing and maintenance. They are then sent for breaking up.

While legislation may protect the environment and improve the welfare of those workers in developing countries, we will have to wait and see whether it brings more ship breaking back to Scotland. I wonder whether we might see the kind of entrepreneurial spirit of Ernest Cox and Tommy Ward emerging in this possible renewed industry? Time will tell.

Cunard's *Mauretania* at Rosyth for breaking up, 14 July 1935.